MW01596517

À ma chère Yb
en lui souhaitant
plaisir à lire ce livre que j'...
... l'écrire avec mon amicale...
Philadelphia 22 Nov 200[?]

MEMOIRS FROM
NORMANDY

MEMOIRS FROM NORMANDY

Childhood, War
&
Life's Adventures

ARMAND IDRAC

EDITED AND TRANSLATED
FROM THE FRENCH
BY
JOANNE SILVER

Beach Lloyd Publishers, LLC
Wayne, Pennsylvania

Beach Lloyd Publishers, LLC, May 2004
Copyright © 2003 by Joanne Silver
Copyright renewed © 2003 by Joanne Silver

All rights reserved. No part of this book, including interior design, cover design, illustrations and photographs, may be reproduced or transmitted in any form, by any means (electronic, photocopying, recording, or otherwise) without the prior written permission of the publisher.

Idrac, Armand, 1928 –
Memoirs from Normandy: Childhood, War & Life's Adventures by Armand Idrac

ISBN: 0-9743158-5-0

Printed in the United States of America

Library of Congress Control Number: 2003110383

Cover design by Book Cover Express;
Computer conversion by Michael Bowe;
Layout and formatting by Ronald Silver;
Photographs by Armand Idrac, Yvonne Idrac, Ronald Silver;
Readability Statistics by Dr. Scott Greenwood,
    Literacy Department, West Chester University;
    Rhoda Kapner, Reading Specialist;
    Microsoft Word 2000.

Line from the song "Madeleine":
MADELEINE. Music and French Lyrics by Jacques Brel, English lyrics by Eric Blau © 1959, 1968 (Copyrights Renewed) N. S. Justinian Music, Inc. All rights in U.S. and Canada administered by Emi Unart Catalog Inc. All rights reserved. Used by Permission. WARNER BROS. PUBLICATIONS U.S. INC., Miami, FL 33014.

TABLE OF CONTENTS

Preface
Translator/Editor's Note
Disclaimer

Charts & Maps

Photographs

PREFACE

Originally, I wrote these memoirs only for family and friends, and did not envision their publication, especially in the United States. I wanted to bring to life details of "my time" which seemed memorable or amusing to me. For some of the people involved, my writings will awaken their own memories, while for others, the settings and events will seem remote. I have added colorful stories gleaned throughout my life.

For clarity, I have chosen a thematic narration; so, you will look in vain for chronological order, and the chapters can be read independently of one another. This is not an intimate work; there are no "family" stories. It is not an autobiography, a more precise undertaking, which I leave to others.

At the outset, I wanted only to tell entertaining stories, but then I felt compelled to add the chapters on the Occupation and the Landing, snapshots of the unforgettable, seen through the eyes of a new, fifteen-year-old "del Dongo," as in *La Chartreuse de Parme*, where the young hero finds himself in the Battle of Waterloo by accidentally riding into it. This unbelievable time, by tacit agreement, transformed me into the new head of the family, whose judgment was respected by my newly widowed Mother and my eleven-year-old sister.

The names of some characters have been changed, but the stories are real.

Because its grandeur has always fascinated me, and distance made it out of reach for such a long time, I decided to devote one complete chapter to the United States. Getting to know Americans was for me a first step towards that different world that I longed to know.

I have placed the "Three Short Stories in Prose," written in a form that I would have liked to develop in my youth, as an Appendix.

My hope is that you will have as much pleasure reading these memoirs as I had in writing them.

ARMAND

TRANSLATOR / EDITOR'S NOTE

It is my privilege to bring to you the memoirs of my long-time dear friend, Armand Idrac. As he states in the Preface, sharing the memorable events and the humor in his life inspired these efforts. His life was defined by humor and all its positive forces, by energy, curiosity, love of learning and adventure, and the desire to help others. Armand needed encouragement to recount the painful memories of being in the midst of World War II as a teenager.

Armand has verified this entire translation. He reads English quite well, and found some of his amusing stories all the more amusing in a foreign language!

Explanatory footnotes are a combination of my own background as a teacher of French, verification with resources, and the wealth of knowledge that Armand so readily supplied in person and by e-mail, in answer to my queries. The Reference section combines my sources with materials that the reader can pursue for further information.

I thank my family for their patience and support during the project. Special thanks to my husband Ron for bringing me up to snuff on the Allies during the two world wars. Thank you to Dr. Dona De Sanctis and Cynthia Lyman for their proofreading of Italian. Thank you to my mother, Catherine Lloyd, for her proofreading and comments. She bore me one month after Hitler marched into Poland, and kept me safe until my Dad returned from the war. Thank you to my sister, Rexanne Morrow, for her proofreading and lively comments.

I lovingly dedicate this translation to my father, Rex Beach Lloyd, a Navy medic among the Americans who landed at Omaha Beach on D-Day, June 6, 1944, when Armand was fifteen years old.

Joanne Shoestock Silver--February 19, 2003

DISCLAIMER

This book is primarily designed to disclose cultural information and events in a subjective setting; i.e., as perceived and experienced by the author. Therefore, establishing a linear chronology and detailed historical events are not primary goals. However, footnoted items are completely factual, and reference entries have been chosen to expand the topics herein.

This book is intended to be multipurpose; it may be read for pleasure, and also viewed and used as an informal educational supplement. The chapters may be read and used separately, or grouped, since they are not interdependent.

Some names have been changed, to protect the privacy of individuals and their families. The author, the translator/editor, and Beach Lloyd Publishers shall be neither liable nor responsible to any person or entity for loss or damage caused directly or indirectly, or alleged to have been caused, from the use of this book.

If you do not consent to be bound by this disclaimer, you are free to return the book to the publisher for a full refund.

CHAPTER I

I WAS REALLY LUCKY

How can you recapture your oldest memories? Those of the "first age,"* when you're eating that French cereal called "Baby Cereal for the First Age"!

Only some old photographs remain, yellowed by time, or the memory of colorful stories heard so often from the mouths of our parents that we recall more from their stories than from actual experiences.

Born one year after the passing of my only brother, Armand, who died of croup at the age of nine, my parents welcomed me as "the miracle child"; but, fearing that I would not be as sweet as the precious one that they had lost, they decided to call me "Albert Jean Armand." Then, after I had, of course, risen in their esteem, they changed their minds, and it was my third first name that became primary. It was also my grandfather's name.

Actually, I have always answered to the two names Albert and Armand, and said "thank you" very politely every time someone wished me Happy Feast Day for one or the other. When I was really little, I was so cute that they also called me "Mimi"! Fortunately, that didn't last long enough to become truly ridiculous. Imagine down at the firehouse: "Have you seen Fireman Mimi"?

My whole life long, to the curious who wanted to know why Albert was also called Armand, I explained pleasantly that the second first name was reserved for the ladies, for it was my mother and my sister who used it most often. Not until much later, having become "Granddad," did I think of combining the two first names, more original than Jean-Jacques or Marie-Claude.

---

* The first three months of a newborn's life.

Besides my parents, I had a grandmother and Aunt Jeanne to attend to my every need. I retain one meaningful proof of that. In a photo not taken for that purpose, you can see my little enameled potty inside the open oven door; it was being warmed, to avoid shocking my behind with a contact so cool as to negate the desired effect.

Before my first birthday, I used this hygienic piece of equipment for other purposes: As a first means of autonomous transportation. Seated and using my legs for locomotion, I could go everywhere, often more quickly than one would have suspected--especially if it was for doing mischief, such as going down the cellar stairs.   (They wouldn't even let me try!) I already had a taste for travel.

At the age of three, shortly before Christmas, I had the surprise gift of a little sister. My young age had not allowed me to choose between a tiny baby and an electric train. For her baptism, feeling intuitively that I was no longer going to be the center of the universe, I tried to keep attention focused on me by endless chatter, and when they would ask me: "What's your name?" I responded invariably, « Gisèle ». Gisèle was the name of a little neighbor girl, older than I, for whom I must have had tender feelings. In vain they told me that it was impossible because it was a girl's name; I stuck to it. Didn't I now have to be a little girl like Arlette, in order to hold everyone's interest?

As much pretty, curly hair as I had--put up on rollers at night--to that extent, poor little sister had a skull bald as a pebble. Fortunately, it covered over rather quickly with a down so soft that I loved rubbing it. Alas! With that, she let loose baffling, howling fits of anger. To justify myself, I said, "I'm not hurting little sister, I'm petting her!"

One day, in the train from Caen to the sea, a lady traveler believing only in outward appearances, not knowing our intimate morphology and finding me a little wild, said to me, "Little girl, you ought to follow the example of your little brother, look how well-behaved he is…!"

Arriving at the station of Douvres-la-Délivrande, in order to unload the bags more easily, my parents passed them out through the windows of the car. At times we used to follow the same route, which frightened our cousin Mercédès a little. She was old enough and big enough to go out through the door.

Armand, age 5, at the steps of the family home in Caen, 1933

In a general way, Arlette and I got along well. From a tender age, she had the good fortune to wear eyeglasses, which served her as protection. "Don't hit me, you're going to break my glasses!" I champed at the bit, holding back the slaps she deserved for her teasing, and she took advantage of it, the little brat!

In 1924, our parents had wanted to have their house built on a cliff overlooking the racetrack meadow and the railroad line of Cherbourg. Cousin Kammer, a renowned Parisian architect, had offered his services to draw up the plans and follow the construction. In that way, he would have a reason to come see us more often.

It turned out that this kind suggestion was a bad idea. At a time when sand still cost less than lime, and the builder was more concerned with economical supplies than he was with strong materials, he went at it whole-heartedly, watched over from afar by this ephemeral Sunday architect, whom he never saw.

To avoid the costly removal of the earth by horse-drawn cartloads, my parents came up with the idea of having it deposited in piles in the angles of the yard, in order to form panoramic vantage points from which events beyond the wall could be seen.

The view of Branville Street was the most interesting, for it allowed one's eyes to follow the rare horse-drawn vehicles and truckloads of military surplus goods from the War of 1914-1918. These old rattletraps had balloon tires and four-wheel drives powered by heavy exterior chains linking gearwheels. In the cab, you could see roughly made levers and an enormous steering wheel, for the cab was door-less and open—no doubt to enable a quicker exit, in case of danger.

The coal delivery people, or those for the Brasserie nearby, were still using horse-drawn carriages. The manure was in dispute between the sparrows and some little neighbors using a short-handled brush to gather it for their garden. Not knowing Chinese customs, we pitied them a great deal. How could their father, Mickey, impose this humiliating task in front of all the neighbors? It seemed particularly awful to us.

Mickey was a nickname. He was a little fellow, dry and nervous, Traction Inspector at the SNCF, whose work was to check the conductors' application of the Security Regulations. Since he was very serious in his work, he was feared. When he wasn't busy "grilling" the agents on their misdemeanors, he was putting fire signals on the track, to simulate an incident. Then, having placed a red flag "full stop" signal at the prescribed distance, he would hide in a trench in order to observe the mechanic's behavior. When the train would stop, he would then leap like the devil himself from his hiding place. That was his starting point before examining the knowledge of the agent by the book.

The young fellows at the depot had quickly baptized this bounding being that caused them so many problems with the name "Mickey" and, so that he wasn't unaware of it, they had even contributed to order him a subscription to the children's newspaper of the same name. Since he was a little stingy, he didn't object—it was a free subscription for his kids. We used to profit from it also when we went to see them, preferably in his absence, for we were afraid of his loud voice, ordering them to do work. Which left us the choice to leave or to stay to help them.

Every morning, we used to see Father Lesomptier, an old man with a beautiful moustache, coming from Bas-Fleury with his horse-cart to sell his milk and cream. He dispensed his wares with calibrated measuring cups that he dipped into large aluminum tubs.

From our observation point, we would watch the year-round merchant lady coming by, pushing and huffing like a seal, with her heavy little vehicle loaded with fruits and vegetables. She weighed the newspaper-wrapped articles with a Roberval scale and old copper weights. She knew how to falsify the quantities in her favor, using its speed to her advantage.

We used to watch the fish lady who came on foot and was inclined to dispose of her most pungent wares in the wasteland at the foot of our wall. They attracted many large green flies from a distance, but also must have distanced the customer, setting serious doubts on the freshness of her product in the air!

The rabbit-skin vendors announced themselves with frightful trumpetings of give-away prices for the poor creatures' clothes, which they hung on bars across their shoulders, like so many trophies. Then they sold them to a secondhand dealer.

We had a few rabbits also, objects of the attentive care of my grandmother. When she found one plump enough, she knocked it out with a cudgeling behind the ears, before taking out an eye and catching the blood in a bowl where she had had the foresight to put a little vinegar, so that it would not clot. We attended these ritual murders in a state of the most profound indifference. Then she would cut off the paws, turn the skin out and fill it with hay so that it would dry stretched out, before selling it to one of those "ne'er-do-wells" with whom she would argue the price all the more bitterly, because the small coin was for my piggy bank.

Grandmom, the second wife of my grandfather, had brought up my Dad; I loved this grandmother no less than if she were my real Grandmom. She took care of the farmyard and the garden, and carried out many other tasks. She still wore the clothes of the past, which I sometimes saw her ironing—long, full black dresses and strange full pants, widely vented between the legs.

This allowed her to urinate out in the yard in a curious manner, like a man. She spread her legs, leaned forward a little, and lightly lifted her dress towards the front. Watch out for splashes!

Grandmom had large handkerchiefs with red and white squares, which she tinted with a brown juice when wiping her nose, for she took snuff. She had taught me how to extend my thumb to get a little indentation at its base, where she deposited a pinch of tobacco. This I breathed in alternately in each nostril, which was enough to loosen my brain when I sneezed. Best not to speak of it to Mom, who did not appreciate her ways and found them countrified and old-fashioned.

Grandmother used to play games with us: *Oie* [Goose],[*] dominoes and different card games. She loved to cook. She used to prepare the soup vegetables and, at the last moment, lift the pot lid to add, in a cloud of steam, some toasted croutons. She had an artistic knack of scraping the white of the Camembert without making the skin collapse. It was she who had to grind the coffee, holding the mill solidly between her knees; sometimes I would try to turn the handle, but not ever staying at it for long—it was too hard for me.

Before winter, she would hollow out a mysterious hole in the garden and fill it with straw, to protect the carrots from the frost. In other seasons, after a storm, I used to gather snails with her. She would leave them to fast in a flowerpot covered with a brick, before pitilessly purging them in coarse salt. They slavered copiously, and it was really disgusting to see Grandmom put her hands in to wash them before cooking them. We would then have a good time putting them back into their shells with herbed butter. Absolutely delicious, as I remember!

Sometimes, she engaged in war against the sparrows that stole the chicken feed, and if we succeeded in catching one in the chicken wire, we twisted its neck without remorse, before plucking it and frying it in black butter--a little treat for my dinner, but difficult to make more than four mouthfuls of it.

She would take us for walks, too. At the level crossing, we used to see the huge steam machines bearing down on us, smoke coming from the whole train. They were so heavy that the ground vibrated frightfully when they passed. With their enormous wheels, they followed the track—fortunately without jumping it—in spite of the small size of the fenders.

When they whistled past us, we noticed that the sound always changed after they had passed; it was the Doppler

---

[*] A board game of that era, played with counters.

effect without an explanation. When we had the luck to see a train brake, the rain of sparks amazed us.

Before the train went by, we would sometimes put one or two pins on the rail, and then retrieve them, completely crushed. We called those spears into service for decapitating flies.

When there were equestrian events, we would go to the racetrack, crossing the Orne River in the ferry *Chez Jehanne*. It was a rather big boat, with masts fitted with pulleys at the ends, running on a cable that crossed the river. When we got on board, the boatman took us to the other bank by pulling in stages on the rope stretched in an arc at the back of the boat.

We also used to go walking on the hillsides of the village called Allemagne, re-baptized Fleury-sur-Orne after the Great War. There we would slide and do somersaults on the grassy hillsides going down to the river. For this outing we borrowed the Avenue d'Harcourt, a road straight ahead at the end of our street. How this unknown road intrigued me, as it went beyond our familiar play area and I could see it end in a hillside straight ahead towards the sky!

Our Aunt Jeanne, who also lived at the house, was a former seamstress, tall and thin. She had a cataract, which, in those times, she dared not let them operate to remove. To keep her busy, Mom gave her old laundry to mend. Making herself useful, she did her best to sew them, which made them useless.

We loved her very much. She would tell stories tirelessly, with a consummate art—marvelous stories that we knew by heart but which we constantly asked for. If she omitted the least detail, we would protest; then we had to recall it ourselves.

Under the window of his room, Dad kept a bed of wallflowers, whose smell she loved. We shared her taste, as did all the bees in the neighborhood on sunny days.

When I was very small, I pulled a terrible trick on her. Since she had been careless enough to give in to my wish to go on the sidewalk in front of the house, I let go of her hand, to wander where I wanted. I shrewdly kept from answering her calls, to the point that she was about to faint from fright. It was the neighbor from across the way, Mother Saoulou, who, despite a frightful cross-eye and little twisted feet, succeeded in catching me. Then she gave my aunt a little lemon balm water on a sugar cube, to help her recover from her emotions. Cruelly, we would recount this scene in our singsong, childish way.

In her bedroom, we had thought up the idea of extending a rope between the window-bolt and the doorknob, using her bedside rug as a frail craft. Then we would slide on the waxed wooden floor, while hanging on the cord. Her little throw rug had become the *Chez Jehanne* ferry.

At Le Havre, our aunt still had some friends among her former business connections, from when she used to be a seamstress. Traditionally, once a year, we would drive her to the boat that crossed from the Seine Bay to Caen. It stopped almost opposite the present fish market and cleared through the turning bridges, doubling back to the canal. We could stay with the passengers on the boat, but had to get off five minutes before departure, when the captain blew on his terrible steam horn. This doleful and prolonged scream loosed a great plume of white smoke that struck me with terror. Maybe I was unconsciously afraid of taking off with the other passengers?

This old boat, the *Emile Deschamps*, was still fitted with paddlewheels hidden under the sides of the hull. It was rather short and its crossing of the Bay was often difficult for those travelers without sea legs. This poor vessel was to disappear heroically off of Dunkerque in 1940. It was never replaced.

The departure of my aunt towards this unknown world did not trouble me and did not conjure up any picture or imagining. One day she left by boat, and some time afterwards, we went to pick her up. She was seated in the same place, so had she really gotten off? However, she really must have left the ship, for she spoke of people we didn't know, she gave news of them, and never forgot to have some little treats for us in her big black travel bag.

One day, invited by our cousins, we had ourselves been to Le Havre to see the ship *Normandie* To avoid the possibility of getting seasick and spoiling the day, we had taken the train. I still see myself in a state of wonder at this boat, whose height and grandeur were spoken of by everyone. We were going along the quay at the foot of the gigantic cruise ship when suddenly I realized that it was actually in two pieces, with two different names, the one being the *Normandie*, but the other, *Ile de France*. I didn't hide my disappointment: "So only this one part was the *Normandie*? It seemed to me about the same size as the other transatlantic. "No big deal!" I said. Was it just a coincidence that our cousins, their Upper Normandy pride hurt, never invited us again?

At home, we shared our parents' room; on winter evenings we took a shovel-full of glowing coal from the fireplace to the stove, to light the Petit Godin, brand name for the little pan that kept our room warm. That would keep things from smoking while we lit still-green twigs with the ends of newspapers.

Arlette had a bed surrounded with metal bars, from which she could not escape. But curiously, it was mine--a folding affair--that they called the cage bed; however, when I was inside, I was not shut in at all.

After dinner, when we were in our little beds in the half-light of the bedroom, we were to await sleep without talking. During this time, the women were doing the dishes in the kitchen, while my father read the newspaper aloud to them.

Through the door, which we used to demand that they leave open for us, we heard with fright the recital of the scariest crimes of the day. In spite of the fear, I could not keep myself from listening until sleep came, followed by nightmares. An unhealthy curiosity prevented me from complaining about it. Perhaps, as a grown-up, would I also like going to see the criminals guillotined on St. Sauveur Square? Grandmom, who had once attended a capital execution in Le Havre, said that it was quite a sensation. She had stayed up all night so as to be well placed for viewing. I thought: "It's a good thing that he didn't get a last-minute pardon by the President of the Republic, or she would have stayed up all night for nothing!"

The newspaper arrived daily at the house, in a strange way. With a string, my grandmother attached the salad spinner to the guardrail of the kitchen window, letting it hang into the alley of the Coteaux. When she heard the merchant coming, she would pull on the cord and the newspaper was caught like a fish. It was *Le Matin*, whose Gothic-lettered title was difficult to read.

Every Friday we also received *Le Bonhomme Normand*, which always included an article in *patois* by Arthur Mary. My father read this with expertise; it was thus that I learned to speak in *patois,* the provincial dialect.

My Dad read with very good intonation because, from a very young age, he spent time during his school vacations playing the role of radio for his father, since the wireless had not yet been invented. For entire days, he was obliged to read flawlessly all sorts of serials: those of Alexandre Dumas, Eugène Sue, Zola and other novelists held in high esteem during that era. During that time, my Grandpop, seated at his tailor's table, made clothing. According to Grandmom, who helped him, he was very strict…and my Dad, at the beginning of every school vacation, would lose his voice.

In 1936, Arlette had to have her tonsils taken out. It was the fashion at the time, to fill the purse of the medical establishment. The eve of the surgery, they had taken a drop of blood from her earlobe, for the purpose of mysterious analyses; it was truly a traumatic event, necessitating at least two candies to stop her torrent of tears. Then my mother accompanied her to St. Martin Clinic, where she spent the night with her.

The next day, Dad drove me to see them. Arlette had already opened the box and was putting on the pearls that Madame Jérôme, a colleague of my father's, had given to her. I expressed my disappointment that she had left nothing for me. "Because you didn't have an operation," they told me. But I had never refused to let them take out my tonsils!

Faithful to their former supplier, my parents continued to have groceries delivered by the "Co-op" of St. Jean Street. Filling out the order, the boy was pointing carefully through the long list of articles with the help of a pencil that he rested on his right ear, where it stayed balanced perfectly. He took it from his ear, re-positioned it again and again, with a steady rhythm. I found this to be very practical, so for hours I tried imitating him, in front of the mirrored armoire in the bedroom--without ever succeeding. Poor kid, my parents wouldn't admit that they had made me in a rush, with pliable ears that stuck out too much to be able to hold a pencil.

They used to stock the boxes of Bouchon sugar cubes on the staircase of the first flight up. I happened to snitch a few cubes, not to eat, but to keep in reserve in my pocket, because I was afraid of running out. That made an odd syrup if my mother didn't check the contents of my apron before putting it in the wash.

Madame Alix came to the house every other Friday, to do the "big laundry." The laundry room became her reserved domain for the day, and I was not allowed in. I could only watch her carry the work out through the entry door, which she generally left open so that she wouldn't get too warm. There was a large cement tub where the laundry had to soak first, and a little tub of hot water on a tripod where she energetically rubbed things on a plank, with a brush called "dog tooth," whose name impressed me. Did it bite?

As soon as she arrived, she would light a low pan in a corner of the room, to heat up the laundry tub, at the bottom of which was located a twice-pierced disk, where she positioned a central chimney, with a sort of mushroom on top to wet the laundry that she arranged around it. I saw her add blue balls from a packet to the linens, so that the sheets would seem whiter, which really surprised me. I would wait impatiently for the hot water to boil up and take off again around the hat.   I was in awe of this thermodynamic phenomenon, which to me seemed inexplicable.

Madame Alix was a tall woman with very white hair. She always wore a blouse and decorated clogs, and a faded blue apron. She re-folded it conscientiously on itself, on the diagonal, so that she would not wet the kitchen table when, at 10 a.m., she came to have her snack.   She had extraordinarily clean hands, deeply lined with furrows made by the laundry water.   She kept her piece of Camembert firmly applied to her bread with her thumb, and the cheese bore its imprint. She no longer had incisors, so she trimmed each piece with a knife, in a very curious fashion, and only at the moment that it entered her mouth.   Grandmom would pour her coffee into a mustard jar, which held up to the heat without breaking.

My parents appreciated this courageous woman of integrity, who lived miserably with a sad individual, a construction worker more inclined to lift his elbow than his shovel.   It appeared that he got nasty after drinking; the expression was *avoir le vin mauvais* [literally "to have bad wine"]. I thought: "Why doesn't he drink Norman cider?"

One day, we had been obliged to go see her in her poor little shack, in the middle of work fields at the town limits. Father Alix was there, very proud of the home that he had built himself with wood "found" on job sites, doors and windows from "remodelings," walls of old 200-liter tar barrels opened and flattened. Without a doubt, the tar-coated cardboard roofing shifted a little when it rained hard--but then, that didn't happen every day.

We could only politely admire his abode, fashioned without an architect. I still see, on the earth-beaten floor, an old rotting piece of linoleum whose holes and floral motifs blended together.

Since the fellow was short and had made the hut to suit his size, Madame Alix always had to remain a little stooped, when she was inside. Without commenting, she listened to her lord and master as he showed us the home. But at our house, she confessed her terror on nights when there were strong winds, when she didn't believe that the sky was coming in, but, more likely, that the hut was descending on her head. She punctuated her tale with: "My sweet Jesus, if you knew!" For she had been piously brought up in an orphanage run by nuns, and relics of that time were with her still.

I would always remember that unusual visit to the home of our laundress; on our return, my parents pointed out to me that I was indeed fortunate not to have been born like their rascal of a son, in that poor home, which made ours, in its modesty, resemble a palace.

At that age, ignorant of all the laws of nature, I still believed that little boys were born in the cabbage patch and that little girls came from roses, so I had to agree that I had been damn lucky.

Yes, I was really lucky! But by the same token, my parents had gotten a really good deal with me!

CHAPTER II

CHILDHOOD

A superb red Calleville apple tree stood in the back of the yard. With an old linen rag, we would rub each fruit before consuming it, to make it shinier and more appetizing. Not all of them ripened. Beginning in the month of June, greenish apples began to fall; we used them for ammunition, to take potshots at each other.

Next to this tree there was a panoramic lookout over the path of the Côteaux, a small street that no one used. Mother Durand lived right across the way, behind a great green door where an occasional gossip would knock.

I must have been seven or eight years old when this simple observation gave rise to an amusing idea. If I hurled two or three apples in a row at the door, with a little pause between each, the neighbor lady, thinking she had a visitor, would come to open the door and would find the street perfectly deserted. Which would make her begin to doubt her auditory faculties.

This little trick worked delightfully for a good month; I would repeat it with equal satisfaction at various hours, and I heard her grousing each time she came to open up, without finding a living soul. Sometimes she would come out so quickly after the "knocks" that I suspected that she waited for hours behind the door.

Unfortunately, I had the bad idea of sharing my fun with some foolish little friends, who laughed loud enough for the victim to hear them. Perhaps they found it even more fun to put me on the spot?

This was an enlightenment for the old lady who, furious at having been fooled for such a long time, screamed into the empty street: "You little rascal, I'm going to tell your mother!" and, coupling action to words, she hurried towards the house. Thus kindly advised of her bad intentions, I took three minutes to prevent her from causing pain to my dear mother.

Our entrance door from the yard was fortunately equipped with an electric bell fed by the main circuit. Well before her arrival at her house, I had already cut off the current. She was, therefore, able to discharge all her anger on the doorbell button, which had become my accomplice.

I have to say that she never came back to complain. Her fury having spent itself, she might have decided that it was a really good joke, or thought that our electric connection was permanently defective. As for me, nothing remained but to discover other healthy distractions.

Since I saw illustrations of the war in Spain in the newspapers every day, they inevitably gave me ideas. I was able to get permission from my father to dig out a corner of the garden for a trench. I piled dirt up around the edges so that I didn't have to dig too deeply and, to add to the scene, I placed an over-turned wheelbarrow on top, to protect the soldiers from aerial dangers. An old stove-pipe, set on an incline and pointing out from the edge of the trench, resembled a cannon and served to observe the enemy, advancing unprotected but freely from the outside.

We fought each other fairly, with fistfuls of earth. I understood quickly that the soldier in the trench, although apparently protected, didn't have the advantage. In fact, to launch his projectiles on the enemy, he had to pull his body halfway out between the handles of the wheelbarrow, which was a handicap for firing and kept him from dodging the enemy's blows.

Generously, I offered the trench, the apparently choice place, to the little playmate who was visiting. We each had an equal quantity of ammunition. However, my missiles, made in advance, had cinders inside, to heighten the realism of the combat because, when they burst on the wheelbarrow, a really neat cloud of dust came up. The buddy in the trench, so happy to be protected from the ammunition, couldn't figure out why he was in a bath of cinders. And he had trouble reaching me because I was free to jump sideways at the right moment, to avoid his missile.

What was the most fun was to put two fighters in the trench at the same time; they thought they would be stronger, there being two of them, but in the size constraint of the hole, they were less effective, they got in each other's way and fought with each other!

Bear in mind that this game of skill was not clean at all. They would emerge with cinder-studded hair and dust-covered faces, especially when they broke a sweat under the sun and the ardor of combat.

I had to renew my combatants rather often, since their mothers did not appreciate this war realism for its true merit. However, they had nothing to complain about: They came back from war trenches in good shape, neither dead nor wounded...

Very close to the trench, Mr. Netzer, the contractor who had enlarged 126 Branville Street, had built a climbing frame for us, with a swing and a knotted cord. Although at that period of my life I had no paunch, my lack of muscle kept me from climbing very high. The swing, which quickly made me sick to my stomach, was not my favorite game either.

Arlette, being more athletic, was crazy about the swing. Since I wasn't always ready to push her, we thought one day of moving over a pile of metal where she could climb up and launch herself. Alas, in her climb, she hit the back of her head on the edge of the frame shaft with such violence that we thought she would become retarded and no longer the best pupil in her class. The future, happily, reassured us.

I, too, hurt myself one day, and it was all the more cruel because I couldn't complain. Since we were having painting done, Mama had temporarily set up her sewing machine in the cellar, warning me not to touch it. But why this restriction? The idea of using it would not have occurred to me. It was a big old Singer, activated by a pedal and set on a cast-iron stand worked in the latest style.

I wanted to place a finger under the needle to see if it was truly dangerous. Turning the wheel with the other hand, I very gently stuck the point of the needle into my finger. To my horror, when I wanted to take it out, there was no way to make it go backwards, and the needle had to go through my finger before it came out. Fortunately, it was not threaded. I heroically hid my pain and the finger did not become infected. I rarely disobeyed my mom, but in all my life I have never again touched a sewing machine.

Armand's mother Marthe; sister Arlette; grandmother Félicité, called Mémé; Armand, age 10; his father Laurent. (1938)

Certain parents complain about the bad company that their children keep, but when the opposite comes about, it's no trifling matter, either. Before building their single home, our parents lived in a little attic apartment at the end of rue St. Jean, with a view of the Alexander III Bridge. That's where they had met Titine and Mademoiselle Leduc.

We loved Titine, who came to share our Sunday meals. This poor old maid, who was an orphan raised very strictly by nuns, had been anti-establishment in her youth. They had made her do embroidery work, and on the dining room wall written in large upper case print was the saying of St. Augustine, "He who does not work does not eat!" She had completed it with a similar thought of her own invention: "He who does not eat, does not work!" The penalty for that were periods of fasting on her part. From that point on, she spent her whole life working there among the sisters, washing and rolling Ace bandages at the Clinic de la Miséricorde. When she found out that I was going into *sixième,*[*] she praised me as though I had been admitted to a post-high school institution, one of *les grandes écoles*.

On the other hand, we couldn't stand Mademoiselle Leduc, an old "dry nurse," who had worked for the upper middle class. She was very proud of having raised the sons of country squires and of a particular fat cheese merchant. To hear her, all lower nobility that they were, she had caused them to lead a hard life, blending more or less consciously a sadistic class struggle with a sincere belief in duty performed.

Without seeming to do so, she gave our parents hidden advice, which was tantamount to criticism of their casual, relaxed way of treating us. She set herself up as an authority having acquired professionalism on the job, to try to indoctrinate them with strong methods, which could have had terrible consequences for us.

In order that we too might benefit from her efforts, she had chosen to come spend every Thursday afternoon at the house, during our weekly time off from school. In nice weather, she would sit on the garden bench, knitting unending layettes for anonymous little ones.

Once, to try to get her to leave, I thought of peeing in a little bottle in which I had collected some red ants beforehand. Then I placed it all in the sun for a week, to

---

[*] Approximately sixth grade in the U.S.

ferment. The following Thursday, having wedged the bottle under her bench, I uncorked it from a distance, by pulling on a string. That afternoon, she definitely noticed that it smelt bad out there, but couldn't pinpoint the origin of the stench. And she stayed put, stoically. I thought that this old "dry nurse" had to be used to this odor already, since it had seeped into her entire professional life.   It was discouraging...

In contrast to most of the other veterans of the war of 1914-1918, my father never spoke of it; however, he had prolonged it by occupying the railways of the Ruhr.[*] He never took us to military parades, and his patriotism was limited to hanging the *tricolore* [the three -colored, blue, white and red French flag] from a second story window on July 14 and November 11, so that no one would take him for an anarchist.

Such was not the case of a close neighbor, Père Marion, an "old World War I French soldier to the bone," as my father called him. It must have been true, for they were called *poilus* [literally, "hairy ones"], and he had hair coming out through the holes in his nose and ears, to say nothing of his long moustache hairs, whose ends he twisted mechanically, pulling discretely so as to lengthen them a little. He would not have missed the least memorial event, sallying forth with a Basque beret decorated with regiment insignia, displaying proudly on his velvet jacket a fully equipped battery of decorations like a set of pots and pans. For those memorial occasions, he believed it necessary to bring all of these out of storage.

During retirement, he had somehow acquired the reputation of being a fine fisherman. We saw him spending almost every day in front of the house, with a collection of bamboo poles, a landing net and his campstool.

---

[*] The territory of the Ruhr, an affluent of the right bank of the Rhine River in Germany, was occupied by the French from 1923 to 1925, after non-compliance with the Treaty of Versailles.

Since I always greeted him politely and occasionally would listen for a long time to his glorious stories, he kindly proposed one day to let me in on the secrets of the art of angling. I gratefully agreed to go with him to the shores of his exploits. Generously, he sold me one of his used lines that he didn't know what to do with anymore, and we went together to the edge of the River Orne on the main avenue, to use our equipment.

It was scientific fishing that he was going to teach me--how to choose the bait, the float with its little feather, the weights that he would crush on the end of the line with his tobacco-stained teeth.

One also had to know about the depths. For this purpose he threw out a special weight with some fat attached. By sounding the waters, he then knew where the holes were located. He would observe the speed of the current, the agitation of the water, the direction and speed of the wind, the depth of cloud cover in the sky--all of which could more or less awaken the appetites of our future victims...

I quickly realized that I had fallen in with a famous professor whom even the fish must now know, and whom they had learned to be wary of, to the point of no longer letting themselves be taken. Which would explain the scarcity of his catches.

Sometimes, to boost his luck, he would visit a familiar hole the night before going fishing, and secretly bait it. Then he would place me right next to this prepared spot and, while I still got nothing, he would sometimes pull out one or two poor little creatures--just to show the superiority of master over pupil and to teach me the use of the disgorger.

While we would peacefully watch the floats follow the light current, my cruel companion would take the opportunity to describe to me terrible weaponry preparations at Verdun before the taking of the trenches by bayonet, and how they had to pull it out unhesitatingly, by giving the enemy a kick in the stomach, so that they could continue on with their bayonets.

Sometimes he had less bloody stories, like the one about the J.P.P. One day, a telegram had arrived at the front: "Immediately send J.P.P. to the barracks in Tarbes." There were a lot of boys, exposed to artillery hail, who were dreaming of other vistas. Twelve of them claimed to be J.P.P., and left immediately. Only upon arriving did they discover the meaning of J.P.P.: *juments présumés pleines* [mares presumed pregnant]. They were sent by return trip to the front line instead of being imprisoned.

When he had told me the same war stories several times, and given the same fishing advice (which was not de-populating the river), I thought that it was time for him to choose another pupil and for me to try my wings.

It came about that, the same day, I caught three perch, of course not at all up to the required size, and bony. They would have had the weak taste of river fish, had I not taken them to the neighborhood storm sewer outlet, where they could acquire that faint, indefinable flavor of cheap perfumed soap.

On this note of triumph, I re-sold all my equipment to another sucker, so as not to be tempted ever again to waste my time at what was for me a fruitless endeavor.

At home, Mom was doing written work for taxes. According to the time of year, the required tasks varied: There were documents to copy, update and calculate down to the centime, with scales printed on great cardboard sheets. Then she had to make out notices to taxpayers. What interested us in this work was that she had to transport the great bound tax registers by taxi, giving us the opportunity to go on an outing and to symbolically help in their handling.

We always called the same driver, Monsieur Lefebvre, who was very accommodating. He also helped carrying the books but, in contrast to his kindness, he had some violent and expeditious ways. He had shown us a regulation pistol that he kept in his car; he was a "Cross of Fire" partisan of Colonel de La Roque, ready to go out into the street with his firearm in his hand. We were duly impressed.

I will never forget that he was the origin of my "fortune," because he was always repeating to my father: "Oh, Monsieur Idrac, if I had ground around the house like yours, I would make garages!" The idea did not fall on deaf ears; it required only about ten years, until I grew up, to take root.

For my Holy Communion, I received the traditional gifts: From my grandmother, the durable rosary in its case and, from my parents, a superb Mass book on bible paper with gilded edge, and a soft leather cover with my initials etched in chrome-colored metal. My aunt had given me a wonderful silver cover engraved A. I., and Titine's gift was a special intention offering of Sainte Thérèse of the Infant Jesus, painted especially for me on parchment paper by a friend of hers who was a nun.

Among the other gifts, I remember that of my Uncle Emile: a bicycle pump and a repair kit. He was definitely not a religious person, so I couldn't expect pious gifts, but I loved my Uncle Emile. I had no other uncle and, moreover, he was my godfather.

Uncle Emile was tall, slightly stooped, no longer young, his nose like a pock-marked potato taking up half of his face, a face punctuated with a salt-and-pepper goatee in the style of Napoleon III. He hid his good heart under abrupt manners and a gruff voice--vestiges, no doubt, of his career as a policeman. There are occupations that leave an indelible mark. From that era also, he had retained the need for an impeccably clean appearance and meticulous habits of cleanliness, like the brave ritual of washing his bare torso in the morning, in every season of the year, at the outdoor water-pump. He lived in the country, on a poor fixed retirement income, raising rabbits and caring for his garden.

I keep the unforgettable memory of having once accompanied him, during the war, to sell his produce at the Saturday market on Place St. Patrice in Bayeux. I thought that was a lot of fun, and I would have loved commerce as a vocation.

During the war, my mother was not really aware of the danger while the English were firing on the locomotives and, every two weeks, she sent me to see Uncle Emile in Audrieu. I took two trains to go fetch a little butter and cream that he had been able to get for us. Usually he treated me to a steak as big as your hand, swimming in blackened butter.

He had become the local policeman appointed by the municipality and, to supplement his income, he had agreed to be the telegraph delivery person. At that time, the telephone was still rare and the post office poorly equipped for that purpose. They had simply provided him with a bell that would ring from the P.T.T. [*Poste, Télégraphe et Téléphone*]* whenever there was a letter to be delivered. Then he would jump into his old jalopy and set off speeding through the countryside, in all kinds of weather, for many kilometers. The most generous people never failed to thank him with a coin, while the penny-pinchers were happy enough to give him a glass of wine or cider.

One particular day, the luck of the messages had sent him out into the heart of the countryside, at the base of a valley lost in the farm of an old fellow whose home maintenance had been reduced to its simplest form. The chickens gathered up the crumbs and got rid of the flies within reach of their beaks. There was a pervading bitter odor in this room—an odor of fireplaces too immense to be cleaned well--and there was always a little fire glowing in the hearth, smoking and treating hams that were hidden in the stovepipe.

On the immense oak table framed with benches was enthroned the traditional carafe of "Calva" [Calvados]* and, next to it, a little footed glass, the measure for it.

---

* Today, *Poste, Télécommunications et Télédiffusion*: The French post office and expanded communication services.

* The very strong apple brandy made in Normandy.

--Hey, Father Emile, you're not going to leave without having a little glass?

--Oh, I can't refuse.

Besides, not accepting would have been an unforgivable insult.

But my uncle was torn between the pleasure of having a shot of "the hard stuff" before going back home, and his distaste for this unique glass that was not only chipped but of a cloudy appearance, bearing witness that it was never rinsed between visitors. But after all, he had fought in the war of '14 and knew that alcohol disinfects. Having taken hold of the notched side of the glass, he said to himself: "The others couldn't have drunk from this side."

And while he was swallowing his Calva, the old farmer looked at him with a strangely ironic gaze, and said: "Careful, Father Emile! You could cut yourself. I don't understand, you're drinking exactly like the mailman, from the chipped side."

With time my childhood memories have also curiously broken off. Certain ones live in my memory as clear as if I were seeing them, others are obscured as though in the fog of a dirty glass, and then there are all the others, like shards of shattered glass, of which no memories remain.

"Alcide," the beloved schoolmaster

CHAPTER III

SCHOOL DAYS

When I was around five years old, my parents sent me to the parish school, and at the end of the week, it was our *curé* [priest] himself who came to give the grades and pass out crosses to the best pupils. Since my mother had not yet decided to cut my very pretty hair, she put it up in curlers at night so that I would have beautiful English style curls. In that era when boys and girls were always in separate schools, the grapevine quickly carried the word that there was now a girl at the Priests' School.

When the Reverend Father Delamazure came to visit the school, he always distributed sugared almonds to the children--the same ones given out at baptism. With a little irony, he would replace the box's ribbon, so as to replenish my wardrobe with hair-ribbons. My father did not like this hairdo at all; perhaps he was afraid that it would lead me one day into aberrant ways? Rather quickly, my parents found a *modus vivendi:*[*] They opted for a Joan of Arc cut, which I kept until my Holy Communion.

Mama had already taught me the letters of the alphabet before I started school. I came to be assigned to the class of the terrible Mrs. Delalande, a stern war widow, very tall, very thin, with a chignon and steel blue eyes that saw every false move. She took to coughing fits and, at specific times, downed medicinal drops, which must have been very effective, because she gave off frightful grimaces of distaste.

I had to learn lists of words, and my mother made me recite them to the limit of her patience. One day, without understanding, I was spelling hesitatingly: *D...I...N...É, DÉJEUNER.* Well, the word for dinner had changed to lunch, but wasn't it still a meal? What was she complaining about? I gave more importance to substance than to form!

---

[*] Latin: [workable compromise].

The pupils were persuaded that the right to sweep the classroom, wipe the blackboard and take care of the stove in winter, were honorary privileges, almost rewards. Generous of spirit, I left them to share these favors among themselves. The long pipes that traversed the classroom contributed to the bad chimney draft; it smoked the room while warming it. The result was headaches and the bitter odor of coal mixed with unwashed children and the ink dye.

There were about forty of us in each class, in somber black aprons, seated on benches in front of inclined desktops, black also so as to show less soil. Knife-carvings showed up brightly. Below was a locker for books and notebooks. On the front of the desk was a small flat section with an elongated hollow for holding pencils, and a hole furnished with a white porcelain ink-holder, which the teacher filled himself with a long-spouted bottle, to avoid spills.

In May, we would gather June bugs, and sometimes would attach a little silk paper to them with a string; but most often, we simply freed them in the classroom through a discrete maneuver: We would open their box inside the desk, then remove the inkwell, creating a hole of light so that they could fly out whenever they wanted. Woe to the one who would take off when the teacher was passing by!

Once, when the windows were open and we had started to release the little critters, the teacher had all the windows shut--believing that then they couldn't get in, since he logically thought that they had come from outdoors. The result was the opposite, to our great delight.

How happy we were the first day that we were allowed to write in ink with a Sergent-Major pen. You could make spots, ink up the ends of your fingers, or draw a little head on each fingernail... And then, what a good defense method it was against physical punishment: It was enough to grasp the pen-holder firmly in your hand, protecting your face between folded arms, so that the teacher looked twice before giving out slaps. Nevertheless, when he told me that "*apercevoir* takes only one *p*, and here's one to remember it by," punctuated with a little clout, he taught me a life lesson. What could he have done for all the words in the dictionary?

Contrary to my mother, I loved chewing gum; she had tried to get a disgusted reaction from me by telling me that it was made from catgut. I was astonished that she believed such a story, which had no effect on me--I loved tripe. She didn't know that her opposition pushed me into finishing the pieces of gum that my friend Duval generously gave me after he had found most of the flavor gone.

I had made a little nest egg for myself in a hole in the wall at the back of the yard; this sometimes allowed me to buy gum for myself at the baker's, for I had found a ten-centime coin. This lady, Madame Zim-zim Baïla, didn't seem to hold it against me that I had made fun of her one day by repeating a joke read in the *Almanach Vermot.** I had asked her:

--Please, ma'am, do you have any stale bread?
--Of course, my little fellow.
--Too bad for you, ma'am, you should have sold it
    yesterday!

We were good customers, usually buying the large (more than four pound) loaf, twice-baked bread for soup, and the beautiful golden custard that Dad made a Sunday tradition of buying, to celebrate the Lord's Day.

At snack-time, I had a slice of buttered bread coated with finely grated chocolate. I envied my buddy Hébert, who ate bread with potted pork while striking sparks with his big spiked boots, which he used to rub on the sandstone blocks of the street. I longed to wear shoes with nails, too.

With my little shoes I would run along the granite edges of the sidewalk, taking care never to walk on the cracks, which would conjure up I didn't know what unfortunate fate. It's amusing to see that sometimes even adults practice this ritual.

Every two weeks, hoping to strengthen our intelligence, my mother would have me share with Arlette a

---

* Similar to the *Farmer's Almanac* in the U.S.

delicious sheep brain fried in black butter. She didn't realize the stupidity of this animal. So I was only an average pupil, favored by the importance given to punctuality and conduct grades. I would arrive on time and keep quiet, preferring to enjoy the uproar that others provoked rather than to let loose myself. My good behavior was rewarded when I was chosen to be in the choir.

I then came into the class of Mrs. Hergon, the wife of the Principal, a big-mouth who made her cry easily, which meant that she had to powder her nose in her little mirror, in front of all her pupils. She was sweet in spite of a very shrill voice when she was calling their son Henry, an awkward, not-very-bright lump of a youth who was one of us, and whom she called "Riri"--which was not to his liking.

Of one whole year of her teaching, I remember only her Natural Science lesson on the tapeworm that one could catch with poorly cooked pork or dirty hands. Without confiding to us how she had caught hers, it behooved her to explain in detail, aided by broad gestures, how she had gotten rid of it by leaning at just the right moment over a basin of water heated to 37° C.,[*] so that the head of the creature did not remain hooked to the inside of her gut. She had brought it to us, saved in a large jar, for our education and enlightenment. It presented itself under the form of a long pale, ringed ribbon, three meters in length. I found this disgusting.

The next year, I was in the Studies Certificate class taught by her husband, a humorless asthmatic who loved doing chemistry experiments. He must have been very knowledgeable, because he always knew how to explain why it never worked according to the book. He was also a visionary, already predicting everything that man would be able to make with plastic materials, in a time when we didn't even have the Bakelite pen bodies that were made later.

On Thursday afternoons, when there was no school, he didn't hesitate to give free shop lessons to the pupils who

---

[*] Fahrenheit = 9/5 Celsius + 32.

would come turn over his garden.   At the risk of disappointing him, I never went, having everything I needed at home, where my father gave me private lessons after he had turned over the earth by himself.

The Principal was not really a mean man, as proved by the unpleasant story of my incident with him. I was the darling of a young vicar of the parish who had said jokingly in the course of one of our walks together: "Your Principal is not Hergon; he should be called Hercon!"[*] It was clever and, since I thought it was funny, I had foolishly repeated it to a friend, who must have passed it on as far as interested ears would carry it.

Hergon summoned me to sign a paper where he had written: "In the Sacristy, before celebrating Mass, Abbey P. told me: 'Your Principal...'". He foolishly believed that, by modifying the context, the joke would appear to be a bigger sin. I refused emphatically to sign these inaccurate facts, and told my father about it. He went to convince the Principal, in other terms, that it was not in his interest to blow the affair up out of proportion, because he risked making himself appear more of a *con*.

The following year, he had transferred to another school.

The third semester traditionally ended with the awards ceremony. My father, who had pursued his studies at the state school of Le Havre, had collected many prizes-- superb books gilded on their spines and meticulously kept in the parlor library, from which they were never taken.

At the Catholic school, the books given by patrons were much more modest. If we nevertheless had many prizes, it was like the Palmes Académiques of Topaze[+]— awarded only for our morals, but tongue-in-cheek.

---

[*] This pronunciation of the second syllable would turn his name into an insult, similar to calling him a jackass.

[+] Topaze is the title and principal character in a 1928 comedy by Marcel Pagnol. He ridicules the honors (Palmes Académiques) accorded to certain elected officials.

So it was that on July 17, 1937, I, pupil of the first grouping of *troisième classe*,* carried off first prizes for: Politeness, Mental Number Work, Arithmetic, Geography, Good Appearance and Metric System; and second prizes for French History and Grammar. I was very disappointed to note that these eight prizes were reduced to only one skinny little book that was of no interest to me, and that my false crown of paper laurels was painted green only on the outside.

The schoolmasters took turns reading the repelling lists of pupils, enumerating the successes of each, finishing inevitably with "nominated ten times." The personalities invited to this solemn awards ceremony were seated in the first row, and gave out the prizes with the appropriate congratulations. The best pupils of each class were congratulated solemnly by the Curé of Vaucelles himself.

The parents, in their Sunday best, were puffed up with the successes of their offspring, and applauded louder when their own were named. Emotions high, like young puppies returning from their first hunt, the little ones brought their prizes back to the family so that they wouldn't get ruined, and so that Mother would congratulate and embrace them through the unpleasant hat veiling worn in those days.

I have always associated the idea of the prizes to that of a vast, dim room where it was very warm, while the sun was shining beautifully outdoors. To liven up this celebration in between the very proper prize announcements, there was some entertainment: One class might stage a small play, another would sing in chorus, yet another might execute a dance. Or we would benefit from a squeaky fiddle number by the pupils of Miss X, who was initiating them into the graceful Arts with private lessons paid as a supplement. It was a way of getting publicity. The preparation for these family shows had occupied the last relaxed weeks of the third semester, except for exams, with the stressed-out pupils taking both the Catholic and the public school Certificate exams.

---

* Approximately eighth grade in the U.S.

After I had passed these tests, my father had me enrolled in the Lycée Malherbe, where I was admitted after a qualifying exam. Since I came from Catholic school, the State could still question the value of my knowledge, despite my official diploma.

Since the time of the Napoleonic Empire, the impressive 18th century restored Abbey had been outfitted for the instruction of schoolchildren. I felt intimidated by the routine, the classrooms designated for certain subjects. As soon as the clattering bell--set off by the campus monitor-- would sound, the pupils would change rooms in joyous commotion. The girls' high school had been appropriated by the Germans, and the concept of co-education was still unthinkable, so we had classes only in the afternoon and the girls had classes in the morning.

I quickly made the acquaintance of colorful teachers, tagged with vivid last names, whose fame I already knew. So I had to take the math course of "Spring-foot," a veteran of the war of 1914-1918, fitted with an apparatus that was too short, made a grating noise, and obliged him to shift the weight on his hips with each step. If my name had begun with a Y, I would have been in the class of "Lice-beard" with the proliferating chain of hair lining his beard--but a much nicer teacher. In German, I was taught by a very fashionable adjunct who, when he was not using Goethe's language, was calling us by the formal *vous* [you] form, or *Monsieur*. At the age of eleven, we weren't used to that as yet.

Our after-lunch lethargy brought him to despair; I can still hear him in our 2:00 p.m. class, saying: "Gentlemen, in French, there are only two words to express the way you carry yourselves: Sprawling and Slumped. You understand me, don't you?" I myself was thinking, without daring to make the remark aloud, that taking into account our young age, only the first expression suited us.

The art classes were taken care of by Garrido, a painter known in Caen Square, famous for his Norman countryside scenes of cows lying under flowering apple trees. To us, he was "Totoche," without my ever knowing why. He had a way about him which he seemed to believe made him more like the artists of Montmartre. It seemed to me a little affected on his part.

For the watercolor course, he would place a jar on each table and fill it with water from a sprinkler-type watering can, so as to avoid spills. A naughty little character thought one day that he would lightly perforate the bottom of the jars. All the tables were flooded, and Totoche believed at first that he had poured to the side. But when he saw the extent of the mess, he guessed quickly—and didn't appreciate--this farce worthy of the so-called painters.

In the schoolyard, there was an extraordinary monitor, not taller than a small pupil, always in a light-colored raincoat, set off with a yellow felt hat. He had such dark-colored eyeglasses that he could see only between his cheeks and the lower edge of his glasses. This gave him a unique tilt to his head, as if he was looking at a perpetual eclipse. I knew only his nickname: « *Beau-citron-gobe-la-lune* » ["Beautiful-lemon-swallow-the-moon"].   He was harmless, perhaps blind.

Before my first Ancient History class with Father Lasnes, I already knew his reputation as a teacher who was ragged by his pupils, so I was very surprised at his stern air and his metal-framed eyeglasses. Next to the podium, the wall was decorated with a magnificent poster of the hills of Posilippo, with an umbrella pine tree in the foreground, and the Bay of Naples and Mount Vesuvius in the background. Looking at it and thinking about it must have given birth to my passion for Italy!

Although that classroom had a very high ceiling, it was adorned with a bunch of multicolored puppets hanging by a string attached to a ball of blotting paper. I really wondered how they could have fastened it up so high. I quickly learned the method, because the pupils were tirelessly completing their work. After having chewed the blotter for a long time and attached what was necessary, they would bend a ruler flat against the edge of the table--the spring-back did the rest. They deserved a lot of credit because chewing up a blotter full of ink really tastes bad.

Since this poor man was deaf, and us being of a pitiless age, when a pupil would raise his hand to ask permission to go to the bathroom, instead of using the ritual formula, the pupil would say: "Sir, may I go make out with your wife?" And when he would reply in his nasal voice, "No, wait a little, until your classmate comes back from there," general craziness broke out, and he couldn't understand why.

While he was lecturing and walking among the rows, we would blow sneezing powder at his back. As soon as he would begin to feel a tickling, he would change rows and threaten to write up the pupils who were disturbing the class with their sneezing. He must have thought that the guilty party would be somewhere in the group. I invented a display against this unfair punishment, the "anti-sneeze" mask, which consisted of putting a little shredded cotton in the nostrils. This efficacious ploy was in fact of little interest, because it was enough to fake a cold when going between classes, for the punishment to be cancelled.

I remember only one lesson from this class, a story of Greek frogs who were giving a concert. He sputtered so well while grimacing during the dictation of the notes, that it was unforgettable.   Much later, I felt emotional when I discovered a certain analogy with the Greek lesson in Fellini's "Amarcord."

The biggest troublemakers among us decided one day to order a layered pastry from several bakers in town, to deliver to the teacher's house at 11 a.m. Then, since we didn't have class in the morning, the imps hid not far from there, to enjoy the show. His wife had accepted the first cake with astonishment, but emphatically refused all the others, which enraged the delivery people.

We had a neighbor named Lamusse, a painter who made a poor living with his Art, along with his devoted sister who, in her youth, had even served as the model for his painting of the Immaculate Conception. He specialized in portraits by commission. When we had asked for one of my father, Lamusse used photographs as a guide, and asked our opinion on the resemblance.

We had to confess that it was not exactly a likeness, but he insisted that we be precise as to whether it was in the eyes, the forehead, the nose, the mouth or the chin, that modification was called for. No, taken separately everything seemed correct, it was only the total effect that wasn't right. The only way he could reassure us was by concluding: "You know, in the end, this portrait will be truer to reality than your memory of him!" The future proved him wrong, for we kept photographs, which were exact.

He was a true artist--far from material constraints, incapable of estimating the cost of his masterpieces, which were of infinite value in his eyes. "How would you have me bill you for the forty years that I have spent studying the human back?" he would say. We didn't ask, but he wouldn't have understood if we had suggested distributing his studies, and therefore their costs, over the entire group of his paintings. It was up to the customer himself to determine the price offer.

He proposed to give me free lessons in his workshop. Under overhead lighting, this large room was loaded with canvases placed in a disorder that was understood to the artist. In the lid of his color box, there was a blue 1,000-franc bill, affixed with push-pins. It was so well done that you would have thought you could detach it; for the first time, I was seeing a *trompe l'oeil* [optical illusion] painting. Maybe he also knew how to make counterfeit money?

He settled me before an easel, placed a Canson drawing paper on a cardboard box, and taught me the art of sharpening a piece of charcoal. He said to me: "My young friend," (this was the appellation with which he honored me) you must hold your charcoal like this, with three fingers, with such light pressure that the Master can, at any moment, pass behind you and remove it without feeling any resistance." Then, while still talking, he executed himself, with ease, what must have been the debut of my studies:

"First you will trace, with raised hand, horizontal, parallel lines, then at the next lesson we will go to the verticals, then to the oblique ones in one direction and in the other, after which we will attack curves. Finally, with raised hand, you will draw a perfect circumference where you will mark the center with your eye alone before measuring with the compass the precision of your estimate."

Discouraged by such a program, I never returned to have my second lesson. Perhaps it was a weeding-out process, which allowed him to recognize true future artists worthy of his instruction.

I liked art well enough, but I wanted instant results. So I went to the class of Sister Lefèvre, a Providence nun who was very unattractive and thick-lipped, but who painted well. She couldn't have used her own head as a model nor been able to teach nude painting, but she excelled at still-life watercolors or *gouache*, and could even teach accomplished painters in oil. I was content to paint on small pieces of cardboard, my pen dipped in wash. The Allied landing on Normandy's beaches cut short my promising beginnings on the bright path of the Fine Arts, to make of me, in a manner of speaking, an artist victim of war!

When school began in the fall of 1942, I had left the lycée to attend St. Joseph's. It was another world. We had classes all day, with daily testing on the lessons and numerous assignments. The system run by the Brothers of Christian Schools had a well-deserved, excellent reputation.

The brothers had profited from a less sectarian French State, and could again wear the three-cornered hat of their founder's time, and a strange black robe with a white bib and a pair of sleeves sewn open, which led to their disrespectful name among the people: the "four-armed Brothers." They were remarkable teachers, capable and dedicated. I owe them everything.

In each class we were taught under the far-reaching gaze of Marshall Pétain, which did not keep the administration from courageously adding to its teachers some members of the Resistance and men who were in hiding, to keep from going to Germany.

Since the premises of St. Joseph's institution had been requisitioned by the occupying army, different rooms in town had to be found. The home of the Sisters of St. Vincent de Paul, on rue de Bayeux, was chosen as base. It was far from our house and, since we no longer could get tires for the bicycles, I replaced the air chambers with old corks, in order to cover the distance. It was a rough ride on the paving stones, but the tires couldn't go flat!

For the first trimester, I had tried taking meals there, but the everyday fare was awful. We ate twelve to a table, in silence. For half of the meal, a reader had to impress us with the works of Jean de Larigaudie; it was edifying in the "totally boring" genre, and did not help us swallow the blood sausage with rutabaga or with Jerusalem artichokes.

To keep from dying of hunger, the kids from the country who lived at school kept secret reserves in their lockers: butter, jam, potted pork, eggs, etc. They renewed the supplies every two weeks, by going home to their dear parents. This gave rise to some traffic with the day pupils, who in exchange posted mail directly at the Post Office without going through the censure of the administration. It was a very serious offence, but difficult to detect.

The Principal was known under the nickname "Alcide," to the extent that certain parents called him "Brother Alcide." He was a wonderful man, gifted with an extraordinary memory. He knew all the pupils and their families by their first names, even after having seen them only once. He was capable of replacing an absent teacher at the drop of a hat, regardless of the class or subject.

At St. Joe's they attached more importance to math than to languages. So in English we had Brother Levante, who had lived in Great Britain without having acquired the least pedagogical aptitude. He was the only one who was really harassed by the kids.

One day, when the noise level was so high that you couldn't even hear yourself, he began to blow a whistle like ten city policemen, saying, "Oh, you like noise. I too can raise a ruckus!" A stupefied air of calm took over. Several moments later, the Principal was there, astonished to find a silent, dumbfounded class. The cause-effect was quickly established; we had found a new distraction: Whistle for the Principal, so that he would come take notice for himself that we were really well behaved.

The second year, Brother Cloarec, "Cloclo" to the pupils (after the character in the comedy *Jean de la lune*), was our main teacher. He had judged it necessary to personally give us an English supplement. It set out with "Practical Words Book," a book where the words were grouped by meaning, two columns per page. We had to learn a new column every day and review five others. He gave us a written quiz every morning, and woe to those who didn't know the words well enough. They had to restudy while walking in the schoolyard during recess. I have retained a huge vocabulary whose usage is limited by its lack of inflection!

In Italian, we had old Father Touchard. He had a South American, bronze head, very fashionable with the white tie knotted at his throat. He had invented a procedure that allowed him to teach any language. So at St. Pierre's, the girls' boarding school, he was under the watchful eye of a nun, whose presence would have prevented him from "picking up" the girls or telling them off-color jokes while he was teaching English. At St. Marie's, it was Spanish-- elsewhere, German.

His gimmick was simple. At the beginning of the year, he had his colleagues point out to him the good and the bad pupils, then he would give just the average grade to the best ones and a miserably failing grade of 2 or 3/20[*] to the others. Then, during the course of the year, all the grading would improve imperceptibly until the end of the last

---

[*]The French grading system is generally more difficult than in the U.S. It is based on 20, but a score of 19/20 or 20/20 is rarely given, and 10/20 could be considered acceptable.

trimester, when the "good" pupils would attain close to 20/20 and the "worst" just surpassed average. Everyone was satisfied with this progress. Of course, there were those who would go for the *baccalauréat (le bac)*[*] testing without understanding how they had earned their grades. Although the exams seemed like lotteries, the students had to catch up elsewhere to have a chance to hit the jackpot!

Father Touchard was replaced the following year by Marbot, a real Italian teacher, a priest-in-training who had attended the University of Pérouse. To get an idea of the level of his classes, he asked to examine several assignments from the preceding year. From the first records, the uselessness of the corrections, and thus of his predecessor, was obvious.

He was young, too nice, already ahead of the times, not wanting to impose any discipline nor to subject rebellious brains to instruction. So he established a *modus vivendi* [Latin: a way of allowing different attitudes to "live" together]: The pupils changed their seats for his class, those who wanted to listen to him going to the first rows, while the others could spend their time as they liked, in the back of the room. One day Guillemette, the oldest student in the section, undertook to give a sexology[+] lesson, which was not yet in the program. Being among the most studious of the students, I tried to follow the two lessons at the same time, but it wasn't easy to take simultaneous notes in the literary AND the scientific realms.

Marbot had made the mistake to confide to us that his young sister was named "Magalie." This pretty name from the south of France delighted us and, at the next written lesson, each of us wrote Magalie instead of his own first

---

[*] This is a month-long series of exams taken at the end of secondary school. The outcome determines whether the student will achieve free entrance to a university. Considerable extra study is required to pass the *bac*.

[+] France invented the field of sexology, and is currently the only country in the world offering a four-semester Master of Science degree that allows you to put the title on your résumé. (*France Today* 2002)

name. Not being able to match pupil to paper, he gave them all back with zeroes. But since he wasn't mean, he didn't record those grades, so that our averages wouldn't drop.

That particular year, we had Vigor in our class--a nice boy with wavy blond hair, which he cared for meticulously. How dumb-founded we were when, after Easter vacation, he showed up with an "egghead." The most curious among us finally got him to confess that his father had drunk too much at a wedding, and wrecked his haircut so badly that the only solution was to give him that sheep-shearing.

After the Liberation, we had "Put Put," a French teacher of Breton origin, which must have explained why for *entièrement* he said *entièrrément*, and for *Atlantique* he ate up the first *t* so that, to our great joy, it became *Alantique*. Since he had noticed all too well our mocking and snickering, he tried to correct himself.

It so happened that they were still setting off mines in the village. One day he wanted to make a point of pronouncing correctly a sentence that he must have carefully prepared in advance: « *Ils traversèrent entièrement l'Atlantique* ». He was answered with a double mine explosion so close-by that the windows actually shook. There was an outburst of general laughter and he couldn't help but laugh with us. But he never used those words again; they had unwittingly and unfortunately caused three deaths.

The Philosophy courses were entrusted to Abbey Louvel, St. Joseph's Chaplain and brother of the Minister, Mayor of Caen. He had a pleasing, lively personality. The day that we were attacking the unit on *La Mémoire*, he asked us by way of introduction to the topic to name for him the works of famous writers of memoirs. For the delight of my classmates, I deemed it well to point out to him *The Memoirs of an Ass [Donkey]* by the Countess of Ségur. But he knew how to turn the laughter around, saying, "That's fine for *you*, Idrac!"

I had other misfortunes with the English teacher. We had to translate Shakespeare's *Julius Caesar* from a text written in the language of that era, and couldn't always find the vocabulary in the dictionary. I had not read the play in French beforehand, and I had to translate the passage of the Ides of March, with his arm struck by burning lightning like twenty lit torches. Not easy to imagine when one has no idea what is happening.

After several hours of effort, I still hadn't come up with a correct reading, when my friend Friley came by. I told him my problems and asked for his help. Not being any better at it than I, he suggested an elegant solution: "Since it's Old English, you only have to translate it into Old French." Which I did, which was not appreciated for its true value. When the teacher informed me that he had given me a zero, I protested, saying that he had given me the same grade as though I had done nothing. He then suggested that if I was not satisfied, I could "take the door"--without telling me where to put it.

This English teacher, an old bachelor and not a brother at all, had imagined that education would take place by arousing curiosity. He would distribute English language magazines of the "Playboy" type, in an era when they were sold in France only "under an overcoat" to those over eighteen. The numerous and suggestive pictures were to augment our comprehension of the text and to help us acquire certain new, modern words. If this vocabulary was not strictly necessary for the *bac*, it could always help us one day or another in our lives, as another language... With the cartoons, whose cryptic balloons were often difficult to translate, we could have learned idiomatic expressions, giving the immediate veneer of an experienced linguist!

Nevertheless, he had shown a lack of judgment, for there were among us enough two-faced punks that Alcide quickly caught on. This original form of instruction hardly conformed to the spirit of the house where, outside of the Holy Virgin Mary, all women were nothing but sources of temptations and sin. It was Alcide himself who replaced this pedagogical method with a less pleasant but more classical one.

Finally, we arrived at the moment of truth: this famous *bac*. They passed only 25 per cent of the applicants at each of the sessions from June and September.   At St. Joe's, we succeeded in more than doubling these scores, thanks to our dedicated teachers and to the remedial courses during summer vacation.

In Caen, the *baccalauréat* was taken in different classes of the Malherbe High School.   There were candidates everywhere, including at the large marble tables of the former monks' dining hall.   The pupils were carefully spaced apart from each other.   There was strict protocol, identification cards before each student, the black folder with the copies glued shut until the last moment.   And the monitors who announced with a certain sadism: "You have no more than a quarter of an hour," or "No more than five minutes."

We had to write with ink pens; some candidates had even brought a second one in reserve.   Everybody used a bottle of Waterman ink to refill the rubber cartridge.   After the second part of the exam, the kids were letting off some steam, and broke their inkbottle on the white pedestal of the statue of Louis XIV dressed as a Roman emperor.   At that time, it decorated Marronniers Square in front of the lycée.

I have no memory of my exams.   I was so tense that I couldn't eat anything that day.   For questions from our courses, we could choose among three subjects and, since there was a little book, *The Annals of the Baccalauréat*, which gave all the tests of the previous years in all the Academics, I had succeeded statistically in finding at least one of the three.   I had focused on only ten or so questions in each subject.   Which avoided burdening my mind for final reviews.

I remember one very embarrassing question in the oral English exam: "Let's see, did you have a bad English teacher, or didn't you work?"   I thought it clever of me to answer modestly: "Oh, no sir, I had a good English teacher and I worked a lot all year, but I don't have a good ear."   I thought it better to play physically deficient rather than mentally weak. Thus I avoided a really bad grade.

GRADE EQUIVALENCIES

(French grades are based on 20 possible points; e.g.,14/20.)

FRANCE		U.S.A.
19, 20		A+
18, 17	"A" range: = excellent, very good	A
16		A⁻
15		B+
14, 13	"B" range: = good	B
12		B⁻
11		C+
10	"C" range: = average	C
9		C⁻
8, 7		D+
6	"D" range: = below average	D
5		D⁻
4, 3, 2, 1	"F" range: = failing	F

(Ghiglione & Pouchol 2003, 198)

CHAPTER IV

VACATIONS IN DOUVRES

In 1930, my mother had wanted an automobile, so that we could get to the seaside conveniently. Since my father was not tempted by the practice of this mechanical sport, they decided instead to acquire a house near the coast. So they began to frequent real estate agents, who took us around in the countryside in search of the ideal villa for the price of a car.

Monsieur Février ended up finding a house for them in Douvres, with two stories and a yard. It cost as much as a car, but included some important renovations. The heavy branch of the pear tree, which entered a ground-floor window and exited through the roof, bore witness to long abandonment. This charming pied-à-terre was three kilometers from Brèche Marais, the nearest beach. The glib tongue of the salesman had sealed the purchase. All we had to do was buy a beach cabana at Luc-sur-Mer, to accommodate mid-day picnics and to shelter us from the sudden downpours that occur there during any season of the year.

Our parents were good enough to push each of us in a baby stroller, so that our little legs wouldn't give out. Our energy was conserved for playing on the sand or running between the cabanas with Jean, in never-ending games of wolf. Arlette, being the youngest, was always the wolf, so that she could never catch us. When she got tired, she just stopped chasing, without letting us know, and we kept running erratically like cretins.

Jean, this childhood friend, was living for the season with his family at the house of a poor fisherman who had ensconced himself in a single room in the house. Luckily, this room looked out onto a courtyard shared with the bread and pastry shop on Grand'Rue. It was a privileged situation, and if we stayed just at the edge of the bake-house door, we could see bread baking and cakes being made. The shop assistant, just three or four years older than us, became a friend who could show off his superiority by grandly giving us, straight from the oven, cakes that were truly too burnt to be sold.

These carboniferous rejects seemed all the more delicious because of their clandestine nature, with regard to the boss. We were not like all the shop-hands, "fed up" with pastries, because we had not been subjected to the brain-washing inflicted by all the pastry chefs when each new apprentice would arrive: "You know, boy, here you can eat any cakes you want and as much as you can." Of course, the beginner stuffed himself during those first days, before becoming totally disgusted for life, and "cured" of consuming these delights.

On the beach, we would play ball, rings and croquet, and organize bass fishing parties. We knew which spots were good for getting periwinkles and mussels, and where we could push the long-handled shrimp net. We would seize crabs with our bare hands, using a special technique so as to avoid getting pinched.

We left it to the older people to deal with the octopi, who wanted only to flee inside a squirt of their own black ink. When the older people caught one, the tentacles would encircle their arms, and they had to kill it right away; then they had to beat the flesh against rocks to make it edible.

When the tide was at its lowest ebb, we would see skilled adults equipped with a large spear, looking for lobsters in holes in the rocks. Others would take a boat, to go on Quillot, a little island offshore of Luc, to look for velvet swimming crabs in the algae. You could also find *dormeurs*--big, heavy crabs who dug themselves into the sand, creating a small opening just for their eyes; it took an experienced human eye to find them.

I remember my surprise, while pulling shrimp from my net and putting them into my basket, at being called aside by a gentleman who wanted to know what I was going to do with those pretty little creatures. "Eat them, of course!" said I. He was horrified--no doubt a "fundamentalist" vegetarian.

The well-prepared fisherman was equipped with a clothespin to remove the little living sea creatures that found themselves caught in the net, for the small transparent fish are armed with triple, retractable, poisonous spikes at the back of the cranium. Getting "stuck" by them is very painful.

Fishing in *La Manche* [the English Channel].

During the tides around the time of autumn solstice, the sand eels were reproducing and digging themselves into the coarse sand of Ouistreham; you could search them out with a shovel. We couldn't find a pattern to explain why, but they would be either quite abundant or rare. I devoted myself to this "gardening" only if the other fishermen would come up with one before turning over ten shovelfuls. As soon as the sand eel came into the daylight, you had to catch it quickly, before it aimed its pointed nose into the sand, to disappear again.

Some friends had offered Arlette an original gift: an English admiral figure in full uniform and a Sioux tent. She settled the grouping on the walkway in front of the cabana and, seated next to it on a folding chair, tallied on a sheet the number of passers-by who remarked on this crazy exhibition. This was a warning notice that she would become an educational counselor—she was already inclined to put people through tests.

At noontime, we would get our main meal at the meat roaster's shop, situated on the seafront. I can still see my parents, pulling the cardboard containers out of the bag and setting them on the camping table--containers with slices of roast beef and the sauce that we unfailingly poured over them, and the bigger container with the fries. We would eat everything quickly, before it got cold.

The meal was complete with a box of Camembert. Its lid, to show the healthfulness of the product, pictured a bald monk himself holding a box of cheese with another monk on it, and I would look beyond the last, smaller monk to see if there could be found yet another monk and his box. This left me open-mouthed with wonder, reflecting on the infinity of the minuscule.

Traditionally, in the month of September, Aunt Suzanne, her mother and our cousin Mercedes came to spend two weeks' vacation at our house. It was a great occasion, marked by a thorough, general housecleaning. For their stay in Caen, we polished the silverware and waxed and polished the dining room, which was hardly used except for these two weeks.

In 1936, Mercedes took advantage of the outing to Douvres to have her hair cut and to have her first permanent wave, as fashion would have it, and as her grandmother forbade it. This aged authoritarian imposed her iron rule on the whole family. The affair had been carried out with my father as accomplice; with Mercedes staying at his house, he could protect her from her grandmother, who wouldn't have hesitated to slap her, although she had reached the age of majority.

I can still hear her screaming: "You'll become a true Girl of the Street! *Une Traînée!** I didn't understand this name-calling. It was evident that my cousin was a Girl, since she wore dresses, but I didn't understand how her short hair would keep her from moving along in the street, and why we would have to drag her as we did Arlette, when she didn't want to walk anymore.

I was not very old, but the memory of this little family drama remains with me, because I was unaccustomed to hearing our parents raise their voices. My father coldly put Mme Lebouteiller in her place; she had to limit herself to a purely verbal, brief correction of her granddaughter.

A few days after that, Aunt Suzanne took a memorable photograph of Mercedes with her new hairdo, between her nephews, with shrimp baskets slung over their shoulders. Arlette, whose eyeglasses they had removed, was squinting a little, and I stuck out my tongue. I stay immortalized as a bad funny person, which I no doubt have never ceased to be.

In the evening, we would come back from the sea so tired that we didn't have the strength to chirp. My father took advantage of this, and said, "We must have gotten the wrong ones at the beach; these children are really good!" That infuriated me, but I couldn't find enough strength to protest.

Mom and Dad, who had rested so well on deckchairs, would push our strollers bravely and effortlessly, while singing marching songs like "Halt there, halt there! The mountaineers are here!" on a road where there were hardly any automobiles, to say nothing of mountaineers. Unfortunately, the Road and Bridge Department always chose this sunny season to renew the road surface, and we were rolling in the fresh tar, which stuck everywhere. Our parents said: "Breathe in that good smell, it's healthy!" In those innocent times, it wasn't yet labeled "carcinogenic,"

---

* Slang for "slut," from *traîner,* "to drag along."

and the mysterious "magnifying glasses" of heating oil on the beaches were still just rare curiosities.

We could have made the trip by the train that served the coast of Luc at Courseulles after it left Douvres. But the distance between the house and the cabana from their respective train stations dampened interest in that transportation mode. Moreover, they weren't State railways, but trains from a private company that had been granted cast-off equipment recovered from the first railway systems.

There still were "Imperial" cars, whose open-sided upper level had a simple chain at the end of the open bench side, so as not to lose travelers en route. Unfortunately, I could never go up there; they were too afraid that I'd slip under the chain, or put out an eye with one of the tree branches lining the track, where only convoys passing by did the pruning.

Picture it: From those blackened benches, you disembarked smoked like ham knuckles, in no-longer-fresh clothes, shot with holes from specks of soot. But I've always loved the smell of this oily smoke mixed with steam, laced with T.I.A. [Traitement Intégral Armand]. This additive to the water was meant to prevent scaling of the locomotives' tubing, and had nothing to do with me personally, despite the name.

The regular cars without a central corridor had a pass-through going their whole length, and a door at either end. When we did ride the train, I loved following the path of the ticket-master, who would go from one car to another-- even when we were at top speed of 40 kilometers per hour-- opening and shutting the doors on the empty between-car spaces while holding onto the side-bars and punching one travelers' ticket after another, after another, without so much as a pause.

It was during this time that I declared that I wanted to be a railroad conductor when I grew up. My parents tried to dissuade me: "If you catch illegal travelers, you'll have problems with them; and if you don't catch them, your boss will give you problems or fire you! Why do you want to be a conductor?" I had just one answer: "To travel!" I still have that feeling today.

One day, to make our trip more fun, my father took off Arlette's ski cap, to pretend throwing it out one window and retrieving it through another. I was awe-struck and, before they could stop me, I repeated the trick. It didn't work. Strangely enough, they didn't scold me; Mom reproached Dad for having lost a hat, although his trick had worked really well.

The trains from Caen to the seaside usually left from St. Martin train station. Before giving the departure signal, the stationmaster would go to the top of the high staircase, to be sure that no one was running on the avenue with baggage. It was there that I rode the first authentic "Micheline," that bus with metal-cast tires that ran on rails, invented by Michelin, whose name served for years to improperly designate all the railcars of the SNCF.*

The green cars sported the flamboyant yellow *C. M.* bull's-eye for *Caen—Mer* [Caen to the Sea]. Once, in Mathieu, I heard a curious traveler ask the stationmaster the meaning of these letters. "That means *Cul Merdeux* [Dirty Rear End], he responded with a loud laugh. I was shocked: How could respectable grown-ups, and this one wearing a gold-decorated cap, use vulgarities that I naïvely thought were reserved for the schoolyard?

The single rail line from Caen to the sea had no signals; it used an economical security system of absolute efficiency—the "pilot staff." Between every two stations there was a single staff bearing the name of the stations, marking off this portion of the route. The mechanic had to have it in order to be able to leave the train station; so, it was certain that no convoy would be met on the track. If two trains in a row went in the same direction, an agent from the

---

* *Société Nationale des Chemins de Fer Français*: The French rail system, including but not limited to the *métro* [subway], its extended lines outside of the center of Paris, high-speed trains throughout France, and the Eurostar under the English Channel to London.

station down the track had to bring the staff back by bicycle to the up-track station. No doubt, that's why they invented the Automatic Block.

In summertime, a railway agreement with the *Caen-État* station allowed the last three cars of train 301 to be routed directly from Paris as far as Courseulles. The poor old machine that had to tow them puffed its lungs out pulling these long, modern vehicles, which gave off ear-splitting screeches on curves that hadn't been designed for them.

In Douvres, the second-floor apartment was our second home. It had been furnished with things from my paternal grandmother, brought from St. Romain de Colbosc when she had come to live with us in Caen. Every year, in autumn, she would spend a month back in St. Romain de Colbosc, to show her independence and to prove to herself that she could always retreat there if one day she no longer got along with her daughter-in-law—which fortunately never happened. She always came back loaded down with a bag of nuts, which she had gathered on "the property." We enjoyed nibbling on them in the wintertime.

It had been decided that the ground floor of the house would be rented out yearly. I can still see my father, lovingly lettering on the back of a dress box: "HOUSE FOR RENT." After affixing an official stamp that he dated and signed, he placed the sign prominently in a window. This proposal, advertised on a lightly frequented street, could have drawn crowds elsewhere, but was not a winning formula here. So, as soon as Mr. Dary introduced himself, he was greeted with relief, despite his five dirty, runny-nosed, ragged little ones, a large dog, and an unclear financial situation. My mother suffered on seeing the littlest kid drag itself on all fours to share the dog's soup near the kennel, and the yard took on the aspect of a gypsy camp.

This first, ill-suited renter was arrested by the gendarmes for having collected honey from the hives of a neighboring town, deserted on the occasion of their patron Saint's festival. What a scandal! And the embarrassment from the Press! Subsequently, we were happy to get rid of him rather quickly, without asking for any back rent.

Old Man Rousin succeeded him. He was retired from the horticultural field, and filled the yard with magnificent dahlias, their heads as big as dinner plates. Supposedly, he was well to do, because he had a motorcycle that could go 100 km. per hour, a Westminster chime that marked off the time without neglecting the quarter hours, and a radio set that crackled loudly, especially on stormy days. He invited us to come listen to it in his house, but we generally profited from it through the floor between the apartments. Because of the inadequate insulation, we shared his strange noises and sneezes; in spite of high blood pressure, he continued to take snuff.

Since we went to Douvres only in summertime, the house was not wired for electricity. In September, dinners under the gas lamp or by candlelight brought the family closer and prolonged the pleasure of cracking open the little green crabs called *enragés*, the fruits of the last tide. You had to count on a quarter of an hour to peel one properly without losing a scrap.

We ate only mussels that we had gathered ourselves, resisting the temptation of those proposed by Maxime, the town bum, who would holler into the street: "Here is the beautiful Luc mussel! Crab-free, crab-free! White as milk! Fat as lard! Crab-free, crab-free!"[*]

We spurned his offerings, not only because we knew that all the mussels--including ours--had crabs, but also because we had seen him urinate on his merchandise, to give the shellfish a false sheen of freshness.

We shopped for food at the grocery-café-tobacco shop at the end of the street. The shop was managed by Madame Catherine, whose husband had lost a leg at the Chemin des Dames, that particularly bloody strategic site

---

[*] Mussels gathered by the sea usually contain a small (2-3 mm in diameter) crab or two, living in symbiosis with the crab, but likely to break a tooth when eaten. Cultivated mussels are "crab-free."

during the final years of World War I. Madame Catherine was a strong woman, with an overflowing bosom and bright red, blotchy cheeks. That's where my father went to pick up his package of shag tobacco. We also bought coffee from her, ground to order in a huge machine with a large crank. The whole grinder filled an entire wall space in the little shop.

On the shelves behind the window, the candies in their jars drew us like flies. One contained pink sweets flavored with synthetic strawberry. You had to suck them without biting, or they would break like glass. When our parents said that we could have 100 grams, Madame Catherine dipped them out by the spoonful and weighed them like gold on her Roberval scale, before pouring them into a newspaper cornucopia.

A paned, double swinging door, one side always open, connected the shop to the heady odor of the tobacco stock, while the café room exuded the anise smell of Pernod[*] and the smoke of blue Gauloises.[+] Escaping from there also, amidst the clicking sounds of dominoes, were vulgarities that our parents would prefer that we didn't hear, although they were pronounced in the *patois* dialect by raucous and besotted, barely comprehensible voices. Our curiosity was definitely aroused; but then, we wanted to enlarge our vocabulary!

Marie Flo, a neighbor who had a knack for acting clueless, arrived at our house one night when we had just lit a triple candelabra. She then made this sententious remark: "If you had 36 candles, that would give you even more light." She must have heard somewhere the remark "to see 36 candles," and it had impressed her. She lavished affection on Arlette, who never made fun of her, and Marie Flo sometimes took her in the donkey-cart to milk her four cows.

---

[*] A popular *aperitif*, a before-dinner drink.
[+] A popular brand of French cigarettes.

I kept busy playing with Joseph and Ernest, who lived in the farm across from the house, where we went for milk, butter and eggs.   We would run through the countryside, and they taught me to make slingshots for hunting sparrows.   Actually, we hit the domestic animals more often than the birds, who were quicker and less tame.

On Sundays, I would watch them play Bouchonne. Each person would place a hole-punched ten-centime coin on a tall cork, and they took turns aiming small stones at this unstable stack.   Each player then gathered up the change that had fallen close to his own stone.   My parents would not allow me to participate in this "money game," so that I wouldn't later be tempted to gamble my fortune in the casinos... Very happy for this rule, I used it as an excuse not to play, because I knew that these experts would have delighted in stripping me quickly and making fun of the "city boy" who was less skillful than they.

I used to love harvest days.   The mechanical reaper would cut the ears, all assembled in sheaves with hemp rope. Then they were regrouped manually into stacks of five or six sheaves and taken up by pitchfork onto enormous carts, to be put into mills as big as houses.

The threshing was even more spectacular, with its steam-driven machine, heated with charcoal briquets, like real locomotives.   It came clambering up to the mills on wide steel wheels like those of the compressor rollers of the railways.   It was tied to the thresher by a drive belt, so dangerous that it was recommended to keep a good distance.

This "spectacle" unfolded successively in the different farms of the village, where all the men gathered to give a hand.   They would pass the sheaves to the farmer on top of the "Machine."   He would cut the rope quickly, to render the ears into a thin layer, in a cloud of dust so dense that his face, eyes protected by motorcycle goggles, was covered in a mask of earth.   While they rebuilt a mill of de-grained straw, a succession of carts drove the harvest towards the barns in sacks of 100 kilos, which a single man managed to carry.

Mid-morning and mid-afternoon, the women would arrive on the work path in a ramshackle cart, with jugs of cider and hefty snacks of bread spread with salted lard or embellished with cold pork—all to sustain these benevolent workers. For mid-day, they spread out a lavish meal. To get them going again, it ended with the *jambinette*, coffee laced with Calvados. You keep topping it off, but only with the powerfully strong apple brandy. At the end of the great table, when the master of the house closed up his folding knife with a rough sound, everyone understood the signal and got up and went back to work.

After harvest, I would attend the long plowings, where for entire days Old Delacour would accompany his two horses, broken in for this work. They had to walk in a very straight line; if they wandered even a little, he would scream at them and pelt them with dirt balls. He had a modern plow, with a double plowshare, which he tipped up at the end of the trench.

As soon as the "city" furnished drinkable water, we had a tap installed in the yard, so that we didn't have to go to the well that belonged to Eugene and his brother. They were two older fellows who lived across from us, in a room where the formerly chalk-white walls were now covered with a brownish deposit from the back-ups of the main fireplace, where a fire was always smoldering.

I see myself in this hovel with my father, pulling his hand, trying to get out as quickly as possible, it smelled so awful. Since he didn't seem to understand, I said to him: "Let's go out! Quick, let's leave. That stinks too much!" He tried discretely to shut me up. Their well was next to a smokehouse, which caused some upsets to the delicate constitutions of the city dwellers, not yet conditioned to a country environment.

We had "conveniences" at the far end of the south garden—probably to take advantage of more warmth from the winter sun. On nice days, there were mind-boggling swarms of blue-flies—so many that the large spiders couldn't eat them all. As soon as the throne cover was opened, an odor of pestilence emanated more violently, which was no enticement to linger to read the newspapers that were pre-cut into usable size. The seat itself consisted of movable planks, to allow the toilet to be easily lifted. You had to sit very carefully, so as not to pinch your backside between the planks.

I had to modify all that in 1969, when I transformed this old house full of childhood memories into two modern apartments. It was then that I discovered, caught in the lime between two stones sized to the keystone over the door, an 1822 Austrian coin, which allowed us to date the origin of the building's construction. Following an old tradition, they would place a coin from that year in the walls.

Under the outside stone staircase, we found a drain where the soil was covered with salvaged tombstones. Being practical, I kept them intact for the base of the heater.

When his wife died, the last renter went to live with his daughter, 100 meters from our place. He asked me, as a favor, to take care of the rabbits while I was working. This went on for some time before we noticed that he had hidden a liter of Calvados under the litter in the rabbit hutch, and that he was feeding himself when he fed the rabbits. This explained how this maverick standard-bearer in Douvres' municipal pipe band could still get drunk without money or cronies.

Madame Ch. had hardly arrived to inquire about the renting of one of the new apartments for her and her maid, when I was apprised of their strange story, unforgettable to everyone in the region. Madame, not being able to conceive, had come to an agreement with Monsieur. He would get the "full-time" maid with child, and they would raise it together.

When I met them, Monsieur had passed away a long time ago. Madame was penniless, but continued to live with the maid, Rosette, whom she still considered her devoted servant. But in reality, it was Madame who helped Rosette.

The collective son, Monsieur R., came every day to see his mothers, to whom he rendered double filial devotion. I had the occasion at one time or another to talk with him.

One day, he unwittingly almost made me burst out laughing. He confided to me that, at the end of a lengthy bout with kidney problems, he had just had an x-ray taken, and they found the cause of his troubles: He had three kidneys. Not surprising, with one father and two mothers...

In less than a half-century, Douvres has been totally transformed. In the 30's, this peaceful town was inhabited only by country folk; the peasants were still living by solar time, one hour earlier in summer than official time. They used to complain about the weather, but had found a reason for it. With their strongly accented, truncated syllables, they would say that the T.S.F. [*Télégraphie Sans Fils* = wireless radio] waves were to blame for altered weather patterns. On the Bretteville "Path," still not called "Road," the chickens would peck in tranquility under the surveillance of the roosters, scarcely bothered by the passage of the horses whose manure they were grazing.

Later, they paved the road and began connecting to city water, electricity and gas—in this two hundred year old town where mice nested in the clay walls, covered with glued-on plaques. The thatched roofs had not yet been completely replaced by factory tiles—*l'ardoise*, that wavy metal that rusts. I remember my astonishment when I saw that the farmhand bedded down on a straw pallet in the hayloft, so as to watch over the horses at night. Because that era pre-dated the automobile, residential construction still wasn't going on in Douvres, which could be considered too far from the sea. My parents, renovating their old shack, had been pioneers, so to speak. Subsequently, my own work there followed the natural evolution.

Today, it has become a small suburban city of Caen, in a sense; some light factories and small malls have even been added. New single homes and housing developments have gone up, old houses have been modernized. It's another world that the horses, and then the cows, have deserted. Some peasants have become rich selling their fields for new construction. With the automobile, everybody has wheels.

For me, therefore, only memories of my youth there remain. The children of yesterday have become parents and grandparents. Joseph is a widower. Ernest now strangely resembles his father; he has exactly the same voice, uses his characteristic facial expressions. In the front of his mouth, he's also missing three teeth and, like his father, he doesn't feel the need to have them replaced.

CHAPTER V

THE OCCUPATION

Television didn't exist as yet, only big radio receivers with tubes, complete with sound interference. We had no radio at home, so that we wouldn't be distracted from our studies. Newspapers were censored by the government, to keep the citizens from losing their sanity. Sometimes when an entire article was taken out, it left a big white space, but there was no price reduction—we could only imagine what it might have said.

In this beautiful month of May 1940, the news was not so great. Faced with the rapid advance of the German armies, we opposed them with "the elastic defense," an extraordinary war tactic, consisting of backing up constantly, so as to draw the enemy further from their bases and make them more vulnerable. It allowed us to surround them more easily, and to divide them into smaller sections.

This also explained the arrival of more and more refugees. When we began to receive those from the right bank of the Seine, and then they didn't want to remain in Normandy because they felt too exposed, preferring to continue towards the South, we began to question our position. Weren't we ourselves going to become the refugees of tomorrow?

Then, the following Sunday, the sky turned blacker than we had ever seen it, so black that we had to light the kitchen lamp at noontime. It was clouds without rain, clouds that dropped fine, greasy dust that stuck everywhere. Were we to become Sodom and Gomorrah? The Army had burned the oil reserves of Le Havre and Ouistreham, to cut off the feeding line for enemy advancement.

The next day, an old dirty soldier asked for civilian clothing, to go home to Thury Harcourt, south of Caen, and avoid being taken prisoner. Was he deserting? He left us his regulation gear: A cap, an empty water flask, and a pair of cartridges. He never came back. Had he been shot?

Pursuing the idea of strategic counter-moves, the SNCF had chartered a railcar to evacuate administrators and their families towards Brittany. We were allowed only one suitcase, but I had added a salad basket full of cherries, a souvenir from the garden. I asked my mother, "What will we do with the basket afterwards?" She answered, "We'll throw it out—it's not important." This answer was so at odds with the principles of economy enforced in our home that I anguished terribly over it. Had the situation become so desperate that we could abandon a salad basket that was still usable?

After an unbelievable trip with our railcar, avoiding bridges prematurely destroyed by the military engineers, we arrived in Avranches. There we saw an English convoy pass by; it appeared to be re-embarking from another site. At that moment, a German plane fired on it. This was the first time that I saw a Stuka with black crosses. The English hurried off into the low sides of the road.

Arlette, at the age of eight and a half, had been surprised by this unexpected baptism of fire, and was crying noisily. We took shelter in a little shack nearby, fearful of a new attack. Then, according to a solidly founded and efficacious maternal tradition, Mother wanted to have the little one urinate, to calm her childish fears, because "she had been so frightened." Except that the lavatory was at the far end of the yard--as much as to say in the line of fire--and, since there wasn't even a chamber-pot, she had to accomplish this in an unforgettable blue-flowered salad bowl, left on the table since the mid-day meal. The plane didn't come back, the English left, and so did we, in search of lodging for the night.

It was Madame Micoin-Saint-Saëns, the grand niece of the great composer, who agreed to keep us. She must have thought us quite clean and polite, and preferable to some strangers that the mayor could have officially imposed on her, in the big house where she lived alone.

We were on the lookout for all the news, more or less contradictory as it was.   It seemed established that old Marshal Pétain had been charged with signing the Armistice, and that a rebel General [de Gaulle] was calling for a continuation of the war from England, where he was inviting them to join in.   This risked the displeasure of the Germans, who perhaps would still like to cut off little boys' right hands so that they couldn't shoot a rifle later.   They were saying that some forward-looking Prussians might have done that during the War of 1870.   I started to look warily at my own right hand, not knowing how to hide it.

Rumor now had it that the enemies were already in Rennes, and were going to occupy all of France.   Therefore, it was useless to continue westward, so the autorail simply took us back to Caen.

The house had not been looted, and in town we didn't find much that was different.   I saw my first two Germans in a motorcycle with sidecar, wearing funny brimless headgear and the large *Feld-grau* ["battlefield gray"] raincoats, which must have made them sweat.   The *Kommandantur* [Headquarters] had already been moved into the Hotel Malherbe, the biggest and the best in the city.   From its façade hung two large, vertical red flags embellished in their centers with the famous *Swastika*.   On the city walls, they had just pasted yellow, bilingual posters, dictating the orders of the occupying army.

To begin with, it was required to turn in all arms, under penalty of being shot.   Since the Germans were well organized, and since they wanted to see how we were accepting them, they had taught the soldiers the question to ask methodically in each house in the city: *Havez-vous des Harmes* ?   [Do you have any arms]?

Alas, the pronunciation left something to be desired, and Bousset, a poor old gentleman living across from us, somehow thought he should answer yes, so as not to upset the soldier.   No one had yet taught him how to deal with the question.   My father, who had occupied the Ruhr in 1919, explained that the old man was a little deaf and not too bright.   Fortunately for Father Bousset, the affair went no further.

I then learned that we ourselves had a small-cylinder revolver in the house.   It was out of the question to turn it over to the enemy; we were not going to contribute to their arms!   Dad wrapped it in a greasy rag before placing it in one of those old cylindrical sugar boxes, which served so many purposes.   He then hid it under the great pile of coal, generously bought a month earlier, to help our coal vendor move his stock.   This fortunate move would provide us with some warmth during the whole war.

At that time, we used to go daily to the neighborhood grocery for fresh milk, which we brought back in an aluminum can.   The can was fitted with a handle allowing it to be turned in a vertical plane, so that, with the help of centrifugal force, the milk miraculously did not spill.   That day, in the shop, there was a superb German officer in bouffant culottes and high cap, rendered even more imposing because he was buying beautiful peaches.   Very kindly, he offered a splendid one to my sister.   Since, despite his insistence, she continued to refuse it, the grocer made her accept it.   "It's offered so nicely!" he said.   Perhaps the officer was a father who would have enjoyed giving it to his own daughter...

I can still picture Arlette, that good little woman, furious that she had been forced to take the fruit.   Hardly had she cleared the front of the store, when she threw the peach to the ground, saying: "For sure it's poisoned, a German gave it to me."   Since I already had a practical mind and was without prejudice against the grocery's peaches, I hurried to devour it.

Then my parents, to teach me a lesson and underscore the heroic refusal of the food-loving little girl, started to agree that the fruit had to be poisoned.   As I began gradually to believe them—for they usually didn't lie to me—I turned whiter and whiter shades of pale.   They themselves had to call a halt to their bad joke, which would have ended with me really getting sick, and perhaps dying by way of power of suggestion!

But this "good" time was not to last; soon we had ration coupons, which were replaced by all sorts of combinations. I learned with astonishment how a grocer "watered down" milk, while this product seemed to me already quite naturally watery. They also said that boxes of sugar pieces were no longer ever full. When I remarked on it to the grocer lady, she explained learnedly—to hide her theft—that this foodstuff commodity had become so precious that the manufacturers were now weighing the packets one by one. I thought that it must have been quite a job for them!

Sometimes, we learned that with the "TZ" or "XY" ticket, you could get something, such as pasta or jam. We always bought it, even if we didn't need it right away, because we could eventually use it. I still remember the extraordinary sensation when my mother brought home a bowl that I believed full of fruit sauce. I dipped my index finger all the way in before noticing with horror that it was hot mustard.

There were secret exchanges, such as when we gave our tobacco tickets to a peasant friend who gave us wheat to feed our chickens. Then I took the hen's eggs to school and exchanged them for sugar. Shoes, clothing, all merchandise was difficult to obtain. It was the era when one found shoes at the butcher shop, as well as sausages at the shoemaker's. The important thing was to know the right address and have an exchange coupon.

The authorities dealt severely with anyone caught dealing in the black market, where you could get whatever you wanted for a higher price. We never bought anything on the black market, out of moral principles; besides, we didn't have much money! Poverty kept us honest!

For something special, sometimes we made crepes. We had to grind up the grain in a coffee grinder, which got more and more stubborn. Usually, we decided not to sift the flour, so that it made more. We still had to crush chunks of sugar on a board with a bottle because, for some unknown reason, our poor rations were always supplied in pieces. Then we got the idea of depositing the sugar on the crepe following a line, which served as the axis for rolling it. This was the best way to be sure of finding a little in each mouthful.

Everything we bought was taxed. The nice farmer neighbors from the house in Douvres agreed to sell us potatoes, but we had to go get them. On each trip, Mom brought back a filled baby carriage on foot, to avoid being taken by the economic control.

And I, each time that I would go to see my friend François Le Roy-Ladurie in Montiers -en-Cinglais, would always bring back a little butter and cream that they sold us at the cost of the tax—but it was a long trip by bicycle!

For Arlette's Holy Communion, in order to organize—despite everything—a family get-together, my mother had raised a sheep with her coffee tickets. That is, for six months, she gave her coffee tickets to the Mayor of Ifs, who, on the given date, supplied her with a sheep. Imagine the party for all those bellies starved for meat.

Unfortunately, nothing could be kept; freezing was not yet available to the public. Therefore, Mom suggested sharing the meat to a discrete neighbor, the mother of a large family. The neighbor refused because she had just returned from Brittany after the death of her mother-in-law, and suddenly having meat would have suggested the unthinkable to the imagination.

At that time, we were like the majority of the French—partisans of Marshal Pétain, whose personality cult had been carefully developed. Was he not our only defense against the occupying Army? His photographs on post cards had been widely distributed. His portrait on posters decorated every official place and even every classroom. Was it not he who had them distribute to us, at each recess, vitamin-enriched casein cakes? I didn't like them, and re-sold them to my friends so that I could buy saccharin ice creams from Gomez's cart, at the end of the main courtyard. *A chacun son goût!* [To each his own!]

For several months, my friend François' father had been Minister of Agriculture in Vichy, long enough for him to take a very popular measure: He gave a pound of bread per day to the farmers, on the premise that those who were producing the wheat ought not to be without it.   This measure was, as so many others, a smokescreen. It was obvious that the peasants had always secretly furnished wheat to their baker, who was freely giving them bread.

Beyond bread and other necessities of life, everything was in short supply, leading to some bizarre measures. Workers pulled old nails from buildings, to straighten and reuse them.   For ammunition, the Germans salvaged every bronze statue, with one exception that I learned of: the equestrian statue of Napoleon Bonaparte, pointing a scornful finger across the Channel towards England.

The Germans had requisitioned houses to move into. Downtown, they could be seen parading impeccably, while singing the famous « Aï! Aio ! » Their Supply Corps moved along in humble, common horse-drawn carts.   They had strange tanks, whose sides were narrower at the bottom than on top, and they were equipped with four wheels, of which the first two pivoted, but the two poor nags pulling them seemed more fit for the farm than the conquering Army.

To "protect" us, big projectors and batteries of German anti-aircraft defense were positioned on the city's high points. The alert sirens sounded three sinister roars to announce the arrival of the planes of the "enemies," our allies of yesterday. We would have had to go to the public shelters, with white paint on the outside doors specifying the number of persons they could hold. Since we didn't live downtown, we stayed at home when the sirens sounded.

By day, we counted the planes passing, and we saw them framed by lightning bolts followed by little black clouds, the firings of the German anti-aircraft defense. A moment afterwards, we would hear the explosions, which reverberated in scattered fashion on the rooftops and flooring. It was no time to be out in the yard. Like other children, I hurried out afterwards to gather up these still-burning war souvenirs, which I have kept ever since.

By night, the passage of the planes assured another spectacle: The enormous parallel beam projectors striped the sky with giant, luminous paintbrushes, seeking targets among the clouds. Woe to anyone found in their rays. All the artillery would open—a real fireworks display, with streaming explosions and ricocheting bullets, a Fourteenth of July* complete with firecrackers. Curiosity and our lack of experience allowed us to brave out this dangerous show.

Later, we would see hundreds of flying fortresses—the big bombers--surveying us at 30,000 feet, leaving white condensation trails. Sometimes the *Flag* (German aircraft defense) greeted them with ineffective cannon bursts. They held to their perfect straight-line formation, going further on to drop the bombs.

Sometimes the Allied bombers dropped pamphlets that we were obliged to deliver to the *Kommandantur* without reading them. Of course, we did the opposite. The Americans sent us little newspapers in A4 format [8½"x 11"], folded in half. The English sent sheets of paper covered very closely with tiny lettering. Knowing nothing of the printing process, I marveled at how printers could be so skillful as to assemble such minuscule characters.

They also dropped odd little bands of paper, metallic on one side and black on the other. All sorts of stories circulated about them--they could have been secret messages that special ink would have revealed. Some people tried unsuccessfully to boil them. We had no way of knowing that their function was more prosaic—to interfere with radar images, the very existence of which was unknown to us.

Only at the time of Liberation did I see the remains of gigantic radar stations in Douvres in the *blockhaus*,+ and the

---

* The anniversary of the storming of the Bastille, French Independence Day.

+ One of the small, defensible buildings that the Germans built, partially in the ground, for defense and as a firing point for their soldiers.

recovery of drawers of electronic material; but the Germans had carefully destroyed the transformers with their revolver shots, before turning them over.

No doubt to avoid awakening suspicions as to the landing site, Caen had been lightly bombed during the occupation, so that when we—for reasons unclear to me— decided to go visit Rouen, we were upset to see the state of destruction of the heart of the city, where the spires of the cathedral stood out. That was our first contact with a badly damaged city, and we had but one wish: to return home as quickly as possible. But we had to wait the whole day, in anguish, for the only evening train.

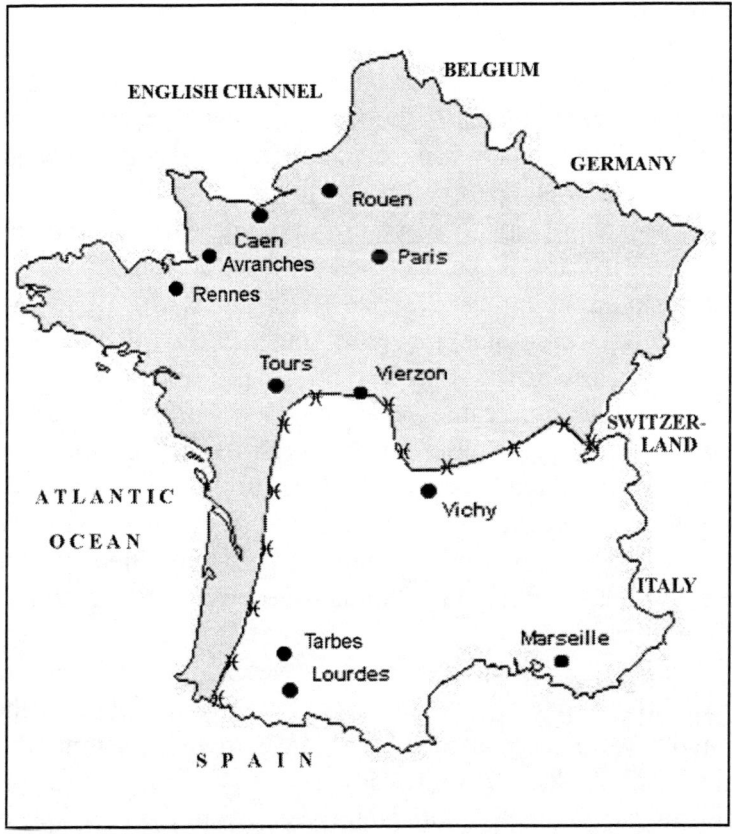

France, 1942, showing the demarcation line between the occupied zone (gray) to the north and the free zone to the south.

On another occasion, despite everything, we wanted to make a pilgrimage to Lourdes. This was no better an idea. Around midnight, a while before arriving at the demarcation line of Vierzon* and entering the free zone, our tickets were checked on the train by a German policeman. We learned that we should have had a date stamp put on our card, at the police station. The policeman made us get off the train, and abandoned us on the platform. After having vainly tried to procure this date stamp at the window of the police station— closed, of course, at this hour of the night—we finished the night in the station waiting room. There, in the early morning, an accommodating railroad worker authorized our cards with a false stamp, allowing us to continue en route to our devotions. The Holy Virgin took pity on us.

A certain Resistance had been organized, especially after the denunciation of the German-Soviet pact. Up to then, the Communists had been rather partisan [devoted to their Communist party], like Thorès who deserted, or Marchais, who went to work in Germany. After Germany invaded Russia and the pact was denounced, they received orders to join in the French Resistance, in hopes of establishing Communist power in France at the Liberation.

To avoid sabotage of the rail lines and telecommunication cables that the Germans had installed along the tracks, the cities had to organize "swing shifts" so that security-cleared men could keep night watch over the lines after their day work. If it came to it, the Resistants had to take them along, or tie them up and gag them before carrying out their sabotage, so that they wouldn't be shot as accomplices.

In the daylight, planes were machine-gunning locomotives, to reduce depot hauling. For defense, the convoys were accompanied by a flatcar fitted with four twin tubes of small, 20 mm cannons. We could see the unfortunate soldiers, numb from the cold and the high speed,

---

* See map, page 69.

looking for the enemy in the sky—the enemy ready to swoop down on them, the enemy that they were obliged to fight.

The mechanics had a cruel choice—either join the underground and leave their families without means of support, or continue to serve as a target. To reassure them, they had been provided with several sheets of metal plating on the back of the cab, which protected them in theory. Some were scalded by the locomotive boiler when it was pierced by bullets. On the station wall was posted the long list of the region's railroad workers who had been killed on the job.

To prevent sabotage of trains bearing their soldiers on leave, the Germans thought of adding a car of French officials just behind the engine. The officials had been offered a free round trip ticket beyond the Rhine, but the short duration of these impromptu tourist trips did not make them popular. Most often, they were the occasion of fortifying drinking sessions, dulling the thoughts of danger.

Offers of employment in Germany in the factories, under pretext of contributing to freeing prisoners of war, had little success, and resulted in some young people joining the underground Resistance.

The railroad men who worked in the marshalling yard or at refilling bomb holes found sugar rolls in concrete, planted here and there between the rails; these provided brief respite.

In the marshalling yards, resistant railroad workers were completing special boxes with sand, for the railroad cars—boxes which, after rolling along for a moment, would become red-hot and set off breakage of the axle, derailing the train.

To head off clandestine landings, the Germans had planted "Rommel asparagus" in the fields. Imagine pyramids made of three staddles, or platform foundations, joined at their heads and tied together at the base, and on which unfortunate citizens trying to position themselves in the grass to free spies or rescue Allied pilots, would be wiped out.   Later, in the harvest season, the practical peasants would dry their grain there.

Gradually, the town was embellished with strategically placed blockhouses, awaiting only the necessary arms.   Located a distance apart in the soil, scooped-out hollows for land mines lay ready for the propitious moment. On certain streets, enormous metallic doors were erected to stop the tanks in their tracks.

It was generally during the milkman's hour that plainclothes police in raincoats and soft hats discretely gathered up the Resistants and the Jews in their homes. They were taken away in black front-wheel drive automobiles.   That's how we saw them take the militant Communist who lived very close to us.

As so many others, we also had our Jewish person to hide, but we had to return her rather quickly to those who had entrusted her to us, because she couldn't remain quiet and out of sight.   She insisted on walking in the daytime in the garden, where she was visible from the apartment building next door.

Armand, age 14, Nov. 1942

We were never decorated for that heroic deed, and I was still too young to be part of the Resistance and too pacifist to be tempted by it.   But I did help a friend who wanted to enter the Movement, by giving him the famous barrel pistol, which he fortunately never had to use, because the barrel—which my Dad must never have greased—was so rusted that it just might have blown off his hand if he had fired it.

The occupying soldiers knew that, despite their ban and the risks, everyone was listening to the BBC [British Broadcasting Company], to access reliable news and to catch the mysterious personal messages. The messages included announcements of parachute drops of equipment for the different underground branches. It ended with them confiscating all the radio sets in our region, ordering that they be deposited in the town halls. The only radios kept belonged to cheats who had not previously declared their radios, so as not to pay the tax. They risked deportation.

I remember a rebellious citizen who, so that his radio would no longer be usable, had attached it to a leash and pulled it on a sidewalk before turning it over to the Special Service in the city. Mademoiselle Fumichon, Arlette's teacher, had recently acquired a superb set, in order to hear the English better, but since it had been declared, she found herself obliged to turn it over. Luckily, I had assembled an old set in a crate at the beginning of the century, which I gave her to declare as a substitution. That's how hers was spared from the fire in city hall, where all the others went up in flame the evening of June 6, 1944.

BBC broadcasts were received on several different short wave frequencies. Generally one among them--never the same--had less interference than the others. That was the one that the Germans wanted to hear.

It was "Radio Paris" which informed us of the tentative landing in Dieppe. This time it was for real, but the English had been effectively put back to sea, with furor and great losses.

Later, I met a French-speaking Canadian who had lost his sergeant's stripes. He was in the second wave and, seeing the fate of friends who had preceded him, responded to the English officer who still wanted to land: "Well, buddy, if you want to, go right ahead." And after having put this courageous but foolhardy officer over the side, he executed a half-turn with their boat. Later, he was only put in prison and de-commissioned; they needed men too badly to relish shooting him.

Life became increasingly difficult with the passage of time, whether in obtaining the necessities or in relations with the occupying army. There was more and more talk of Resistants being shot, imprisoned or deported. The situation had come to a head, and there seemed no way out other than an Allied invasion. Although we were only fourteen years old, my friend François Le Roy-Ladurie and I tried a little strategizing: This fervently-wished-for landing, where could it take place? After the failure in northern France, where the coastline had to be particularly well defended by the Germans, what remained across from England? Le Contentin was too narrow. Brittany, a little wider, was nevertheless too far to provide a battlefield. Our mutual conclusion was not at all optimistic: It seemed obvious that Calvados had all the pre-requisites for becoming the site of heroism.

During the course of one of these conversations, I confessed to François that we had no place to take refuge. Without hesitation he said, "In that case, you'll come to our place in Villeray." When the landing came about where François and I had predicted—very close to home--my father was no longer living. He had died of a heart attack in 1942. There was an unspoken agreement that my distraught mother would look to me to protect her and my little sister, so it was my decision to leave our home in Caen and seek refuge. I never forgot François' words, and we did eventually present ourselves at the Château. There we were welcomed with open arms, to spend with them those unforgettable days from the Landing to the Liberation.

CHAPTER VI

THE LANDING

At La Bagotière, the German soldiers had hung branches of lime trees to camouflage their trucks and tanks. The drying leaves gave off a bitter smell that I still recognize among all other scents. After so many years, imagine remembering that odor, mixed with the lingering smell of battle powder and the sweat of exhausted men. Then move to the picture of the men covered with ochre-colored dust from the gutted paths.

For me, the perfume of the dying foliage is all that. All that and much more, from the first day of the landing, June 6, 1944, when the roaring of the Navy artillery had begun at dawn, like a gigantic and distant storm. Could this really be The Landing? The joy and the agony, were they indeed meant for us?

After the raid at 1300 hours, which blocked the streets by razing houses and prevented the access of German reinforcements, entire families left Caen. They passed in front of our house to go into hiding in the old subterranean stone quarries in Fleury-sur-Orne. Some left in a crazed state, taking nothing with them. Perhaps they had already lost everything? Others were loaded down with bicycle trailers and little kids' cars packed with bizarre and sundry piles of mattresses, coverlets, etc.--What? There was a child pulling a cage of canaries. A grandmother was moaning in a wheelbarrow, while her son-in-law, in a strap like a head collar, was pulling between its handles.

Along their passage, the fleeing were hanging onto broken telephone lines, spread out in tangles on the ground. They invented new passages, circumventing the bomb craters and the hills of debris. Under the destroyed houses, they sometimes thought that they heard the weak voices of those buried inside.

I had made a simple shelter in the henhouse, with old tables. This actually constituted an even more dangerous refuge, but here we would go to spend the night and get through a long bombing. We had the idea that they would try to destroy the railroad bridge at the foot of the cliff below our house. The planes proceeded in successive waves. After four passes dropping bombs, they made an observation tour, and the waltz towards the still-standing metal bridge began anew. Four small bombardment runs and one bomb-less run, during the hours of one endless night. We could see in the yard as though it were daylight; it was illuminated with a strange apocalyptic light, shining curiously from the north. This was the whole city burning, its red flames reflected on clouds of smoke.   Little fake suns hung from small parachutes, lighting up this unreal decor with magnesium whiteness and delineating the bombing zones.

Sometimes the bombs came from very high, whistling with infinite slowness; at other times, they arrived in quick, screeching breaks, making us instinctively draw our heads into our shoulders.   The explosions became deliverances, shaking us from head to foot like gravel in a sieve. We weren't dead yet! We mistakenly believed that the volley of blows coming to us then were no more than amusing showers of metallic hailstones.

Finally, it was calm. Ravaged with fear and fatigue, we collapsed. When we awoke, it was full daylight and the house was still standing. But since we had left the windows open to prevent their breaking, the house seemed to look at us with great sunken eyes. The railroad bridge was still intact. Was it all just a frightful nightmare?

No, it was real, because the wind still bore the bitter odor of flying cinders with half-charred ends of papers, and the calm was punctuated with the frightening sound of crumbling houses.   From the street came the confused murmur of a phantom-like procession of fleeing, shaggy-haired individuals, including the wounded, lightly bandaged with already-dirty rags. They were leaving, going they knew not where. And the dogs, all the dogs in the city, answered each other, screaming at death.

Yes, they had really landed--the immense Armada beating the beaches baptized with new names: Sword, Juno, Omaha, Utah. Paper decrees dropped from the sky and ordered us to leave, saying that our city was now condemned!

Mother agreed with me: The grave dangers on the road seemed safer than staying in our home. Nothing to be done but reduce our affairs to one load and run towards uncertain tomorrows. Would we come back one day? Would we see our house again? Before leaving, I yielded to the impulse to bury our last two, old bottles of Médoc* in the yard. I spotted each with a stone, but we were never to find either bottle. Did they furnish the last pleasure of the anonymous soldier who bloodied our staircase? Did they fortify the bomb disposal experts when they came by?

By noon, we were fleeing towards Les Moutiers-en-Cinglais, pushing our old, filled-to-overflowing baby carriage. We hadn't agonized over whether to take the works of Dante or Shakespeare, but more prosaically chose the last jar of blackberry jam. Holding Arlette, Mother and I relayed on the single bicycle. Towards evening, exhausted from a trip of 25 kilometers, we reached the road to the Château de Villeray. Horrors! A column of German reinforcements was hidden under the trees. Since they prevented passage, we were forced to complete the trip with a detour of three kilometers, which seemed the longest segment of the journey.

Our friends Le Roy-Ladurie welcomed us warmly and gave us a room on the second floor, where we moved in before dinner. That evening, there was a marvelous dessert of wild strawberries, the first of the season. Right from the first day, we were integrated into the family. Mom helped in the kitchen, and I shared garden chores with François. We began by mulching the strawberry plants with straw.

---

* Bordeaux wine made in the Médoc region.

Omaha Beach today, with the English Channel at low tide

Before noon, the first bomb arrived and broke the château windows. I was thrown to the ground nose first in the yard, the impact stopping my pocket watch, a treasured gift from Dad. It was 11:20 a.m. We swept up the broken panes in the house—shamefully, as if we were at fault, as if bad luck had followed us there.

At the château, where the ways of the city meant nothing, life had maintained a decorum to which we were unaccustomed. Gabrielle, the cook, announced the meals with the bell. At the first ring, we had to converge from different points of the estate to wash up and change. At the second ring, we went to the dining room and waited behind our chairs until Grandmother Le Roy-Ladurie was seated. Then we all sat, and she played out her role as mistress of the house.

She was a tall and noble lady, dressed all in black, and very proud to say that each of her three sons measured not less than 1m 85 (1 meter 85 centimeters)* in height. Around her neck she wore this little band of black velvet; among the aristocrats, it was meant to hide the mark of the guillotine, my father had told me as a joke. Although I never believed in this macabre make-believe, I secretly entertained the thought that without that black velvet band, her head would fall off and we might see traces of glue.

She moved about with difficulty, with the help of a silver-capped cane. To cleanse her intestines, she would make three tours of the main yard after lunch. But her memory began to betray her; she would lose count and do extra loops.

Her fear of modern war methods was equal only to her courage. We were all at the dining room table at the time of the terrible bombardment that annihilated Evrecy. So that we could not see fear drain the color from her face, she said with much dignity, while hiding her head under her napkin: "This way, my children, if I die, you will not see my disfigurement."

---

* 1 meter = 39.37 inches; 1 centimeter = 0.3937 inches

Despite her youth, Cécile, François's little sister, tried with her comments to comfort my poor mother, who was demoralized by the circumstances. She affectionately called her « *Maman Idrac* ».

Château de Villeray, where the Idracs first took shelter during the Landing. Descendants of the Le Roy-Laduries own the property today.

At Villeray, generosity was limitless; often, they received people from Caen en route to distance themselves even further from the battlefield. One day, M. Etterlé passed by with his whole family. He was a well-known and important entrepreneur of public works in Caen. With age, and perhaps for some other reason, his voice had become frighteningly deep, and he said to me: "Do you hear those cannons beyond the valley of the Orne?" I had grown accustomed to the sound of the cannon fire, but not yet to the sound of his sepulchral voice, which reminded me later of Malraux in his speech on Jean Moulin.[*]

---

[*] Jean Moulin (1899-1943), a French Resistant born in Béziers and buried in the Panthéon in Paris in 1965.

Sometimes we thought we heard a train passing on the abandoned line from Caen to Flers; it sounded like rattling rails, with the valley responding in echo. But it was instead a convoy of tanks hurtling down the sunken lane extending from the other side of the Orne towards coast 112, which had to be taken and retaken so many times.

Ironically, we were near the battlefields and knew nothing at all of the battle outcomes. Transistor radios were not yet invented; we had one crystal set that worked without current, but the sound was very weak and it was difficult to regulate. Of course, there were no newspapers.

During the occupation, we used to receive occasional pamphlets from planes passing overhead. Now the Allies no longer took the time to give us their news. All we could do was attempt translations of the information bulletins that the Germans posted at their camp entrances. Even while doubting their credibility, we would find names of towns we knew, and tried to figure out where the Allies were advancing.

During a calm interlude, we would go onto a high area near National Route 162. In clear weather, we could make out the area of Caen, where columns of black smoke were climbing high into the sky, and in cloudy weather we saw the streaks of cannon fire. But these morbid sights told nothing more.

In Caen, enormous red crosses had been painted on the rooftops of the Church of St. Steven, the Lycée Malherbe and the dwelling of the Little Sisters of the Poor, where civilians and wounded had found refuge. After the bombings, every able man—including youngsters as young as I—were charged with searching for the wounded and the dead among the ruins. They evacuated the wounded and set aside the dead, for burial.[*]

---

[*] Late in August, when we returned to Caen, I remember certain streets at the foot of the Château of William the Conqueror, as well as in the center of town, where the ruins were two to three meters high. The foul odor of decaying cadavers emanating from them was to last for several months.

The needs of the civilians in Caen were becoming urgent. Madame Le Roy-Ladurie tried to organize a convoy of wheat for them, but no one in the village dared venture onto the road with a wagon and horses. She declared that if it came to that, she herself would go on June 22nd, so several men were shamed into going with her. We left with shoulder lanyards full of sacks of wheat. I went along to see the state of our house, and to try to bring back a change of clothing, which was badly needed.

The morning that we set out, the weather was overcast, the low clouds dodging machine-gun fire. Before Laize-la-Ville, a long German ammunition convoy had exploded and burnt; at the edge of the road, the sheet metal trucks—already rusted—gave off lugubrious grinding noises at the lightest breeze. Cartridges of all kinds were spread on the ground; they would have made a great souvenir collection for amateurs. I held so little hope for surviving this ordeal that I did not gather any.

Having seen so many houses destroyed, I was really worried about the fate of ours. Oh, joy! It was almost intact, hardly ransacked. I gathered some clothes into an old potato sack, and then rejoined the handcarts at the home of the Little Sisters of the Poor. For the return trip, they had already loaded several bags of salt, which would eventually allow us to preserve the meat of animals killed in the war.

In the afternoon, the weather was very pleasant, and the bombings had started anew. On the route to Falaise,[*] at the exit from Caen, enormous craters made the passage even more difficult than the artillery, with its random bursts of gunfire threatening to render this zone impassable.

The road to Harcourt seemed calm by comparison, but the towns of St.-Martin-de-Fontenay and May-sur-Orne were already completely destroyed. In St.-Martin, a cabaret owner had set up a sort of café under the ruins of sheet-metal roofing from his house. Out of consideration for her

---

[*] The birthplace of William the Conqueror, Duke of Normandy, who defeated Henry II in the Battle of Hastings (1066).

"working crew," and following the rules of etiquette, Mme Le Roy-Ladurie offered a *café-calva* to everyone. Only Père Lemarrois, who didn't like to drink, claimed to be in a hurry and continued on the road. His bay horse was pulling a covered wagon bearing a white flag of truce.

During our stop at the bistro, we had heard a short machine-gun burst. Alas, on the road at the end of town, we found Lemarrois. His horse and he were dead, the wagon riddled with bullets, torn to pieces despite its pathetic white rag hanging mockingly on a shaft of shattered hope. The poor man was beyond our help.

The next challenge was to clear the valley of the Laize. There was a steep decline before the bridge, followed by a rather rough coastline—a site where it had been hoped to attack the convoys, with planes that surveyed the route constantly. Curiously, that was where bandits used to attack carriages, in the past.

We managed to pass this place between two volleys of bullets. On the downgrade, we were thrown into the trench. I can still see Mme Le Roy-Ladurie lying in the grass in front of me, holding her big pocketbook against the nape of her neck. For her, this was the most essential point to protect. Lacking this accessory for imitating her, I simply crossed my fingers on my skull, so as not to die an idiot.

By pulling back, the Germans were chasing farmers, settling and then fighting from their lands. That was how Victor came to us. He was a small farmer from nearby, who had quickly rediscovered the response of his ancestors to duress: Solicit the help of the *Seigneur*.[*] His exhausted old horse pulled up with the family and a few old clothes in a tipcart, and his four cows following. Poor Victor was so upset when he entered with this entourage that he noisily overturned a front gate support--unfortunate entrance for soliciting shelter. He tried to explain to Grandmother, who generously and vehemently assured him: "My poor man! We can replace it." It was the best that she could say.

---

[*] From feudal times: the lord and master of the estate.

They were allowed to bed down in the barn, joining the group of refugees already there. Victor was energetic, and had offered his help, so they put him to work using steel wool on the parquet flooring of the château. Dying of the heat, and with no regard for the nobility of the place, he took off his shirt. When my friend saw him, he couldn't resist the temptation to hide the shirt. And soon we heard the poor devil running through the château hollering, "Someone stole my shirt, my only shirt!"

Then the Germans decided to turn Villeray into a country hospital. All refugees had to leave, since they would tolerate only the owners. For a few days, they placed us in an abandoned village house; then we found refuge with Raymonde, guardian of the Château de la Bagotière, who was too afraid of the troop to sleep in his own home. It was there that we saw the German army up close. They occupied the entire château, hiding the automatic machine-gun in the park area. These shock troops* could be denied nothing.

One day, a young S.S. officer amused himself in front of the children by putting their little cat in the mouth of his German shepherd. Granted, the dog didn't hurt it, but the kids were screaming with fright and the poor little animal was terrorized. What was the point of this cruelty, when we could all die tomorrow?

At any given moment, they might come into the house to ask for butter, eggs or "milk cream." Since we had no inclination to serve them, they didn't hesitate to take out a persuasive pistol. We learned not to be afraid, just to open the empty cupboard doors, and they would leave with no problem, sometimes discharging the pistol on the weathervane of the compass card, for no real purpose.

I still think of those men, who one last evening before mounting the attack were harmonizing so melodiously in the park—singing *lieds* [German songs for solo voice and piano]

---

* Troops especially suited and chosen for offensive work because of their high morale, training and discipline.

of their country, accompanying themselves with harmonicas. I never saw any of them come back.

It was during that time that they set up three enormous 220 mm cannons in the woods of la Hoguette, 300 meters from the Château de la Bagotière, where we were staying. The cannons would all fire at the same time, setting off a terrible shaking of the house. On the walls, the great *oeil de boeuf** and the picture frames jumped, ready to fall, and all the dishes clattered in the buffet cabinet. The artillery of the Allies answered. We heard the shots initiate, and we recognized the responding batteries by their sound.

Sometimes we could even see a high explosive shell pass like a shadow. By their whistle, we could distinguish those that would go further from those that would land nearby.

We ended up getting accustomed to the agony!

Every day, we would go see our friends in Villeray, but that meant passing near the battery of la Hoguette. We had to plug our ears when they were firing. The artillerymen had hidden their reserve shells in the hedge at the edge of the path. One day, when we were passing by, fearful as usual, a plane dropped one enormous bomb. We lay down in the grass, expecting the worst. Wouldn't that set off the munitions depot? Then we realized that this thing was not headed for earth in normal fashion, but was drifting down in a strange horizontal plane. To our great comfort, it landed without exploding; it was only a reservoir of fuel, released by a plane. Of course, we hadn't known that such a thing existed.

During the whole occupation, we had made it a point of honor not to talk to the Germans; now, the dangers that we had in common brought us together, and we exchanged words. They weren't all firebrands, especially the older ones. Some showed their family photos. "War is horrible," they confided to us, and they were sincere. Without admitting it, some began to realize that the situation was not

---

* Here, an old-fashioned wind-up wall clock, marked in Roman numerals.

in their favor. Under bombings and machine-gun fire, they seemed more fearful than we; of course, they had more experience with the dangers, and knew that they faced a greater personal peril.

From the outset of the Landing, they had lost mastery of the air space. For them, all planes were enemies, and they had to hide from them. In the park of Villeray, in the middle of a flowerbed, there was a lovely 18th century statue of a cherub looking up in the air. An officer with a sense of humor had put a whistle in its mouth and hung a sign around its neck, saying « Luftsperre » ["aerial barrage"]. The statue had become the watchful guardian angel of the soldiers of the Grand Reich.

At la Bagotière, an officer had use of an amphibious Volkswagen equipped with a radio. One day, when he was looking for a station, I just had time to hear: "The tricolore* flies over the ruins of Caen." So our city was now freed, but destroyed.

Quick to interpret the least signs, we really felt that the enemy was losing ground. Now, in the lull of the heavy cannoning, the wind sometimes bore the sound of the machine guns.

A calculating farmer lady was able to supplement her farm animals when the soldiers were pushing a large herd before them; she opened the gate just at the right moment, and captured a good number.

And the time came when the soldiers would amuse themselves, shooting and trying to chase me in the fields. I forced myself not to run, to hide my fear; then I found that they were firing blanks.

Bombs had destroyed their battery of huge, deafening 220 mm cannons with no more noise than one of their salutes. Now, they were evacuating. On the vehicle at the head of the convoy, the real Luftsperre, whistle between his teeth, was poised to give the alert, as he searched the sky for

---

* The three-colored (blue, white and red) flag adopted after the French Revolution.

the pursuing bombardiers of the R.A.F. (Royal Air Force).
They were to loom into view before long.

Our days were unparalleled, divided between fear
and misery. Property was a senseless concept, since we
lived for no more than one essential goal: not to die!

That particular morning, the troop had not returned,
and la Bagotière was strangely empty. A *Feld-Webel*
[sergeant] ordered us to remove some items left behind; there
was still a washbasin in back, covered with cigars.

I don't know why, but I played the farm boy and
wanted one. The task finished, the soldier began to count his
cigars. He was missing three: « *Drei Zigaretten !* » ["Three
cigars!"] He frisked the valet, who had been careful to leave
his jacket at the farm with his booty, while I secretly
disposed of mine in the half-light of the barn. We had
foolishly fallen for their pre-meditated temptation, which
allowed them to abuse us verbally and with their boots:
"Little French swindler!"

It became obvious that we would be leaving before
long. We began to finish off our bottles of hard cider and
old Calvados, drinking both at every meal. After an
alcoholic lunch, I smoked a retrieved cigar. It made me sick,
justifying the proverb, "Ill-gotten goods seldom prosper."

Monsieur Jacques Le Roy-Ladurie, whom everyone
called « *M'sieur Jacques* », was a captain in the
underground. He arrived unexpectedly, to order the
evacuation of the town where he was Mayor. I can still see
his head emerging from the secret vault of the château,
where we were helping him hide his most beautiful books,
the dishes and the silverware. His face, illuminated from
below by the light of a candle, gave him an air of conspiracy.
In fact, weren't the Germans looking for him?

Then he led me to his wardrobe and offered me the
choice of three ties, any that I would like--but only three--so
that we wouldn't be unnecessarily loaded down. He spread
out an armful on the bed, two or three hundred perhaps.
There were ties of all colors—those that he had worn when
he was Minister of Agriculture, others that he must have

worn only once. I was flabbergasted to be faced with such a choice, astounded that one man could buy himself so many ties.

Early in the morning on the 25th of July, our carts loaded, we evacuated with the whole village, about fifty kilometers out, to the Château du Jardin in Giel, property of Count Dauger, father of Madame Le Roy-Ladurie. M'sieur Jacques couldn't bear to leave the Gobelins tapestry behind, so he used it as a beautiful tarpaulin.

In Tournebu, a plane hit by the D.C.A. [French anti-aircraft] fell in flames not far from us. Then we crossed the still-smoking ruins of Falaise. Out of all the rubble, I remember especially a radio set that had been hidden behind the metal curtain of a fireplace, now enthroned in plain view, above a heap of ruins.

Château du Jardin de Giel (13th century). The refugees hid on the (center) tower's dungeon staircase during the last major bombardments of the Landing.

At the Château du Jardin de Giel, the war had not yet arrived. We poor refugees, with our dusty load, brought its first indecent picture. Here, the birds were singing and you could no longer hear the rumbling of battle. Their reception was rather cool, but we couldn't blame them; there was no food for extra guests. We asked to be put up where we would be the least trouble.

It was there that I agreed to grind false coffee and make grilled barley for the German field kitchen cook. To thank me, he generously offered a moldy loaf of brown bread. But at night, how good it was to eat a little when hunger kept me from sleeping.

Our family received some special treatment: Instead of bedding with the others in the straw of a barn, we were lodged in the unused roof spaces in the castle, where the genealogical tree of Monsieur le Comte was located—for some reason, on the reverse side of funeral announcements pinned up in the spaces.

Although we had avoided the squalid lack of privacy of the barn, where the villagers were thrown together, we did share their meals at a potluck table. Cider was served from a bucket by Léon, a grimy dwarf who plunged in his brown, snuff-taking hand with the ¼-liter goblet that he used to fill our glasses.

The idea of war, with its bombs and shells, soon caught up with the premises' inhabitants, and marvelously improved the consideration of our hosts. Wouldn't they themselves soon be refugees? A pilot came by, machine-gunning so low that we could see his head at the controls. Cartridges rained everywhere, goading the enormous bull in the middle of the lawn, and making him quite furious.

The next day, while I was admiring the wheeling of the "Lightings," those double fuselage fighter-bombers, I realized that I was in the axis of the heavy machine gun shooting at it. That's how a 20 mm shell planted itself in the soil at my feet--without exploding. Which would have deprived you of this story.

I can still feel the cold of the sleepless night of the last attack, when we all thought we would die under the shells from the tanks. We were on the steps in the old stone dungeon, with its enormous walls. Calm returned only at dawn.

Later, in front of the stable at the farm, four men were firmly holding a splendid racehorse, while the veterinarian tried to extract shrapnel. Since the flow of blood on his hide was making me nauseous, I set off for a walk, heading to the edge of the park. A German guard sprang from the ditch, taking aim at me: « *Wer da ?* » ["Who's there?"] I raised my arms and returned peacefully to witness the end of the horse's operation.

The hedge of the *Terres Noires* [Black Lands] was burning, ignited by the shellfire. From the main road, beyond the trees, came the uninterrupted noise of a convoy. Later we learned that they were cordoning off the sector of Falaise. Would we really be liberated?

A reconnaissance jeep arrived in the château courtyard, with men dressed in other uniforms and other helmets, and weapons in their hands. They seemed in a hurry, nervous. We stared at them, not believing that this moment, so fervently hoped for these four years, had arrived. They were looking for Russian soldiers of the *Wehrmacht* [Armed Forces] in their hideout. Proudly we accompanied the voluntary prisoners, who joyfully give us their last cigarettes of powdered tobacco. But the Allies welcomed them roughly, frisking them while at gunpoint, as though they were enemies just the same. They loaded them into trucks and, with heavy hearts, we saw them leave, feeling as though we had betrayed friends. The extermination to which they were delivered on returning to the U.S.S.R. confirmed our premonitions.

Later, we ventured as far as the route to Argentan; the tanks and the curtained cars advanced slowly in a continuous wave. The vehicles were so close together that it was impossible to cross the road. This convoy—of which we had not seen the beginning—seemed endless. How had they been able to disembark with all that equipment?

The torsos of the leaders of the tanks emerged from open turrets; they were very serious, with their radio sets on their ears, until the moment when we noticed that they were listening to music.

Suddenly, this unimaginable parade, the beginning of which we hadn't seen and the end of which we couldn't know, stopped. Over there, beyond the hills, had they met with resistance? No, they did not go into defense mode, did not re-buckle their war helmets. They came down from their vehicles to settle at the roadside with stoves and mess kits. They were British and we were at the sacred tea time!

These brave soldiers wanted to eat, like everybody. They shared food with us-- slices of bread of an unfamiliar whiteness. They offered chocolate, chewing gum and packets of "blond" cigarettes, the odor of which hung on their uniforms. They even had a condom with every ration.

In the ditch, a dead German soldier was in full decomposition, swollen and black. In the eyes of the peasants, he symbolized the enemy; they spat on him, while marveling that a "black man" could be in the German army. The next day, the orphanage in Giel celebrated a dignified burial Mass for him.

We had just one mission—to return and gather up whatever of our heritage the war had left us. As soon as possible, we took the road of the liberated territory, to discover a new world where everything was surprising. We no longer feared being attacked, but everywhere there was this mixed odor of fire, powder and rot.

Dead soldiers were still lying out in the fields, their guns in their hands. Had they been killed by land mines? Arms and munitions from the two camps were strewn everywhere. In a ditch, a whole crate of Panzer-Faust was fraternizing with scattered English rockets. Dead horses and cows, swollen like toy balloons and covered with flies, poisoned the air with their stench.

The bomb disposal experts had unwound their red and white bands, delimiting their action zone, "Off Bound!"

Behind their Ariane's[*] string, in the fields without animals, the grass had grown very long. Who would dare risk it?

Trees blown into a leafless state had taken on winter silhouettes. Elsewhere, the shells had simply marked their passage in the foliage with very round holes, which stood out against the clouds like aspirin tablets.

We learned to recognize other arms, other uniforms, other trucks. The engineers maneuvered machines never before seen. We discovered the first Bulldozer. Bridges that could be taken apart by the engineers were slowly replacing the destroyed stone bridges.

We saluted the convoys we met, and used two fingers to form the Churchill V for Victory, suppressing the thought that this could also be V for Victim. On the rear of the vehicles we translated, without understanding its importance, the reminder painted there: "Keep Right!"[+]

Now, some British occupied the château of Villeray, which had fortunately been spared. They seemed at ease there, and agreed coldly to let us sleep in a barn. Who could prove to them that these nomads, accompanied by their followers, were the legitimate proprietors? Couldn't we be former collaborators or German spies?

The next day, we continued on our return towards Caen, discovering the virtues of hitchhiking. Mom fainted when she saw that our home was roofless. We were taken in by more fortunate neighbors, whose house was intact. They had feared that the city would assign undesirable refugees to them, so they wanted us to occupy the premises instead—which we did.

Near the old washhouse, we could cross the Orne on a pontoon bridge. It dipped each time a car went over it, threatening to throw us into the water. In the midst of the

---

[*] Ariadne in Greek mythology. She left a string, threaded through the Labyrinth, to help Theseus find his way out, after he had accomplished his mission of killing the Minotaur on the isle of Crete.

[+] The British, who drive on the left side of the road, needed to keep right, so as not to collide head-on with the French and the Americans.

ruins, new rail tracks were born. Some wall sections conjured up images of entire streets, with their little shops, of which practically nothing remained. The homes left offered new perspectives, astonishing one's memory. Even distances seemed changed. It would take months to substitute these new images for those in our memories.

At home, only the high roof had been destroyed. We recovered enough intact tiles to repair the lower part and retain the use of two rooms: one for living, the other for salvageable items.

After each downpour, we would go to the second story, sweep the water as you would from the bridge of a ship, and make it run through the holes of shells, into basins placed on the ground floor. After the storm, a strange odor floated down rue Branville: a mixture of fresh tar, wet ivy and the pleasing (to me!) scent of Players Navy Cut.[*]

That day, on the Cours Sadi-Carnot, the British gun crew of a D.C.A. joyfully brandished a sign made from a broken door, where they had written with a piece of plaster debris:

"PARIS IS DELIVERED"

It was the 25th of August, 1944.

---

[*] A brand of so-called "blond" cigarettes that the English smoked after the Landing. On the box of 20 is the head of a bearded British sailor, encircled by a lifesaving ring.

EPILOGUE

What remains today of those horrible, tragic, deafening days? Vast cemeteries under the silent vigil of the moon. I think especially of the American necropolis of St.-Laurent-sur-Mer, which I know best. On this grand, impressive site overlooking the sea lies an immense carpet of perfectly-tended grounds, the final resting place for nearly 9,000 tombs. The Carrara marble crosses and stars of David are in perfect alignment. The site is never without visitors.

Often, French schoolchildren come to lay flowers on the tombs, offering their small bouquets of gratitude to the soldiers who, without realizing it, died for them as well.

Today, after so many years, I returned to the Château de Villeray and its powerful emotions and memories. The Le Roy-Ladurie children, having now grown to be parents and grandparents, are its proprietors. Marie, my friend François' sister, received us simply, as if we had returned to pick up a conversation interrupted the night before.

We found the magnificent entrance hall just as before, with its superb mosaic flooring intact. Still hanging on the wall was the large Gobelins tapestry that we had saved in 1944, and used as a tarpaulin to secure possessions on our cart. In the dining room, the monumental fireplace still stands, with its light yellow licks of smoke left by ill-burning damp wood.

In the parlor, next to the immense grand piano stands the harp that I had so admired when I first saw it. There, the family assembled every evening with the château workers, to offer prayers. Fear had deepened religious fervor.

And with a single stunning blow, the memory of the Fear comes back: the Fear that gripped my belly for days. It was a cramp, the size of a fist, centered constantly in my solar plexis.

Today, in these rather empty, grand rooms, I see again my dear friends, all the friends who have disappeared. And I want only to weep.   ARMAND—October 4, 2003

CHAPTER VII

HYPNOSIS, MAGIC, MYSTERY

By chance, I had found a remarkable book on hypnosis, enhanced with descriptions of numerous experiments. It captivated me, but the fear of not being able to awaken my subjects had prevented me from carrying out exciting experiments.

That year, I was in Beginning Math, next to André Langlois, whose father had a fishing boat at Port-en-Bassin. He was a fine fellow, with a round, rosy face, where a peach-fuzz beard was beginning to show. He spoke slowly, with the drawling accent of his locale. He was one of the best pupils in the class, and was later admitted to the Naval Academy. He was a good buddy, in whom I had confided that, at the moment, I was interested in this type of reading.

At the beginning of one afternoon, when we were in Study Hall, I was observing him with an amused and ironic smile as he opened his eyes after a postprandial doze. He seemed strangely afraid and questioned me: "Hey, did you just hypnotize me?"

The idea seemed so funny to me that I preferred denying it in an ambiguous way, so that he remained persuaded that I had put him to sleep, and that maybe I had ordered him to commit reprehensible acts. With a subject so disposed, it would have been a shame not to try something. I quickly came up with an original idea and solicited the help of my friend François Le Roy-Ladurie, who lived at school as André did, and shared the same dormitory.

That night, my friend François would be the last to leave the classroom, secretly taking André's history book, to put it on his night table while he was sleeping. The next day, we had a history composition. After the test, I asked him how it had gone for him, adding: "You must have reviewed last night, right?" He looked at me speechless and confided that, in fact, this morning he had found the history book next to his bed, and he was sure that he hadn't put it there.

Then I explained that during the night, I had commanded him to go look for his book in the classroom. Not happy at all, he said: "Not surprising, then, that I sneezed when I woke up, and I feel like I have a cold. With your idiotic tricks, you made me get a chill." Then he added: "So, you could also order me to kill someone?" I explained that the outcome was uncertain, because that would be immoral, but the experiment was worth trying.

A few days later, I had a new accomplice—Lerosier--who simply had to ask many times in the course of the day to go to the bathroom, as if he had a problem.

When class started, I asked André for my glass tube. "What tube?" he asked. I made him go back to his room and find a small tube in his desk, which I had put there without his knowing. It was half full of a white powder—some sugar in this case.

I told him of my disappointment: He had only partially obeyed the command. In order to know if I could make him poison somebody, I had ordered him to pour a laxative in his neighbor's bowl at breakfast, but now the effect would be insufficient.

Dédé went crazy every time he saw his victim again ask permission to leave the room, saying to himself: "To think I could have killed him, if you had wanted me to!" In his eyes, I started to become a dangerous man. So I swore him to absolute secrecy as to my methods and obligated him to be in my good graces.

Again it was he who inspired the next experiment. He didn't want to be the victim every time, preferring to set up someone else. Shamefully, I profited from his ignorance of hypnosis, to show him a new farce.

The next day, we had synchronized our watches with François. During a study hall, two minutes prior to the agreed-upon time, I stayed motionless, my hands extended towards my accomplice—and I assure you that two minutes with nothing happening seems a very long time. Dédé was beginning to doubt that I could do it, and I myself began to wonder if François would hold to the starting signal. But he was a precise guy and, with a single movement, got up to ask the proctor if he could consult André's dictionary.

I can see him now, his eyes fixed vaguely ahead of him, his pace purposely slow and deliberate, halting and uncertain. He didn't have time to ask for the dictionary, because André handed it over on his own. He opened it upside down and threw me a furious look, accusing me of having put him to sleep, before returning to his place at a normal pace.

That night, after class, to dazzle some followers, I asked them to put six objects on the table and, in my absence, one of those present had to touch just one of them, and I would be able to tell when I came back which one had even been just lightly brushed. I had repeated the trick many times, to the astonishment of everyone—or almost.

For a moment, just for effect, I wanted to get André to ask me to hypnotize him. I must point out that he had been chosen, because he was so earnest, to be master of ceremonies at the chapel of the Institution. He was charged with sounding the clacker to have the attendees stand, kneel, or be seated.

Our chapel was too small for all the Holy Communion pupils and their families, so the ceremony took place at the Abbaye aux Hommes, the biggest church in Caen.

The night before this important occasion, I feigned great embarrassment and confessed to André that I had ordered him to give fifty blows with the clacker at the time of the elevation of the Holy Host, but now, reflecting on the scandal and the problems it was going to create for him, I was feeling great remorse.

My victim was not only dismayed at this revelation, but also touched by my contrition. So, what to do? I had to put him to sleep again, he begged. It was the least I could do.

The French School System & Approximate U.S. Equivalents

Age	France	U.S.A.
	Ecole Maternelle	
2-4	*Petite Section*	Preschool
4-5	*Moyenne Section*	Preschool
5-6	*Grande Section*	Kindergarden
	Ecole Primaire	
6-7	*11è=Cours Préparatoire (CP)*	1st Grade
7-8	*10è=Cours Elémentaire 1 (CE1)*	2nd Grade
8-9	*9è =Cours Elémentaire 2(CE2)*	3rd Grade
9-10	*8è =Cours Moyen 1 (CM1)*	4th Grade
10-11	*7è =Cours Moyen 2 (CM2)*	5th Grade
	Collège	
11-12	*6è =Cycle d'Observation*	6th Grade
12-13	*5è =Cycle'Approfondissement*	7th Grade
13-14	*4è=Cycled'Approfondissement*	8th Grade
14-15	*3è =Cycle d'Orientation*	9th Grade
	Lycée	
15-16	*2nde (Seconde)*	10th Grade
16-17	*1ère (Première)*	11th Grade
17-18	*T (Terminale)*	12th Grade

SOURCE: Giglione, Margaret and Carol Pouchol, eds. *AAWE Guide to Education*. (Paris: AAWE 6th edition, 2003): 198

For two months, I had the time to carry out other "hypnotic" experiments, and to appreciate just how far his naïveté could go. My tricks became easier every day, as the number of pupil accomplices grew; but they also became less amusing, and the utter confidence of my victim was prickling my conscience. I was making him look like an idiot in everyone's eyes, and he really wasn't. Also, because of the magnitude of all this, it could reach the ears of Alcide, the Principal.

I resolved to stop the game by Pentecost break, but I had a hard time convincing him of the truth. He was afraid that I didn't trust him anymore, that I feared he would disclose my marvelous gift. In his drawling accent, he assured me so touchingly of his absolute discretion, that I had to be very strong not to continue to fool him right up until we took our *bac*, or even for the rest of his life. Today, I still wonder if he wouldn't have preferred to continue believing in the occult.

As a beginner at the SNCF, I found myself in the same office as Jean Le. He was also a real conjurer, complete with a business card. He had even chosen a rather pretentious artist's name; so, modestly, he called himself "Magic's Son."

To him I owe the secrets that allow me to swallow knives and to make objects disappear, and some other tricks that have made me the only one of twelve uncles to my sixty nieces and nephews, to have such strange powers. They are so justifiably proud that they've invited their buddies to join us, so that they could show me off as a curiosity.

But what strikes the youngest children speechless is not so much the disappearance of objects as their reappearance on their back or in other unexpected places, and their inability to see them coming back.

Sometimes we are surprised at our own talents. One day, for example, I was having fun making something disappear—the personal tennis ball of Bora-Bora, my son Laurent's dog. The poor animal had seen it vaporize before his eyes. His expression showed complete bewilderment. I didn't repeat the trick, since the animal was gifted with olfactory means that would have placed him in the realm of the "fantastic."

"Magic's Son" had among his relatives an illusionist friend who made his living with his art. He had invented a procedure to charm foreign customers in Parisian cafes, where he would show up with his wife. Having his wife guess the Passport number, he secretly let her know the nationality of the Passport holder, which allowed her to add a little phrase of welcome in his or her native language. It was quite impressive.

Every year, this rather Bohemian artist would tour the movies in France. At intermission, after several thought transmission demonstrations, he would sell horoscopes with his partner—all the easier, with the audience still stupefied.

This particular evening, after having dined at Jean Le's on a meal well complemented with liquids, which could have dulled their faculties if the artist and his partner hadn't been so well trained, my friend drove them to the Majestic Cinema for their presentation. He himself remained in the lobby, smoking a cigar.

Shortly before the artist's exit, a young man came up to them, visibly excited. He hurried towards them, almost shouting: "Madame, Monsieur, I'm a psychology student. I didn't used to believe in thought transmission, but now that I've seen you, I believe in it!" They thanked him; the artists also knew how to play it "cool."

That year, my friend François Le Roy-Ladurie had been given the responsibility of organizing the local festivities of the Moutiers in Cinglais, where his Dad was mayor. To liven up the festival, he had invited « Le Mage Dirca » to perform a few extraordinary tricks. He hadn't strained himself finding an anagram to my name. I've always regretted not having kept a poster as a souvenir of that festival.

I made my public debut with my partner Jean Le, who insured logistic support for a phenomenal number memory technique. I had had to learn by heart the 1946 Petit Larousse edition, in order to recite it from any point. To eliminate all trickery, the spectators gave random numbers, and after a foolproof calculation, he would pull out one, which I would have to say. For example, give the fifteenth word on page 432, with its definition. The people would then look in the book, which had stayed shut up to that point, and they could verify the accuracy of the response.

To spice up the affair after several intellectually exhausting demonstrations, François would ask me for the twelfth word on page 727. I had to feign embarrassment, and then, at his insistence, end up telling him: "Sorry, sir, but that page pictures foreign flags; the twelfth flag is Ethiopia, which has (such and such) colors." Everybody was satisfied; I could have sold them horoscopes by the wheelbarrow.

Many years later, I had to lend my help at a Christmas Eve party for the elderly people in the neighborhood. I thought of asking the assistance of my friend Vong Koth, a Laotian refugee prince, whose head I found particularly appropriate for the role of Hindu fakir. He kindly accepted, amused by this collusion. He thought it unnecessary to rehearse. I can still see him in his exotic costume, topped with a splendid feathered turban, its cabochon shining like a real diamond.

We began with "The Magic Pendulum." He had to stand before the audience with his eyes covered; on his back was a huge clock without hands. Specifying a randomly-selected time with my naturally magic ring, I would always ask the same question the same way: "What time is it?" Then, without being able to see it, he had to say the designated number.

Horror! Clothes don't make the man! Here's my neophyte fakir, panic-stricken and incapable of answering. I had to save the situation. I hurried to the front of the stage to rail against my audience, although I was perfectly calm. "Dear spectators, this thought transmission process is particularly delicate; if I do not obtain absolute silence from you, I will regretfully not be able to continue my demonstration. I will try it one last time, but I must not hear the least noise." This had given my partner time to get hold of himself, and all proceeded perfectly. That made it all the more real!

Then, I executed a trick that I'll briefly describe to you. You distribute about twenty identical envelopes with sheets of paper, on each of which volunteers write a first name and the name of an animal, keeping it secret or showing it only to immediate neighbors. Then they seal the paper in an envelope, and the fakir presses them one by one to his forehead and decides what is written inside. The spectators, who are not accomplices, are speechless when the fakir guesses what they had written in secret.

He who has gifts of magic is often tempted to practice them for everyone's pleasure; alas, the results don't always measure up to one's good intentions.

In 1960, we were in Crete, and had taken an excursion to the foot of Mount Ida, in the high plateaus of Lasithi, to see one of the numerous caves where Zeus was born. At this time, there were hardly any tourists in the area; in fact, we were looking for a pretext to go to the interior of the island and meet "natives." We had borrowed the mailman's bus, the only means of transportation in this lost region.

There was no restaurant, nor the least shop in the village, but only a poor café managed by a widow. With the help of the phonetic pronunciation of *Le Guide Bleu*,[*] we had managed to order fried eggs. I can still see them, floating on an oil bath as black as the oil change from my car.

The poor woman was attending to our every need. Evidently, it was the first time that she had welcomed V.I.P.s in her modest establishment, and didn't know what to do to show that she was up to the occasion. I had noticed, hidden

---

[*] One in the series of French guide books, an assemblage of maps and site information.

like a treasure under her kitchen buffet, some aluminum table settings wrapped in tissue paper.

She stood watch over us, ready to respond to our least desires. And spying by the open door were fifty village kids, who had been following us all morning. Proud of her guests, she had declined to chase them; they had so few distractions!

Suddenly, I thought of offering a little of the supernatural to these people. I didn't hesitate a moment before her and the pack of curious little villagers. I swallowed a fork.

The reaction was immediate and surprising: The children ran away, and the good woman, who had initially taken us for noble strangers, now believed instead that we were henchmen of Belzébuth, the prince of demons. Terrorized, she signed herself piously three times with three fingers, as the Greeks do. And Christ the Creator, who watched over the whole room from His frame on the wall, came to her aid, to protect her from the works of the devil. We didn't disappear in an evil-smelling cloud but, without her knowing how, the fork was again on the table. God had triumphed over the Devil.

About ten years later, we were at the house of some American friends in Pennsylvania. They had arranged an extraordinary visit for us, which included an invitation to the house of their uncle, a retired mechanical engineer, and their aunt, a talented sculptress and former friend of Grace Kelly.

They lived outside of Philadelphia, in northern New Jersey, in a magnificent home of wood and glass, nestled in a cluster of trees at the edge of a lovely lake with a lush island. The entrance to the house was wooded, with a private stone driveway. They heard us drive in, and welcomed us on the doorstep.

Since the weather was nice, they had planned a luncheon on the terrace, at the edge of the water. Tame fish, that no one had ever tried to catch, hurried over for food as soon as someone approached the edge. It was an American style reception, where one goes to a lot of trouble to grill hamburgers on the barbecue and then serves them on deluxe dinnerware.

At dessert time, I thought I would amuse them by swallowing my knife—with no bad intention, of course. But I immediately read serious worry on the face of our hostess, who was too well brought up to protest. I then realized that the heavy knife in my sleeve was solid silver, a valuable piece that she would not want to lose. We didn't give her too bad an impression, but you can never trust the French! Fortunately, I was able to return the knife promptly and in perfect condition.

Back in France shortly thereafter, we attended an official dinner at the Préfecture when, opposite me at dessert-time, there was a chic and conservative gentleman who obviously wanted a souvenir of that evening. He calmly took the dessert spoon and put it in his handkerchief. I was a witness; if I said nothing, I was an accomplice. But I couldn't cause a scene, either. My dessert before me, I fortunately had an original solution at hand. I proceeded to swallow my dessert spoon and, to their astonishment, asked the question that would set up my own response: "And now, where has it gone? Into the handkerchief of Monsieur!" There was nothing he could do but give it back. He shot me a furious look, probably thinking it was I who would be bringing home a souvenir that night.

This great story so amused Gérard Gorcy, the National President of the Society of St. Vincent de Paul, that he pressed me one evening to repeat the trick, to surprise the members of the national Bureau. I asked him beforehand to put a coffee spoon in his pocket. Oh! Of course, it was just a modest self-service spoon. As soon as I had swallowed mine, I asked Gérard to "find" it in his pocket. The one that he took out was awkwardly twisted. A wise observer dared to declare that it was not the same one. I questioned him immediately: "Have you ever swallowed a coffee spoon?" He admitted that he was not so gifted. "Of course," I answered, "If you had ever swallowed any, you would know that it always twists them a bit."

My curiosity about the unusual led me to read a manual on divination and to try a few experiments. I know an astute diviner who had set himself up as a well digger. He was a little more expensive than the others per meter of depth, but he guaranteed success based on the estimate. "No water, no bill to pay." He had to be certain of the results, to safeguard his status as a diviner.

This search into the unknown relies on the "power" of the artist.   Personally, nature having given me only modest gifts, I didn't pursue it for long. However, one day I was able to conduct a most satisfying experiment.

At this time, just after the war, Anne-Marie, a university student, was lodging with us. We had no means to heat her room in the winter. She had brought along an oil stove that was from the last century. It worked with a wick, like a lamp. This ancient device was hard to regulate and gave off little specks of soot, which escaped from the apparatus with the heat. They fell at random throughout the room, making black spots that were difficult to remove.

When she periodically filled the reservoir with oil, she had to be careful not to spill any; a single drop, as it evaporated, would have stunk up her room.   She even preferred leaving the five-liter metal can outside, on the edge of her window.   Now, the day after a night storm, it had disappeared.   Nor could it be found under the window in the embankment of the Coteaux path.   In these difficult, post-war times, would a passerby have stolen it?

What a great opportunity for me to show my talents! With my divining rod and a map of the city, I found the oil can very quickly, at the house of a neighbor, Père Letellier, an honest and friendly railway worker whom I knew well. I had only to go to his house to verify the result of my experiment.

Anne-Marie, until then extremely skeptical as to the possibilities of divination, had declared that if I really found the oilcan, she would completely change her mind, and I would have convinced her of the effectiveness of this science.

Several minutes later, I triumphantly returned, can in hand. From that day, she has believed in divination.

However, I have only a weak claim to the credit. That very morning, I had met Père Letellier, who let me know that he had brought the oilcan to his house, so that no one would take it.

In *classe de première,** I idolized Victor Hugo. Throughout the entire year, I read his complete works in prose and in verse, as my only free time activity. (None of my classmates were doing this, and my own children have never chosen Hugo's work as a hobby!)   This led to knowledge of the phenomenon of levitation, with the table rising and descending, "knocking" as it did so: two blows = yes; three blows = no. But the procedure became very long when you had to spell out letters while counting knocks, before you could form any words.

This particular evening, we had met at the house of a friend who had a three-footed table. Since we had just taken practice baccalaureat exams, we had amused ourselves asking Hugo himself—in a manner of speaking—how we would all be classified in the grading. He could give us the right information, and we would verify it afterwards, since the tests had not yet been corrected.

It certainly was impressive when, having formed the circle with our hands, and placed our fingers barely touching the table, we felt it hit the ground as it went down and came back up. The séance lasted a good hour, and we came out exhausted. But what a triumph to share with our friends!

For such a séance, there's a technique for asking questions. Since I had just told this story to my friends from la Bagotière the night before a fishing party, they wanted to ask how many fish we would catch the next day. The table knocked three times and we expected to catch three fish, but

---

* Approximately 11th grade in the U.S.

it meant "no," telling us that we would end up empty-handed. Which happened. We should have thought to ask first if we would catch anything.

My friends were convinced that it was I who made the table perform, with a subterfuge that they had yet to uncover. Knowing myself that I wasn't cheating, it effectively proved the authenticity of the knocking. When they were convinced of that, they didn't want to do it any more, since they thought they were communicating with the devil. Picture the night: Out in the middle of the country, in a room poorly lit with a single candle, the storm outside blowing the trees wildly and a branch rubbing against the window while the high wind screamed—enough to give you shivers.

Could that be why I never again made tables talk?

When the nice old women that I had visited regularly for a long time could no longer light the fire in their dilapidated apartment building and socialize with their neighbors, I felt under moral obligation to have them admitted as quickly as possible to an old persons' home. Since openings were rare, I was happy to get them admitted the following week to Hospice Pont-l'Evêque.

Alas, because of the distance, I couldn't assure them of a weekly visit now, so I asked Dr. DEG, a retired physician who lived there, to visit for me. He carried out this mission very faithfully, and when I went every two or three months to see my old friends, it became tradition that, afterwards, I would return to the doctor's place to have tea and listen to his extraordinary stories.

When he was young, he was in a Jesuit middle school when the laws against the Jesuits were declared and, to continue his studies, he had to go to the Anglo-Norman islands, where his school had taken refuge. He was good at composition, and knew English as well as Latin and Greek.

During the occupation, he had been a Resistant and had been deported to Buchenwald where, as a doctor, he had courageously helped the other prisoners. He had been among the rare ones to return from this death camp, but tuberculosis had reduced him to a skeleton. Miraculously cured, he made a vow to go to Lourdes by bicycle, a promise that he was able to fulfill several years later.

As a retiree, he had undertaken to write his macabre recollections in a flawless style that he was endlessly polishing to perfection. They came out under the name DEG, his initials. I never dared tell him that it was a poorly chosen *nom de plume* [pen name], because my daughters used to love using this short form to point out something they thought was *dégoutante*, or disgusting.

DEG was an excellent storyteller, but I preferred setting him onto professional or unusual subjects that were less horrible than his deportation; he excelled at these as well.

He recounted that, before the war, a nurse who was raising children on Public Assistance had come to him for a consultation. She brought him a small child with impetigo all over his face. He wrote a prescription for silver nitrate ointment, the only known treatment at the time. Two weeks later, she brought the child back, but he was even worse than before. After an initial improvement, the condition had been seriously aggravated. The doctor admitted that he could do nothing more, but advised her to try the pilgrimage, which was done in those cases.

There was a strange custom in practice: People had to take up a collection for bus fare to make the pilgrimage to St. Laurent de Clarbec. Just one small coin per request came in, so requests had to be repeated and repeated... The pilgrimage having been finally accomplished, they washed the child's face with water from the spring, and the cloth was left on a nearby tree. Strangely, the child was cured, although he was still too young to respond to the power of suggestion.

Among the doctor's patients, there was also a patient dying of an idiopathic illness. This woman had come to believe that she was the victim of a spell, so she went to Le Havre to see a spell-breaker, who told her this: "You've consulted me too late to save you, but I'm going to turn this fate against your sorcerer neighbor, who in a week will die like a dog, without seeing a priest or doctor, or even his/her own children." She reported back to DEG, who spoke to his friend, the parish priest. Together, they searched for the identity of the evildoer.

A week later, the doctor was called out of consultation on an emergency, to see a patient that he recently had cured of pneumonia. The fellow lived in a cottage at the top of a coastline. To his astonishment, he saw the man in his nightshirt at the edge of the path, gesturing wildly. Barely out of the car, he said to him: "You're crazy, being out here in the cold in your condition," and the poor old man explained: "It's not me, it's my wife. You're too late, she died like a dog, without seeing the priest, or the doctor, or her children!"

The coincidence with the words of the spell-breaker was so stupefying that they checked in the neighborhood. It was learned that, every day, the deceased would see a little girl, the daughter of the bewitched person, going to get milk, and she would ask each time for news of her mother, so as to follow the progress of her evil spells.

In the region, there were also miracle-workers like Arthur, a rather crude peasant, who had kinesthetic-type gifts. This particular day, seated at a table behind the window of a café in Touques on the road to Trouville, he suddenly exclaimed: "Hey, you see Joseph arriving with his cartload of apples? He still owes me money for treatments. You'll see, he's going to pay me today!" These comments left the audience cold; no one seemed concerned. Joseph then actually stopped his team and entered like a bomb, shouting: "Quick, boss, a *café-calva*; the boat for England won't wait for my apple delivery." At that time, there was a lively exportation trade to some British jam factories.

Then Arthur intervened: "Hey, guy, didn't I cure your horsc? But you still haven't paid me." Joseph recognized the facts and promised to pay him his due, "but not today," he was in too much of a hurry. Arthur responded: "Well, I'm telling you that you're going to give me the money now."

Joseph, without answering, crossed the street to continue on his way with the load. But the horses stubbornly refused to get going again, and neither coaxing nor slapping had any effect. People outside were uncomfortable with this cruelty to the animals. Among the witnesses, there was one who advised Joseph to go ask Arthur what was going on; we could see him laughing behind the bistro window. That's what Joseph finally did.

Arthur welcomed him with the reminder: "I told you that you would pay me today!" Joseph handed over what he owed, grumbling. But as soon as he left the café, even before he had time to cross the road, his horses had taken off without him.

Doctor DEG was not naïve, and in the course of his career had seen many extraordinary things that science cannot yet explain. Like the stories of my pulls and sprains.

On the way to work, I pulled a muscle. I went to see the Railway Service doctor, who x-rayed the ankle and gave me a three-week leave from work. That very evening, a friend phoned to invite me for an outing and a walk that I really wasn't up to, and I told her about the injury. She knew a good bonesetter in Falaise and offered to drive me there. He was a little 85-year-old man, but still strong. He warned me that it would hurt and, while he did the maneuver, I bit my scarf so hard--so as not to cry out--that I broke a filling. So I was cured and had leave to go to the dentist.

When I returned later to see the SNCF doctor, he seemed surprised that I was so much better. Not wanting to undermine his practice, I offered no explanation.

Two years later, I again had a sprain—the other ankle—so I asked a friend right away to drive me to Falaise. I remembered the approximate address and arrived in the neighborhood, where I asked a passerby exactly where Monsieur Anne lived. "You mean Madame Anne, because Monsieur died last year," was the reply. I explained the reason for my visit to this helpful Falaisian, who then told me: "Monsieur Anne used to make people well, but the treatments were painful. You'd do better to go see Juliette in the house down below, on the turn in the road. She'll do you just as much good without the pain."

My friend didn't believe in this kind of treatment any more than I, but believing seemed unnecessary. I again picture myself leaning on his shoulder to go down the three steps leading to Juliette's residence. She made me take off the bandage before passing her hand about a centimeter above the ankle for two or three minutes. It gave me a localized sensation of heat, and strange shivers in my chest. I was cured, and could walk and climb the small staircase with no help.

Juliette had had time to tell me her life story. At the time of the Liberation, she was running a café-restaurant, where she would receive workers who were rebuilding the city.[*] Among them was a stonecutter who had the healing gift. One day, when she was in pain due to osteoarthritis of the shoulder, she asked him to treat her. At that time, he told her that she had the same healing power as he. Alas, this gift is often accompanied by alcoholism, so she decided not to do any bones that were old.

For my third sprain, I had to call on Madame Aubert, a healer from Reux, next to Pont-l'Evêque. She used to live below Route A13, in a charming little Norman style house with false beams, carefully painted.

The front of her house presented an expanse of lawn decorated with garden dwarfs and a statue of St. Theresa. Her flowerbeds were bright with rare flowers. Since she was very pious, she completed her healing moves with the sign of the cross and a short prayer. Without ever asking for anything, she collected whatever money her clients wished to forget on the corner of the buffet. She prescribed no medication and gave no opinions on medical treatments that were already in progress. So she was perfectly legal.

---

[*] According to American veterans of the Landing, 75% of Caen was in ruins after World War II.

I liked talking to this simple woman, so happy to make people feel better with her gift, which had been revealed to her under strange conditions. During a pilgrimage to Lourdes, she had met an old healer, a priest who had disclosed her power and exacted from her a moral obligation to use it to care for others.

She had dared to treat all sorts of sufferings, gradually enlarging her range of activities. She cured sprains, burns, rheumatisms, etc. Then, after having tested herself on a neighbor's goats, she realized that she could also cure animals.

Except for Sundays, she received callers every afternoon. The patients followed one another in and out of the courtyard, in their cars. By exercising her faculties, she had observed that they were developing further, and on Monday mornings she felt so recharged with energy that she had to use it.

People sometimes came from a distance to see her, but the strangest phenomenon came about when she tried to treat people long-distance, by putting her hands on photographs. It seemed impossible to her, but she had to acknowledge its effectiveness. Her little four-year-old son, on vacation in Vendée with relatives, had taken advantage of a moment of inattention to put his hand on the still-warm electric barbecue within his reach.

While the child was screaming, they put him on the telephone, and she succeeded in lessening his pain by working on his photograph. Even before being taken to the hospital, he was already feeling better. The doctor was very surprised by the unusual aspect of the burn, and the little boy healed very quickly.

Later, I sent her a friend who had been cruelly burnt on the hand with a blowtorch. She succeeded not only in eliminating the pain, but also in effecting a rapid healing. He has only a minimal scar now.

Although it's not part of her current activities, she has also been involved in finding lost persons by using their photographs. Sometimes she would receive information in a flash, enabling her to localize or visualize the place where the missing person could be found.   She gave the example of her friends' rat terrier, missing for three days, no doubt in pursuit of some small animal.   He was stuck in a pipe under a path in their park.   On her advisement, they broke the conduit and he was saved *in extremis.*[*]

For practical purposes, I asked her if she had ever happened to have sudden insights into the results of upcoming horse races.   She seemed rather shocked at my thought, which seemed unhealthy to her, and assured me that she had never experienced that.   A pity, perhaps!

---

[*] At the point of death.

CHAPTER VIII

APRIL FOOLS' JOKES

I enjoy this tradition, this business of April Fools' jokes, or *Poissons d'Avril*. For me, the joke is not an ill-intentioned one; it should leave even the victim with a pleasant memory. The ideal would be that one could enjoy one's own reactions, but these two conditions are not easy to achieve together. Sometimes, despite precautions, it also happens that someone is surprised by indirect or unexpected consequences, or the lack of humor in the "jokes."

For the school year 1967-1968, we had taken in Chris, an extremely nice American student, whose parents were of Sicilian origin. They still had family in Sicily. He was a handsome guy, rather fussy about his appearance. For his first haircut in France, he went to Brazard, the best hairdresser in the city, who engaged in styling competitions and had won many prizes. Now, this hair-styling artist found an unusual thickness to Chris's hair, and offered to coif him free for the year if Chris would serve as his model for the next competition, scheduled for May 1, 1968, on the isle of Jersey.

Alas, several months later, our student received this letter from Caen:

April 1, 1968

Dear Friend,

We have just received details for the preparation of the Jersey Competition. Towards the goal of a uniform presentation of the models, we are required to have them all wear a rather special form of beard, which we will also trim. We therefore ask you, from this present time, to allow your beard to grow as you wish, and then we will proceed with a first shaping within two weeks.

In addition, it has also been required of us that hair should be dyed a vivid, very modern, true red, to allow easy recognition of the Competition models for their trip on the Island. We are confident that you will not be inconvenienced by these small details. We also request that you come to our Salon promptly, to receive a first experimental application of the color.

Of course, after the competition, we could, if you wished, trim your beard or do away with it, the choice being up to you. We could also return your hair close to its original shade, should you so desire.

In anticipation of your next visit, dear Friend, we extend to you our very best wishes.

Signed, Brazard

Chris was dumbstruck.   Soon, during Easter vacation, he was to travel to Sicily with his parents, to visit family. With such a beard, he would no longer look like his passport photo, and having bright red hair seemed unacceptable to him. He never would have entered into this bargain if he had known the conditions. He wanted to go straightaway to see Brazard. Re-reading the troubling letter didn't help; he still didn't notice the famous date, also celebrated this way in the U.S.A.

Yvonne, my wife, kindly advised him to wait until I came back, to ask my opinion. This would leave him time to discover the trap and also allow me to enjoy my joke. Around mid-day, I had him re-read the date. The tradition of the date continued, adding a new "victim."

This trick must have inspired my friend André to trap his wife's colleague, who used to tell the office all the details of her private life. She couldn't go to her hairdresser without everyone being alerted, and she had the misfortune to go there on March 29.

On April first, André called the chatterbox at his wife's office, pretending to be the proprietor of the hair salon where she had just been, and he said something like this:

"Madame, how are you? The day before yesterday, we applied a color toner. We're so sorry, but we just received a telegram informing us of an error in the composition of the product. This error would cause hair to fall out after several days. Are you beginning to lose it in clumps?"

After her denial, he signed off by saying:

"Don't upset yourself, we have every reason to believe that the hair will grow back normally and, in the meantime, the salon would be happy to offer you—free—a superb wig in the color of your choice. And this will allow you to appreciate the effect of a new hairdo!"

The next day, the "victim" was absent and advised her office that the doctor had ordered a one-week absence for a depression following a severe fright. Ironically, Madame André had to take on her work, in addition to her own.

Not discouraged, the following year André asked for my collusion for another *Poisson* of his invention. His brother-in-law from La Baule had the bad habit of making important household decisions totally on his own. André, knowing that they were planning to change their black and white television set for a color one, asked me to play the TV salesman on the phone.

I had to call the sister-in-law at a time when she would be alone, to make the following proposition:

--Good day, ma'am!   May I speak with your husband?

--He's not here right now, but would you like me to take a message?

--He just stopped by the store to buy a new color TV set, but he wanted us to resell the old black and white. Well, we just found an interested customer, but we would have to show it to him right now. If you agree, before we deliver your new set, I have a favor to ask. For the color reception to be excellent, we have to replace your antenna cord with a new model cable. I'm sure you have a measuring tape at home. Would you please measure, as accurately as possible, the length of the present cable, so that I can bring you exactly what you need to replace it?

At that moment, she realized that it was April first.

The telephone allows some excellent jokes. But it isn't always a success and, unfortunately, the visual effect is lost. The answering machine is a very important ancillary that I have used for a long time. Unfailingly, I consult it after an absence. One night, we came back from vacation to find that the machine had recorded more than thirty messages, several from the same person.

One of my renters from #126 was reporting that the toilet was plugged up. Then another call came in, reporting that the situation had worsened; someone who was unaware of the problem must have used it. Then another: "Monsieur Idrac, this is an emergency, the back-up is awful!" And a woman's voice in the background, prompting my caller: "Tell him that it's overflowing!"

Dropping everything, I hurried to 126 with the necessary tools. Seeing my equipment, the renters feigned surprise: "No, no, Monsieur Idrac, everything is fine. Nothing has happened."

There are *petits poissons* (little fish) that can truly take on the savor of a real fish. So, one year, I searched the whole Caen train station for a carful of compressed air cartridges, to recharge the air bubbles in the spirit levels that we used for checking horizontal surfaces.

Another time, I had placed on the "service aisle" in front of the window of my office, a worn-out, disposable lighter attached to a fixed point with a strong nylon string. I can still see the head of the first "victim," who, believing that he had found something for nothing, leaned over discretely to recuperate it. When he noticed that it was attached, he glanced around quickly, saw our hilarious faces behind the windows, and left.

I hardly had time to camouflage the string again, when an Arab came by. He was strong, and succeeded in detaching the line with a single pull, then went off delighted with a fuel-depleted lighter that still sparkled like new.

Shortly thereafter, a third "victim" arrived, the best one. Having been told about it by the first person, she came to look for the lighter, wanting to carry it off at all costs, but it had just been taken.

The following year, I suggested to my renter that I install a pool in the yard. The proposition didn't seem to entice him.

--What do I want to do with it, give my dog a bath?

--No, but you'd always be able to put your *Poisson d'Avril* in there!

He hung up coldly. I really felt that he was not impressed—neither with my suggestion nor my response.

Arlette's greenhouse, placed at high noon on top of the garages, could easily reach 45° C.[*] This gave birth to the idea to mount it on rails to laterally cover the pool that I would build next door. Our daughter Béatrice made us happy by believing in this plan for forty-eight hours.

If we're traveling on the first of April, I come up against bigger obstacles, but, with imagination, they are not insurmountable. I remember the year we were in Corsica. When the hotel agent gave me my change, I refused a bill, telling her very seriously: "Madame, didn't you listen to the news this morning? This bill is out of circulation, starting today. You'll have to take it to the bank."

I recall another adventure, which could have been a beautiful *poisson,* but it was only February. I had to spend the afternoon at la Chaise-Dieu in the Massif Central, visiting that magnificent abbey church and the surrounding region. Then, on Sunday, I'd be off to see Puy. Alas, since it had snowed 25 cm[+] and I had only street shoes, I found myself limited in visiting that monument.

Given the snowy weather, I was the only person for the 3 p.m. visit. I was inclined to prolong it to the maximum, not having the option of doing anything else; so I was asking the guide whatever questions came to mind. At the twentieth

---

[*] Fahrenheit = 9/5 Celsius + 32.

[+] 1 centimeter = 0.3937 inches.

question, he pointed out that he was capable of answering me and of then picking up his presentation where he had left off, without having to begin it over again. I explained that I had absolutely no intention of complicating his life, that I appreciated his abilities, but I would have been truly surprised if he had felt obliged to begin over again.

The choir of the church is decorated with many 16th century tapestries; I had never before felt captivated by this form of art, but that day I was sincerely interested. This meant even more questions put to my cicerone. It was the end of the afternoon, and getting quite dark--meaning that the visit had to end--when the guide said to me: "Monsieur, you have asked me a tremendous number of questions, and you could see that I always knew how to answer. Would you allow me to take a turn now and ask you one?"

--Of course. And I'll be happy to answer, if I can.

--You are the Inspector of Historical Monuments, correct?

Since it wasn't April Fools' Day, I humbly confessed that I was nothing of the sort, but told him how much I appreciated his extensive knowledge and the interest he took in his work.

At the least, I had built his self-confidence for the day when the real Inspector would come. As for me, I had won his friendship and he lent me his personal documentation on the Abbey church, allowing me to spend a long and pleasant winter evening.

I could have related many other *Poissons d'Avril,* but I thought it better to limit myself to this little shish-ka-bob instead of giving you indigestion from fancy fried foods.

CHAPTER IX

CONSTRUCTION PROJECTS

As a youngster, I already had a taste for building; my father had given me a corner of the yard along the fence wall, to build a hut. To make it solid, I used a mixture of mud and stones, but I had neither joiners nor grooved timbers to make it very high.

Even reduced to less than a meter of ground, I had equipped it with a phone. In this case, it was an old water pipe, which made an excellent acoustical tube leading to the outside. It also allowed you to surprise the person on the other end with a good puff of air in his ear.

The wall on the Coteaux path had been destroyed during the Landing, so I later persuaded my mother to rebuild it five meters into our property and to create in its place seven garages, the first ones in a long series.

Our yard was situated between two streets of different heights, so I used the terraced plot to increase the number of excavations in the yard, and to bring all the soil onto the level of Branville Street. This opened the possibility of subsequent buildings, which my mother wouldn't hear of at the moment.

The following year, my mother agreed to have two garages built, leading onto Branville Street, in place of our henhouse—one for the car that we were going to buy and one to pay the cost of maintaining it. This time, Company C. refused to work under my conditions, and presented their own estimate; I considered it unacceptable, so I persuaded Mom that, for that price, I myself could build the garages plus four others. The deal was made, and I added another two above those on the Chemin des Coteaux.

Since we now had oil heat, the useless coal cellar was easily transformed into the garage for our Renault 4 CV. Then, I used another lost space under the house, for yet another garage. It was the seventeenth that I built for Mom.

These rather simple edifices had opened my horizons and given rise to other ambitions. Observing that the north wall of the property was 3½ meters from the blind side of the house, I dreamed up a project for building a three-room apartment that would need a short length of wall. This was accomplished in less than a year's spare time. But everything had become more arduous, necessitating a roof framework, a tile roof, everything for the second structure: doors, windows, floor, plumbing, plastering, electricity, carpeting...

I had found it money-saving to use "seconds" for the flooring, placing slabs in a rather free-form pattern, after having broken them one by one with a quick hammer blow, which cracked them in an easy-to-assemble triangular form. We mixed in several shades in planned proportions, adding blue and white touches to brighten up the total effect.

I still see myself helping Cocorapide prepare the mortar for the sealed surface. He worked to the accompaniment of a song by Edith Piaf: « Comme un air de 14 juillet. Padam! Padam! Padam ». At each Padam, we would turn over a shovel-full. Try working to that rhythm!

I had also recruited Arlette to put pieces of the flooring on the fresh mortar surface. You had to negotiate regular, medium-spaced spaces in between. No piece could be placed backwards; there's one in the W.C. that got by me, and every day I regret this negligence! To avoid placement problems, you have to follow a convex line of work.

In the course of the icy winter of 1954, the ten meters of the old wall of the Coteaux Path, spared during the War, had collapsed. I asked my mother for permission to construct four garages in this area, but now for my own benefit.

At that time, 75 cubic meters of earth did not justify using a mechanical digger, so I called on a team of Sicilians who would work for a fixed rate. They were giants, and very thirsty; every day I offered them a case of Mascara wine, which they complained about, because they weren't used to wine that was 13% alcohol. It made them a little dizzy, but they could neither drink less nor cut it with water, to adequately quench their thirst.

During a downpour, they taught me the game of "Mora." The players throw a hand on the table with a certain number of fingers outstretched, each player shouting his guess at the sum of all the fingers held out by the players. Winner takes all, and then it starts over again. It's a pastime of bandits and cheats, and often ends at knifepoint.

Since we were playing without money, the game held no melodrama. The excitement came at the settling of our fee, when they tried to collect more than their due. I held firmly to the signed contract. My mother was horrified to see me, all alone, confront these four pairs of muscular arms, but, solid in my rights, I wasn't afraid. Moreover, they didn't insist in a nasty manner; they simply wanted to try out their complaint, for the sake of the gesture...

Being only a "pencil-pusher" by profession, whose daily work ended up sooner or later flung aside or in the archives before its final destruction, I experienced a drunken euphoria in filling empty space with solid edifices that could last for decades. But when my niche as joint proprietor reached saturation point, I had to go looking for other sites.

In 1958, the abandoned park of Monsieur Lamusse (my art teacher for one day) came up for sale. It was a stretch of land at the foot of a cliff, separated from the rail line of Caen-Cherbourg by the access path two to three meters below. This site, hardly propitious for the building of a bungalow, suited me. I sold my four garages to Arlette in order to acquire it.

The city architect required that I include planting trees in the project, because the terrain was within the protected perimeter of the Grand Cours. Our survey map showed the land contours, so that we could reduce the movements of earth. Since the access ramp to the interior path had to be straight, I made a scale model, in order to study it carefully.

The basic terrain work, 500 cubic meters, was accomplished with an enormous Michigan earthmover whose bucket picked up more than a cubic meter of earth with one scoop. Fortunately, we were able to deposit it, free of charge, in a huge ditch nearby.

I found myself in old rock quarries, a former loading bank for cartloads. This presented 50 cubic meters of rock, against which the teeth of the Michigan were useless. Explosives were forbidden, so I hired « Bouboule » to break the rock by hand.

« Bouboule » : I had never known him by any other name. He was a strange little fellow--full of energy, muscular as a wrestler, and a former quarryman. He lived with his large family in emergency city housing on Armand Marie Street. That year, during the month of June, I would pick him up every morning at 4 a.m., and later drive him back to his regular job at 7:30 a.m., to begin a full workday there. I profited from his best working hours. Although he had episodes of heavy vomiting, we attached no importance to that.

Sometimes we fell onto fissured limestone, but there were also relatively hard rocks that had to be attacked with the pick and freed from the mine pit. So that he could use all his strength on the mass with both hands, I had to hold the tool that we stuck into the rock. Not without a certain apprehension; it reminded me of the movie « *Jour de Fête* », when the "cross-eyed one" pounds in the circus tent pegs. Fortunately, his vision was clear at that hour, and the powerful blow was sure.

When he dug out nice-looking pieces of rock, I lined them up, with an eye to using them in the construction at a later date. The refuse would be used for leveling. If Bouboule extracted a large block, he carried it on his head, walked it further off, and split it. Educated in trade from the ground up--no pun intended--he had learned on the job, with his father.

Repeatedly, he told me the strange story of his sister who, after the Landing, had married a very rich American officer who had wanted to help him realize his one dream: returning to the earth. Bouboule saw himself as a farmer, surrounded by all sorts of animals. Later, I learned the ending of this true fairy tale: The American had come with his wife, had seen Bouboule's miserable home, and immediately retracted all his promises. Alas, Bouboule despaired of reaching the farm dream, and died disillusioned, with no dream to replace it.

We needed 30 cubic meters of concrete. Since "pre-fab" didn't exist at that time, a construction friend lent me his concrete mixer and a spreader. At the last minute, the concrete mixer was unavailable, and he supplied eight Arab laborers in its place. The spreader was a sort of super-wheelbarrow, one cubic meter in size, with a rear-guiding engine situated under the driver. This required him to execute inverse maneuvers, so that a turn to the right went left. This very dangerous engine has since been outlawed.

At the hiring, the driver of the spreader was missing, so a mason kindly volunteered to replace him. He gave it up after two swerves that frightened him as much as me. I had to go get the real driver at his home in Flers, in order to unblock the construction site.

Rémy was handling the installation of the garage doors, and he enlisted the help of his brother-in-law, on leave from the psychiatric hospital. But the door closing system was unique, and Rémy lacked the expertise to attach the upper rail, which fell again and again under its own weight. He went into a fit of anger. At the height of his exasperation, he hurled a panel to the ground, hollering: "Hang your goddamn doors yourself, wherever you want. I give up!"

While I was reflecting, not on the different places where I could have "hung" them, but on their means of fixation, the scene was extraordinary. The patient was trying vainly to calm his brother-in-law and also to reassure me with words that he must have heard directed to him at the hospital: "Don't be afraid. You musn't hold it against him. He isn't mean. It's going to be okay..."

It was Père Poutard, a good mason, who carried off the hanging of the doors after having made a simple gauge to hold the upper rail in place long enough for quick-drying cement to harden. These doors were quite satisfactory, and I was flattered when I caught a real finish carpenter copying the model.

When the garages were done, they still had to be rented. But they were located a bit far from downtown and classified ad newspapers didn't yet exist. One morning at dawn, I stuck 250 fliers on the windshields of parked cars. The garages filled up quickly.

After our third child, Agnes, was born, we started to feel cramped for space; fortunately, the land adjoining our property was for sale. I sold the group of small homes there and built, parallel to our house, three rooms, with a garage and a cellar underground.

In excavating, we discovered several fossils in the shelly calcium deposits, one of which was a fish remarkably well preserved. We were in a quarry backfill and found rock outcroppings characteristic of three or four centuries earlier, formed by the dumping of wheelbarrows full of earth.

The most delicate operation was the resumption of work on the old fence wall. Some of our blood had ended up in the timbers before I entrusted this patience-demanding chore to an elderly worker. When I expressed concern that he was using a pick so twisted that it almost folded back onto itself he assured me that his own personal tool was no better.

That was how I hired Tonio. He had trained on worksites as a mason. It was he who opened the wall to link up the two sections of construction. Our daughter Béatrice protested: "Stop, Monsieur Tonio, you'll break the house!" He was a born artist, playing guitar perfectly without even knowing how to read music. When he was young, he used to perform in dance orchestras. That was how he met his wife. Alas, she was too jealous, no doubt rightfully so, to let him continue in this iniquitous musical activity...

At the age of 14, during the Spanish War, he had been sentenced to death *in absentia*. Paradoxically, I had to obtain French citizenship for him so that he could return to his native country for some vacation-time, with minimum risk. His wife was very nervous that, in the euphoria of the trip and its reunions, he would express seditious views in public. Franco was not yet dead!

The following year, back in Caen, Tonio asked his sister to come and visit. She had never left her Andalusian countryside of Aguadolce, and for nothing in the world would have accepted such modern experiences as being shut up in an elevator or riding an escalator. At his house, she asked for the bathroom, and was surprised to find it installed in the house itself and not in the back of the yard. He showed her the little chain for flushing, but omitted the explanation of what would happen. As soon as she pulled it, she jumped out in a panic, wondering what flood she had let loose.

My friend Totor installed central heating in the extension. He was a former Navy volunteer, who had survived three torpedo attacks, and had saved the life of the man who later became our Minister Messmer. Taken prisoner in Indochina by the Japanese, he had come back with a curious malady: He would fall asleep unexpectedly. Many times I had to wake him when he was working late and having dinner with us, for he would stop eating with the soup spoon halfway from the bowl to his mouth.

His sleep troubles brought painful spells of insomnia, with morning drowsiness. One day, when he had to take the 6 a.m. train to Argentan, he hadn't heard the alarm, and tried to catch up with his work crew by hitchhiking. A kindly driver picked him up, and offered to buy him a cup of coffee when he arrived at the work site. Leaving the flow of traffic, they found the car surrounded by policemen, who took the driver to the station at gunpoint. According to them, this accommodating driver had just committed a robbery and, in his flight had run over one of them, which they did not appreciate at all. According to their information, the bandit was alone, so Totor's presence surprised them. To clear himself, Totor had to have the mounted police call up his boss and explain why he was not at work.

Totor had a very good heart. After the war, he had married a girl who was leading a hard life, in order to make things better for her. They had been living in an SNCF apartment building where everybody knew everybody's business. A good buddy considered it his duty to inform him that, in his absence and with his young children there, his wife was entertaining a boyfriend. He immediately broke two of the little informer's teeth. A week later he apologized, then asked his wife for a divorce. After that, the guys would call him names, but never to his face, for fear of getting beat up.

One year, when he had answered an irresistible ad for a summer rental in Yugoslavia, they showed him such a hovel that, in his words, "It couldn't have served even as a henhouse." He then recounted without embellishment everything that he had witnessed in this Communist "paradise," which upset those workshop pals of his who were members of the Party and wanted to keep their dreams and the popular legends alive.

When I went to his house, I never accepted anything to drink, but on this particular day, he was treating himself to a dish of sea snails, eating them cold with a dark brown sauce. He served me a small plate of it and, while he recommended that I not smell the sauce, his son advised the opposite. That's how I discovered Nuoc'Mân, a sauce from Indonesia made with decomposed fish.

To cut back the workforce of the SNCF, a decree had come out that favored the anticipated retirement of railroad workers who were war veterans. Totor wanted to take advantage of the offer, but he fulfilled only two of the three conditions. Cool as a cucumber, he had gone unannounced to see Messmer, shaking up the bailiff, who was astounded to hear his Minister praising the intruder immediately after the incident. [Remember, he had saved his life!] But, despite the Minister's letter passed through the general administration, Totor was unsuccessful. We felt sorry for him.

A little later, to maximize the benefit of my newly acquired land, I undertook the construction of four garages on the Chemin des Coteaux. For the earthmoving, I had employed my neighbor Père Maison, who usually was a charming fellow. His wife, who had lost all gratitude for the Germanic paternity that he had assumed (although he was a prisoner in Germany at the time), treated him very badly. She was so mean that she affixed this sign to the entrance door, under her husband's name: "Beware of dog."

In his youth, Père Maison used to spend Sundays participating in bicycle races. When he would see Yvonne pushing Laurent in his baby carriage, he always said to her: "Oh, Madame, how proud you will be later, when your son wins village bicycle races!" Laurent did nothing of the sort.

A developer wanted to transform the gardens in the Blot housing development by adding apartment buildings. Just across from our house, he had placed a billboard to sell two badly situated lots in the shade of the large unit that he planned to build. These land parcels were separated by partially ripped out metal fencing. Together with my father-in-law, I bought one of them, to build garages there.

I had envisaged placing garages around a central courtyard, which would have been advantageous for my neighbor, sheltering him from the north winds. And yet he had refused to agree to it, under the pretext that he didn't want this type of proximity. So I had to build them at an angle in the middle of the land, to stay five meters from his property. This plan reduced considerably the required wall surfaces, but meant that two rather inconveniently angled entry/exit lanes had to be added.

The seventeen lintels had just been completed when Michaud, the neighbor, went up to his house. I was watching carefully to be sure that he also would respect the five-meter distance between our properties. I noted with horror that, with no warning, he had destroyed the separating wire fence and reduced the access path to a width insufficient for the ingress and egress of cars.

Information in hand, he had had property limits verified by a surveyor, and declared that the fence had been positioned inaccurately. The business agent, acting as negotiator, succeeded in getting back my indispensable strip of land by giving him the double of it on the other side of his plot. At my own expense, I had to establish a low dividing wall. With these troubles, I felt the first signs of hypertension.

My friend Printemps participated in the labor according to his availability,. He was an Italian from the Frioul, a tall blue-eyed blond, which cast him as a typical Austrian. I had known and appreciated him from the era of the first garages; he used to work as an unskilled laborer for his cousins, the owners of Company C. They had brought him over after the War, for the reconstruction of Caen. They were relatives, but had taken him in as a boarder at nearly the sum of his salary. Taking advantage of their family relationship, they paid him no overtime hours, and he was at their beck and call.

This intelligent man quickly learned the trade, and from a simple unskilled laborer became an excellent all-around mason. He understood that it was in his interest to find independent housing if he wanted to bring home a salary. As soon as he could, he returned to Italy to marry his beloved, a schoolteacher, who came back to France to live with him and bear him ten children.

He had feelings about leaving his exploiting cousins, who had hired him when he was unemployed in Italy. His wife had the impression of betraying Italy if they asked our nationality, and learned that he was not working for Italians. European prospects paving the way, I succeeded in convincing them to become French in order to be hired by the city bus company, and to benefit from the many advantages reserved for large families.

Printemps was very courageous. He had fought in the war in Yugoslavia, charging with a bayonet to the cry of « *Savoia !* » He possessed uncommon strength, and had even once lifted a carriage single-handed, to free a boy who was trapped. Printemps was a real Jean Valjean.[*]

Sometimes he had bizarre ideas. He wore work boots with reinforced toes, guaranteed to withstand 800 kilos[+] of pressure. One day, he put his foot under a small truck, which must have been around that weight. The vehicle passed over without crushing his foot, but the shoe burst from the ordeal. It must have been at the end of its warranty.

At the table, he didn't leave his place. When he took salad, you had to serve him in the salad bowl. Plums, he swallowed with the pit, while complaining about not being able to eat many at one time, because they inexplicably gave him stomach problems. For a party meal at his house, they prepared a kilo of meat for each guest.

He liked to illustrate his comments with colorful Italian proverbs. He had simple tastes; for him, happiness lay in this one saying: *Acqua fresca, vino puro, castro duro.* [Cool water, pure wine, a firm sofa].

After the birth of Laurent, we needed another room, so that each of the four children could have his/her own room. Urban rules prohibited adding on in an "L" shape, so I had to enlarge the house by its length.

Several embarrassing problems came up. First, the soil of the four garages was 80 cm higher than the level of the existing house. I thought of establishing the new enlargement on two levels: One at 40 cm would include the entrance door and the bedroom facing the street, the other at 80 cm would be just above the garages, and include the central room facing the yard and the third bedroom. For the façade on Branville Street, the entry door was set back and preceded by an arched porch, to avoid an impression of misalignment.

---

[*] In Victor Hugo's novel *Les Miserables* (1862), fugitive Jean Valjean unveils his identity when he uses his extraordinary strength to single-handedly lift a carriage and free a man trapped underneath.

[+] 1 kilo(gram) = 2.2046 pounds

Then, so that the roof of the new, higher construction would not go beyond the existing wall, I had planned for two sides opening onto a central gutter.   This arrangement allowed a glass-paned cover on the entry hall.

Later, I found a solution that would also provide the ideal natural light in the living room: This roofing was oriented to the south, so shade was necessary from springtime to autumn. Following the slope of the roof, two gravity-driven sliding panels and a counterweight easily raised them again. The ceiling had been fitted with double blades of glass, to avoid condensation.

There also was my inheritance to consider: the property at 16 Chemin de Bretteville at Douvres. I wanted to remodel it into two modern and comfortable apartments, complete for each renter with a garage big enough to include a cellar.

It was painful for me to transform that early 19th century house that held so many happy childhood memories. I thought of the Austrian coin dated 1814, embedded there according to custom, that we had found in the lintel over the doorway. At first, I wanted to preserve the old part of the roof, with its pretty tiles, but certain imperfections of the roofing worried me, so I took it down.   That was wise, because healthy-looking chevrons crumbled when we tossed them into the yard.

We re-distributed all the openings of this southern-exposure house, then installed bathrooms, toilets and central heating. My slightly tipsy team of masons worked badly. After having put up the scaffolding, they tried to charge me a prohibitive flat rate for the façade. The plasterer put me in touch with Marcel, a mason who managed to be hired after they were underway. I leave you to judge their reaction when I told them to get their building materials out of there!

A considerable amount of earth had to be moved to conform to the urban building code and set the garages back from the street. Lesommier, with his mechanical shovel, took on the responsibility of the work. We got along well during that time; he seemed to have a certain admiration for the work.

With all this barely done, Lesommier let me know that a sizeable acreage in the industrial zone of Douvres was up for auction. It included a large unfinished house, built without a permit. I had no more liquid assets, and didn't want to borrow. A childhood friend who lived in the Paris region was looking to invest, so I let him know about the opportunity. He bought the land at a great bargain price, and proposed financing all the work himself, with me directing it on site, and us splitting the profits 50/50.

Quickly, I closed up the property and, after considerable reflection and guidance, built—with his consent—camper storage and boatsheds. This legalized the existing structure, which would become an office and lodging for the watchman. I went to Fécamp to buy all the necessary doors and windows at a liquidation sale.

Our research showed that, for financial reasons, it really was important for us to become incorporated. My childhood friend wouldn't hear of it. Watch out for your real friends! Had he hoped that, with him being sole owner, I would work for him as if he were the King of Prussia, annexing lands for his glory? Thanks to his wife, I was reimbursed for my first investments, but our collaboration stopped there.

Lesommier was upset that this golden opportunity ended badly for me, and said: "Your friend is a crook, be careful not to deal with him. Right now, I am creating a plot in Douvres, a land parcel where you could be in charge of development. You'd be able to use the doors and windows that you just bought and I'd give you the foundations free." That was how I came to create the villa of Sorbiers.*

---

* *sorbier* = sorb or wild service tree, any of several Old World trees bearing bunches of apple- or pear-like fruit, eaten by the birds. The sorb trees in this story bear red bunches of apple-like fruit.

Up to this point, I had always had constraints because of what was already in place, whereas now I could work more freely. I was inspired by one of the housing projects of type F5 that the Equipment Company puts at the disposal of builders, and conceived of a spacious single dwelling on a partially-below-ground basement level where there would be a large workshop-garage, a [wine] cellar, a heated laundry room, and a completely independent extra room.

Lesommier not only did the promised excavating, but also lent me his theodolite [surveyor's instrument] to measure all the horizontal and vertical angles for leveling, plus a work shed to store tools and cement. After excavating, he had prefabricated concrete delivered for the foundations and slab.

Marcel the mason would ride with me from Caen to Douvres. En route, he and I would philosophize; he was a convinced Communist, who awaited the Great Tomorrow. I finally told him that if I had believed in it myself, I would not have given him any work, and would have chosen to place my money elsewhere. He was open to this reasoning which, in his mind, must have simply postponed the coming of the "singing tomorrows."

In the group of houses going up at Sorbiers, ours was the first to appear above ground level; that is, above foundations. We still appeared to be working in an open field, because only the roadway had been established. When we heard the Offertory bells in the church of Douvres, Marcel never failed to comment: "The curé is happy, he made a good collection, he's ringing the bells!"

Alex, the wood-worker, had brought in a carpenter friend to help build the roof trusses. I can visualize them again, tracing the roofline in the earth, trimming it exactly at the sides, then assembling it there before we all put it up together. I have a fond memory of each time the bradawls fell into the heart of the oak, making holes for the brads and screws.

La villa des Sorbiers

We erected a four-sectioned, flat-tiled roof, laid on bituminous felt to keep snow out, in case of a storm. This very elegant roof was heavy, and took a lot of wood.

I had an old, experienced plasterer who worked for a flat fee, because he had his own ways of saving time. Before beginning a ceiling, he would fashion a scaffolding of such a height that the plaster-holding lathes were 5 cm higher than his cap. This allowed him to plaster without raising his arms any more than necessary.

In his large wooden trough, he would mix an entire sack of plaster with water, then smoke a cigarette while waiting for it to begin to set. After a moment, as if to accelerate this, he would pull from the bottom of an almost-empty bag, one or two fistfuls of what looked like plaster. This he mixed with the rest of the troweling, before beginning to spread it out. It was, in fact, fertilizer, meant to give him more time for the setting of the final job. This trickery also allowed him to put up the ceiling perfectly while using much less plaster, saving time and easing labor.

Printemps, who had observed this maneuver, had fun one day replacing his bag with another, identical but actually containing plaster. It set up in normal time, and the troweling was partially lost. The plasterer was dumbfounded and furious.

The painting and carpeting work was considerable. I couldn't refuse Marcel's request to hire his unemployed son, who did this work as his trade. One day, arriving on the work site unannounced, I looked everywhere for my painter. I discovered him hidden in the cellar where, by a string through the window, he was controlling the descent of a trap to catch thrushes.

It was in my interest to keep a close watch on my artist. Another time, when he had been absent from work, I received a call from the prison when I arrived back home. It was the social worker, who asked if I knew a certain Loison O., and could put up 400 francs in cash, for he had been fined and detained and, lacking payment of this sum before the close of the work day, would spend two weeks in prison.

So I went to free the convict, and I assisted at the lifting of the bolt. Loison had definitely lost his haughty attitude, and found himself profoundly humiliated. The guards, who had seen others in his situation, were rather amused by his demeanor. The head guard asked what he had thought of the noontime soup. A while before, he had confessed to me that he hadn't been able to swallow anything, but he assured the head guard that it was excellent, and that he would have liked soup that good when he had been a prisoner in Germany.

On the drive back to his house, Loison told me his story: He had lent his car to a buddy, who was cited for driving on worn tires. As the owner, Loison was responsible, but the summons didn't stipulate the reasons, and he hadn't responded until that very morning. At the station, they had demanded the sum of the fine, refused his settlement by check, and denied his request to go home for cash.

When the renter moved out of my old family home at 126 rue Branville, I went ahead with a complete renovation. I transformed the whole, including some very old sections, into two apartments and five furnished rooms. This meant central heating, showers and toilets. The wood-worker completely renovated an attic room, covering the ceiling and carefully insulating the entire area.

To provide work for my unemployed friend Philippe, I asked him to make a greenhouse for my sister, Arlette. This became a superb veranda and the largest room in Arlette's house—nearly 30 square meters—with an extraordinary view over the meadow and the city.

This is not the place to speak of all the maintenance work, nor of the smaller "add-ons," nor of the magnificent land that my in-laws gave us at Montlouis, where I immediately planted trees. The whole family now good-naturedly calls it "the hedged farmland." My health did not allow me to build on it. Everything ends.

*Il ne nous manque qu'une petite maison de
rapport avec six locataires qui paient bien.*
[What we need is a little investment property with six
good-paying renters.]*

--Céline, *Voyage au bout de la Nuit*
[Voyage to the End of the Night]

CHAPTER X

THE HAPPY LANDLORD

I must have been born to be a landlord, like my
father. This aspiration flows from a spirit of foresight
blissfully ignorant of taxes and heedless of maintenance
work, the frequency and timing of which are as
unpredictable as the costs are unforeseeable.

Of course, the ideal situation implies that the renters
pay regularly and that neither they nor the neighbors pick
quarrels with you that cause you to lose sleep. For this
investment would then become a catastrophic affair.

Dad was a good landlord; after having collected the
fee and glued the required fiscal stamps on the receipt, he
would offer a little glass of cassis to his renter, la Mère
Morin. After her children had left and the house became too
big for her, my father suggested that she rent a room from
him. He tempted her with a false ad, which I have kept:
"1939, THE YEAR YOU HAVE TO BUILD!"

So he had three new rooms built, to make a modern
lodging with a bathroom, tub and indoor toilet, all connected
to the sewer system. He even had an electrical outlet put in
the kitchen, to allow, if one wished, listening to the
"wireless" [the radio] or doing the ironing. This was the last
word in domestic comfort. Each room was heated by its own

---

* Author's note: An amusing coincidence! At one point, I actually had a
small rental property with six apartments, but having the tenants pay well
was sometimes a challenge!

fireplace, finished in salvaged marble. Dad even had a cellar put in under the new section, to store wine, food supplies and coal.

Netzer, a small independent businessman and an Austrian political refugee, was in charge of the work. Since it was well along, my father did not refuse to sign several bills in advance, for debts that would fall due upon completion at the work site. It was precisely at that moment that the work was interrupted. We had just declared war with Germany. Netzer was drafted with his truck, for military transportation.

Two weeks later, the government discovered that our builder came from an enemy country. They took his vehicle from him and he was placed in a concentration camp. My father had no choice but to honor his signature and pay a second time, for sub-contractors to finish the jobs.

Let's pass quickly over the war, the semi-destruction of the house in 1944, its difficult reconstruction, and the blocked rents; all this changed a rental into a sinecure for the occupying forces. It was only about thirty years later, with this house in arrears for my inheritance, that I was able to profit from the departure of the renter to transform it into five rooms and two separate furnished apartments, dividing up the risks of the insolvency of the renters. For in spite of all the care taken to select good renters, and a certain experience in the matter, only the actual live-in period tells if the choice was unfortunate and if they might move out with no forwarding address.

I remember this nice young couple who did not mention that they had been having serious relationship problems. They fought like cats and dogs and promptly broke everything, beyond the total of their deposit. I was forced to replace the shower and the sink, totally repaint, and buy new carpeting.

Another time, I took pity on an old, alcoholic couple who smoked constantly and had cancer; no one else had wanted them. They had raised eleven children who, alas, came frequently to see them. Some were homeless, so the couple had converted their little cellar into a miserable bedroom. All the sons had been in prison, and it showed on their faces. One used to terrorize the other renters with a perfectly realistic, fake plastic pistol. When I finally got rid of them, the tobacco smoke deposit was so thick that I had to wash the walls.

I also rented to a "musician" who worked by day at a lettuce-shredding plant and, in the evening, staged modern dance programs with stolen speakers. I had to make him leave before the neighbors became as deaf as he.

After running a "For Rent" ad in the newspaper, I never concluded the deal without considering the applicant in person. Even so, we found that the loud, convivial life style of some did not make them the renters of our dreams. Sometimes, when the family was large, I was tempted to pretend that the apartment was already rented.

I was approached by a madam who wanted to rent all my rooms so that her girls could work there--impossible, the location was in a different zoning category.

One day, however, I did have my self-employed worker, who did not present herself by that title. She was not unattractive, but her glass eye must have brought down her price a little, and led her to have promotional offers. I found out what was going on only much later, through my friend David, who also lived in the house. Arriving home one evening, he crossed paths with an acquaintance, who burst out laughing and said: "Oh, this is funny; I didn't know that she had your business, too."

I also rented rooms to Turkish workers who, all in all, didn't create any problems. But the story of one among them stands out. He was a well-brought-up lad who had satisfied his military service in the National Guard of his country, and he was a wood-worker held in high esteem by his employer. Luck would have it that I was also renting to a pretty young girl employed at the General Treasury.

They cried when they told me of their plan to get married, asking me to be their witness. For this event, Ali's employer had given him the necessary wood to make a superb dining room.

A week before the wedding, I met the happy fiancé, who looked gloomy, and said to me: "Oh! If you knew what happened to me. I really wonder if I should get married. My fiancée just now told me that her brother has been sentenced to life for theft and murder. I hesitate to go into such a family." I comforted him, assuring him that this was not a contagious disease. Then I attended their wedding.

They divorced a year later. Benefiting from her married name, she had found a new companion of a background more similar to hers, with whom perhaps she had omitted to speak of her brother, who would yet live in the shadows for a long time to come.

Another time, I came back from the office to a renter who informed me that a girl was locked up in the Turk's place, in the upper room, and that she was calling for help. If she's calling for help—*au secours*—we have to call the police, right? This I did, promising them that I would also be on the premises. We arrived at almost the same time.

With some effort and their convincing voices, they succeeded in having the door opened. We found the young girl perfectly nude. The Turk, however, was still dressed. The cops immediately demanded his visa and working papers. Although they repeatedly asked the girl to get dressed, she did not. At their insistence, she finally confessed: "I can't, he locked my clothes in the armoire!"

Then we understood that we were intervening in a business dispute. She was asking 50 francs, the equivalent of about $10, for her service, and he wanted to give her only a box of powder and a tube of lipstick.

The young person, finally dressed, had no ID to prove that she was not a minor.

--Where are your papers?

--At home.

--Well, we'll drive you home. Where do you live?

-- With the nuns!

I myself did not attend the scene at the convent. The Turk, his curiosity aroused, tried his best to keep her with him. But the police were insistent, and made it clear that if she was a minor, he would pay dearly. The next day I put him out, with no resistance, for having dishonored my house.

Shortly after the arrival of Gobbois, I had noticed an abnormally high rate of electricity used. He had an electrical heater, which was not allowed. I reminded him diplomatically of our regulations, noting with interest the large world map he had posted, with itineraries penciled in.

I discovered that this bachelor was an avid traveler and photographer. A craftsman, he subcontracted for electrical wiring in homes, he said. As soon as he had rebuilt a nest egg, he would be off again for other horizons. Speaking several languages, he had accompanied expeditions as a photographer, driver, interpreter, etc.--which allowed him to travel at reduced rates.

I invited him to dinner, so that he could show us his slides of China. They were remarkable photographs; afterwards, we received him several times, with friends, in order to have more people there to appreciate the show. In response to our curiosity, he extended himself, and his commentaries on the photos became better and better. He had quality photo equipment and an excellent projector. Being very accommodating, he even came to put on a program for our parish house *soirée*, benefiting the Society of St. Vincent de Paul.

After his return from India, he had come to dinner with one of my friends, a judge at the court of Assises in Caen. The judge was a native of Pondicherry, formerly the French colony in India. Later, when this tenant had left my home, we stayed in contact; he would let me know when he came back from a voyage, and I would organize an evening of slide projections.

Arlette was at my home when Gobbois returned from Australia and phoned me. My sister had just planned a photo evening for the following Saturday at her villa in Hermanville, and she invited him. But Gobbois did not come, and did not take the trouble to call with an excuse. This was not like him; his manners were those of a well-brought-up gentleman. So I advised Arlette, in order to avoid hard feelings in the future, to send him a note in this vein: "Last Saturday we finally sat down to dinner without you, hoping that nothing had happened..."

Alas, the poor man had indeed been involved in happenings—unfortunate ones—reported by the press the next day. His garage had been burglarized, but not completely emptied, and the police found TV and High Fidelity sets taken from "Super Stores," as well as arms and explosives. They weren't particularly surprised, because Gobbois was a repeat offender. He had been recently freed for good conduct, after 16 years of hard labor: As a very young man, he had killed a police officer in a robbery that had turned out badly.

After a couple of weeks, an investigator came by, wanting to know how long he had lived at my house. My sister, compromised as she was by her letter, received a summons by telephone at her office, to present herself the next day at the police station. The secretary who took the message expressed doubts as to whether her employer would be available, since she had so many appointments; but they made it clear that her employer could not decline, and that it was up to the secretary to cancel the appointments. The astounded employee truly wondered what her superior could have done, and if she would ever see her again.

My dear sister underwent an interrogation loaded with pitfalls. They pretended to look for Gobbois' first name to see if Arlette could be manipulated into saying it, in order to measure the depth of their relationship (*cherchez la femme*). Then they asked if she would submit to a house search, which they carried out without conviction. They took so long with the search that, if there had been any traces of a possible complicity, she would have had ample time to whisk them away.

At home, Gobbois had to clean up his image; he had never tried to fence the products of his illegal activities.

Now we understood better why, after so many years in prison, he really wanted to travel!

When I next saw my judge friend, I asked him to pardon me for having had him dine with such a guest. He responded very kindly that it was exactly that sort of person that he kept company with professionally, every day. I never saw the prisoner again, so I couldn't ask for his impressions of that evening with the judge.

The apartment renters aren't the only ones with savory stories; the garage renters have their share. Obviously, when I had 28 garages to rent at one time, I couldn't be too picky with the clientele presenting themselves.

That's how I became involved with a novice insurance salesman, who rented a garage in hopes of underwriting fire insurance for all of them. He asked me to grant him the favor of a meeting with him and his supervisor, to discuss life insurance. I had told him that I would not be signing up, but he wanted to demonstrate his techniques for his boss.

The demonstration must not have been very convincing, because he gave me back the garage the following month. He had already insured his whole family, his friends and relatives, but then was booted out for insufficient sales. So, he opened his heart to me, spilling out all his negative thoughts on that worthless insurance business.

I also rented out a garage to a painter, to store his equipment; he paid me only the first third. He was known around as a sponger. As a beginner landlord, I went to ask advice of a bailiff friend, who confided to me: "You won't get any back rent from this disreputable character," and he knew him well. "I'll tell you what you have to do, but it's perfectly illegal: Put all his things on the sidewalk, change the lock and ask him to come and get them." My renter was furious; as a precaution, I kept his fishing lines, which he had chosen to leave behind.

We had rented a garage under Arlette's house to an old friend, a big-hearted woman who had taken pity on an old guy, a former printer abandoned by his wife. Without saying anything to us, she had given him a key to the garage, where he had made up a pallet. Like her, we also shut our eyes, until the night when he burned an electric cable while passing flaming newspapers between the ceiling joists—"to chase away the bugs," so he said. His dt's[*] were becoming really dangerous.

During this period, I had some customers for whom a car was an expensive luxury, the dream of a lifetime. One that I remember was Barthélemy, a worker in the Normandy Metallurgical Company. He had traced concentric circles on the almanac map with a compass, to pinpoint the post offices around our city, showing how far out he could go with 10 or 20 francs worth of gas in his tank.

There was "Johnson Polish," whom I remember only by his nickname. We called him that because he spent his Saturdays polishing his car with a product of that brand name. Then, on Sunday, he would take his wife out for a rather short, economical ride, but long enough to justify another half-day of cleaning. It was he who had observed that in Caen, the rainwater was so hard that a little ring was deposited around each drop.

A problem presented itself when he put his car in the garage: If he left the doors shut for a week, the airtight joints would be compressed, which was bad for them and, if the doors remained open, dust would get into the interior of the vehicle—insoluble problem.

At the moment of going into retirement, garage renter Père Letellier let himself go hog-wild. Since they were a two-income couple, and his wife was doing housecleaning at the Renault factory, he decided to buy a 4CV and take off for Brittany, for the trip of their lifetime. Upon their return, the recounting of this adventure was worth its weight in lightly

---

[*] *delirium tremens* (Latin): violent tremors and hallucinations brought on by prolonged alcoholism.

salted butter.   It was as if they had explored a primitive, unknown country.

They must have believed the good Norman jokes about their neighbors in Brittany: "There are no staircases in their homes, because they don't know how to go down them. They don't know about plates, but eat their thick soup from hollowed-out spaces in the massive tray in their table."

They were full of praise for the friendliness of the Bretons, and told us: "Don't believe the stories that on the coast they don't have villas as beautiful as ours...Their roads are tarred...They have electrical lines and phones, even out in the country...All told, we didn't find so many differences from here, but we learned a lot on the trip..."

Another customer had wanted to make a trip through Morocco.   He had found the country splendid, but he was afraid for his car, because that country is full of Arabs, more than here...

"Doctor" Leblond, a former nursing aide at the hospital in Bayeux, had always felt the need to care for his fellow man and, to be more effective, had promoted himself to healer.   He received the sick in his apartment, full of pious images, which must have inspired confidence upon arrival. He had studied doctors' deportment, and had acquired the art of opening his wallet to show that it was full of bills, a gesture calculated to favorably impress the client.

In order to expand the benefits of his practice, he wanted to start up a laboratory of homeopathic preparations, for which he rented three garages from me—for he had a lot of equipment.   He also wanted to hire me as Commercial Director, to launch his products.

Having become competitive, he was now being pursued for the illegal practice of medicine.   Bankruptcy followed.   Since the merchandise in his garages had been deemed worthless by the authorities, it was I who had to remove it and try to resell the bottles and flasks, to recoup my expenses.   Which was not at all easy to do.

On another occasion, I had a customer who wanted storage for "something other than a car," and when I pressed him to be more precise in his plans, he asked: "Would it be a problem if it were bags of coal?" I saw no problem there, if he would leave the area clean on his departure. And the contract was signed.

It wasn't exactly coal that he wished to store; the premises were regularly frequented by a city employee, who would leave with five-gallon cans in his saddlebags. Since he had to taste what he was distributing, an odor of apple alcohol wafted into the area, and his cycle swerved. At Christmastime, all my suspicions were justified when he offered me a bottle of old Calvados. I ended his contract without giving a reason, and he left without asking for his balance.

I must also tell you the strange story of what happened several years later, when I rented garage #7 to the Prince of Corsica. A mutual friend had asked to keep his car there, because he was living in Paris and using a château in the south of the *Département** du Calvados*. To avoid tiring himself, he had planned to come by train to Caen, where he would pick up his vehicle and then go to the château.

He had mailed me his contract, but I had never seen it. Every four months, I sent him a reminder, but he regularly forgot to pay. This had been going on for months, when he phoned one day, furious. "Several times," he said, "I've suspected that someone was using the car in my absence. Well, now I'm certain of it, because the police photographed it exceeding the speed limit on Pentecost Saturday, in Mamers, while I was in Paris. I'm coming to Caen tomorrow, to see the Head of Police." Being a personal friend of President Chirac, he thought that this would expedite things.

From the tone of his voice, I had the impression that he suspected me of using his property. I suggested waiting for him at the train station, with our mutual friend. All day I tried to figure out why someone would borrow a car and

---

* French territory, whether in France or overseas, is divided into *départements*, each governed by a general council and a prefect.

bring it back each time. For liquor traffic? (Drugs were not common at that time.) To commit robberies? I found no other explanation. And then, to borrow it during Pentecost holiday, not knowing if the Prince might come to spend a few days in Normandy?

At the train station, our mutual friend presented himself. He had gone to lengths to assure the Prince of my honesty, and the Prince was quite friendly. He was a gentleman "of a certain age," with eyelids marked by spots of cholesterol. And he was accompanied by the Princess, a ravishing young woman.

She hastened to tell us a similar but unlikely story, which had happened to the husband of one of her friends: "He had to unexpectedly leave his office at the Ministry, and on his way to the parking lot to get into his car, he saw the borrower bringing it back. The borrower even had the nerve to encourage him to have the brakes fixed, saying he thought they weren't working properly."

That very evening, we had to take the train to Paris. Barely settled in the compartment, I thought I saw the Prince and Princess go by in the corridor. I hurried up behind them, to inquire how it had all turned out.

I did find the Princess a little further up in the car, but the young man with her was not her husband. I returned to my seat without daring to ask anything. I never found an explanation for this curious affair, which must have given the Princess quite a fright. At the next billing period, they gave me back the garage, saying they had no further need for it.

I just posted an announcement for a rental; an applicant is ringing the doorbell while, at the same time, I have a phone call. What's going to happen next?

CHAPTER XI

ADVENTURES WITH
SAINT VINCENT DE PAUL

I've been a member of the Society of St. Vincent de Paul for more than fifty years. The Society was founded in Paris in 1833 by Frédéric Ozanam, a young college student, whose intention was to organize a group of Christian friends to extend brotherhood and help to needy persons. This movement, fulfilling a real need, grew very quickly in France and throughout the world, and the first United States Conference took place in 1845. Today it is the oldest lay persons' movement in continuous activity for more than a century and a half.

Around 1830, there existed in Paris *Conférences d'Histoire,* which brought together students interested in these goals. Taking inspiration from this nomenclature, Ozanm baptized his group *Conférences de Charité*, and soon afterwards placed it under the patronage of St.Vincent de Paul. Thus, the group took the name of *Les Conférences de St. Vincent de Paul*, the members forming not a union of lecturers--as the English translation would indicate--but a fellowship, united by the same charitable principle.

The choice of this name was all the more appropriate because there was a nun within the Sisters of Charity--generally called "The Sisters of St. Vincent de Paul"--who first pointed out needy families that the Sisters could visit in the Mouffetard quarter.

In our last year of high school, our math teacher had suggested forming a *Conférence* to visit elderly persons whose finances were insecure. In addition to our meetings, we went two by two to see the elderly in our neighborhood. With Dupont, I went to see Mère Gueitte, a poor old lady who had never signed up for a pension fund, and was living miserably in the attic room of a state shelter. Each time we visited, we brought her some canned goods, beans, rice, sugar, etc. She spoke to us of her youth, of her husband who had disappeared, of her children who had left...

Later, when I had begun to work at the SNCF, I joined the parish group of St. Vincent de Paul, where my father had belonged before me. Our fifteen members met twice per month to update the situations of the persons whom we were helping, and to study new cases that were proposed. Traditionally, Father Buet, who had educated numerous children, acted as family advocate, while Father Courtil pleaded the case of isolated elderly persons. We let them battle it out in vigorous but courteous debates, to end up with arbitration in the best interest of the poorest persons.

Our good priest of the moment, a miner's son, was politically a little wet behind the ears. He would come to every other meeting, where he would assume an attitude of spiritual reflection and interest in our activities. This particular evening, unemployment being much less widespread than we would see later, he was criticizing the system for allowing retired persons to take up a second career, while young people were having problems finding work.

This was exactly the case of Father Courtil, a former military man who, to complement his warrant officer's discharge, had found a small job in an administrative office. Right or wrong, Father Courtil had taken the criticism personally, and declared that he would not attend any more meetings, so as not to meet this "red priest." The priest was upset and asked me to try to straighten out the misunderstanding.

It was always difficult to talk to Father Courtil for, not only did he have the reputed hard head of a Breton, but he also reasoned in a fishbone pattern. The subject of the debate was the vertebral column: It split at the first bone, then came back to the column, before going off onto the second bone, and so forth, to the tail, which could never be reached.

For the most part, the devotion of the fellowship improved everyday lives. In the fall, we were able to get potatoes at a terrific price from generous farmers. They brought them on trays pulled by tractors that were almost impossible to drive through certain small neighborhood streets. Under the friendly jibes of the growers, we ourselves awkwardly carried the bags in, on our backs. It was a survival food which they consumed in quantities unheard of today.

With the help of the coal-dealer's pickup truck, we collected donations of coal to deliver to our friends for whom this was the only means of heating. They also gave us fire-starting matches made from defective Camembert cheese boxes. This meant that the part in between the round, outside pieces, otherwise wasted, was put to use. This went on for years, until they started fabricating the panels of conglomerate particles. For those whom we were helping, that was a necessary loss, but the fellowship was freed from a real task.

Wanting to respond to all distress is a very pretentious ideal, always leaving you dissatisfied with the little that you can do in the face of so much misery and all sorts of problems. Moreover, we have to be generous and vigilant at the same time. People who might have been unjustifiably helped always have imitators showing up, pressuring with the argument: "You're helping so-and-so!"

I remember, around 1950, this old couple who were disaster victims, still living in a former stable, awaiting the reconstruction of their house. The fellow claimed not to have applied for his veteran benefits. I had obtained the paperwork, and had undertaken to put together the rather complicated application. Then, just before sending it off, I wisely asked him to sign it himself. Only then, fearfully refusing, did he finally confess that he had indeed received that money.

Sometimes, too, we stumbled into amusing situations. Like the little mother who had succeeded in getting herself the offer of a pilgrimage to Lourdes with her rather slow-witted, young gigolo. A real honeymoon trip! Everyone can't go to Venice, it would get too crowded...

As for Mademoiselle Chopin, when she found out that she was expecting a son, her neighbors suggested calling him Frédéric. And she agreed. "Yes, that's a good idea. Frédéric Chopin, that has a nice ring to it!" Doubtless, she had heard the association of these two names somewhere. I hope that the poor kid was a good musician!

I also remember the Sainlots, who lived in a group of huts in emergency housing, with a tiny yard that housed their three constantly barking dogs and some fish crates. Since he was occasionally a warehouseman for the fishmongers, he was paid in kind with articles, which, if they weren't frankly rotten, shouted by their odor that they had long since passed the "expiration date."

They had lived in Cherbourg during the war, and had insisted that their son fight against the Bolsheviks. They then used his recruitment bonus. Denounced and judged at the time of the Liberation, they served two years in prison, plus a prohibition on residence in the Cotentin.

Upon the Liberation, their soldier, rather against their wishes, had been sent to clear himself in the Foreign Legion, where he found friends with whom he could speak German. Later, I was present when he came back home. Actually, he was better for it, having acquired some artistic skills over there. He played the trumpet, blasting the neighborhood senseless, under pretext that he had signed up with the neighborhood band. No one dared protest—he had established a reputation as a tough guy. With his parents, he gathered the "holy reeds" for Palm Sunday, and the lily-of-the-valley for the first of May, occupations that, from one year to another, bought them wine and left them plenty of free time.

Forty-eight hours after a blow to the head, the old man died. According to the official version, he fell from a tree while gathering reeds, a weakly credible explanation, given the height of this bush in our region. Certain well-informed neighbors let it be known that during an evening of boozing it up, the son hit his father on the head with a bottle of beer. Finally, they obtained permission to bury him in the Catholic Church. Better not to delve too deeply into such sad circumstances.

We always saw domestic violence in this emergency housing development. This included alcoholics who fought daily when they were drunk, before making up as their heads hit the pillow. With Yvonne, I went to see this one couple and, while the old man was vilifying the woman, she was imparting similar confidences to my wife, showing her the battle scars. They would have liked furniture; their lodging was essentially bare. Most likely, the least-damaged furniture had been bartered for drink.

A certain Mlle D. assured me that she was still a virgin, although she was now "of a certain age." One day, she insisted on showing me the new orthopedic corset that she wore for her scoliosis. Moreover, she was always inviting me to lunch at her house--without my wife, who was supposed to stay home and feed the kids. My wife never gave me permission; I forgot to ask. On the other hand, from time to time, we invited her to eat with us. The day that we served her a glass of Mascara, the name of that city in Algiers unleashed unexpected souvenirs for her. Her parents had met there, and she told us about it with much enthusiasm:

"My father, a military master of arms, had to go into town for a photo ID, and my future mother was there, standing on the sidewalk, waiting for business..." My curiosity was piqued, and I asked about the young lady's occupation. She said that it was just a little haberdasher's shop that her future mother ran. The gentleman who would become her Papa rolled the ends of his finely pointed mustache and, seeing this beauty on the sidewalk, said to himself: "Goodness gracious, if that woman is free, I'll make her mine"! Which bore witness to a pretentious machismo, as well as to the high morality of this officer, all to his honor and that of the French Army.

Sometimes, her reminiscences were pious. She claimed that, for the Armistice of 1918, they had sung the *Tantum Ergo* at St. Steven's in Caen, to the tune of *La Marseillaise* thus marvelously substituting the holy words of that Latin chant for the bloody words of our national hymn.

To offset her depressed personality, I invited her one evening to come watch a television play that I had announced as very « *spirituelle* » [full of spirit, witty]. The play was « *Dans les Vignes du Seigneur* ». Steeped in devotions, she believed that she had been duped by this title, having expected quite a different sort of *spirituelle*. Deciding that this was the image of our society, she was scandalized by the play, whose aim was to make the viewer laugh. Not true in her case.

Some time afterwards, to somewhat exonerate myself, I invited her to come over to watch the re-broadcast of the coronation of Paul VI at St. Peter's. It went on and on... When I came home for lunch,[*] she was kneeling before the screen, where we usually saw so many other shows. Eventually, I had to turn off the set, assuring her that now they all had to go eat, like us.

When you are in the bosom of the Society of St. Vincent de Paul, you never know where it will lead you, and how an impatient, thoughtless gesture can have unforeseen circumstances.

In the course of our meetings, we had a spiritual reading or we listened to our priest. The plan was to also read a page of our Ruling--wise precaution--so as not to lose sight of it. Alas, it hadn't yet been brought up to date, and its obsolete 19th century terms often caused gales of laughter among the young people whom I had brought with me, who were not given to melancholy. The old Ruling was more or

---

[*] Even in modern times (2004), lunch is traditionally the main meal of the day, when many people take a relaxed two-hour break from work to go home and enjoy a several-course, hot meal.

less well respected, but it was soon to cede to a necessary rewriting.

To avoid the aging of the supervisory staff, the Presidents could remain in office only five years, renewable once, and could not be over seventy years of age. These arrangements, valid for all levels of responsibility, have always been difficult to respect, but seem indispensable. Sometimes tired presidents hang onto their title despite everything, under the pretext of not being able to find a replacement. They remain on the task until their death, which is not for the good of the Society.

So it was that our Departmental President of the moment was already quite elderly when he was, by a pious euphemism, "called to the Father." There was no one to replace him; his Vice-President, as old as the President had been, was moreover a little daft.

Under these conditions, the General Assembly that convened to elect his successor was not properly prepared. No one had been approached and asked to take over. With all Department members present, this gave way to a long debate, with barrages of polite expressions bounced back and forth among the parties in charge of the different *Conférences*: "Let's see, M. X., you are doing such a fine job at your local level." To which the person addressed would reply: "But why not you, M. Y.? You who run the *Conférence* of V. so effectively." The Assembly sought to find someone who would offer the least resistance to the pressure in the room, and would allow himself to be nominated. At the end of a seemingly interminable period, M. Letouzé, a Bridge Engineer responsible for our group in Vaucelles, raised his hand. He was immediately elected unanimously, with a palpable feeling of relief.

Now, the same comedy began again, for electing a Vice-President. That threatened to develop into a debate as long as it was grotesque. To avoid this, and naïvely believing that this position, incorrectly filled by the predecessor, amounted to nothing, I followed the example of my local President, who had just been elected, and courageously suggested myself.

I was immediately accepted, with enthusiasm. "A young person! The change in the old order that we've been waiting for!"

Later I learned that the Vice-President has to be up-to-date on everything, assist the President, help with important decisions, and stand in for him unexpectedly. Moreover, I had not foreseen the royal lineage, meaning that I would replace him when his terms expired. Which would happen to me several years afterwards.

During my presidency, our Vaucelles group created "The 3 x 20 Years Club," a neighborhood meeting center to help older people combat their isolation. This idea led to important developments, because the city of Caen itself then created other meeting places with the same goal.

Pickup and delivery for the Food Bank

It was also during this period that we joined up with the Little Brothers of the Poor, who used to organize spectacular meals for the elderly who would have been alone on Christmas Eve. At the beginning, it was not easy to find these isolated persons, nor to find those places that would donate space for the dinner, plus enough volunteers to drive them to the dinner on that special night. This activity still goes on today.

We also founded the Food Bank of Calvados, with six other charitable and humanitarian movements, modeled on the Bank that had been set up a year earlier in the Parisian region. The basis was to gather food which otherwise would have been wasted, to be redistributed to families in difficulty. We still participate in managing the Food Bank and, twice yearly, collect foodstuffs at the doors of the largest stores. In exchange, the Bank furnishes us with food for the families that our Society is helping. We were able to redistribute more than 900 tons of merchandise in the Department of Calvados during these last few years, at a retail value of one million six hundred thousand francs.[*] This necessitated a complete transformation of our *modus operandi*.[+] We needed local depots, freezers and vehicles.

Thanks to my replacement, Michelle B., a particularly capable and devoted Vincentian, the Department Seat of our Society has been created, bringing subsidies as well as places of welcome, and distribution centers.

In 1972, the Congress celebrating the fifth anniversary of the Society was held in Strasbourg. I attended, in order to represent Calvados. It was there that I met the envoy from Guadeloupe, who would become my friend Saint-Ange.

At this time, the Society was creating "Twins" between different city Societies, to promote friendship and to establish exchanges of information on our reciprocal activities. This also would give rise to direct material benefits from the richer Conferences to those of the Third World. Although Guadeloupe, a French Department, could

---

[*] Approximately six francs = one dollar.

[+] Latin: [method of operation]

not be considered in that category, Saint-Ange saw in a twin relationship the opportunity to receive funds for developing his activities. So it was decided that Caen and Guadeloupe would become Twin Cities.

During his stay in France, Saint-Ange and his wife had been our guests and, one or two years later, we accepted their invitation to spend two weeks with them. We paid only for our transportation, while our friends provided lodging.

Before our departure, Amin de Tarrazi, the National President, had asked me to extend our trip to Martinique, to meet several of our many fellow Vincentians there. After we returned and I reported to the National Council, he asked me to be Regional Delegate for the Overseas Departments and Territories. For 25 years, this involved correspondence and several trips to the French Antilles, two trips to the island of Réunion, and one to New Caledonia.

The arrival in France of the refugees of southeast Asia led to our working more closely with Catholic Charities, who welcomed them and provided temporary housing in an old château. There, the refugees took health exams, were cared for, dressed, fed and taught French. Later, our role was to provide furnishings for the lodgings that Catholic Charities had found, and to find work for them.

Under the generic term of Southeast Asia refugees, we had grouped together Vietnamese, Cambodians, Laotians and Hmongs. All these people spoke different languages and, we later learned, had certain prejudices against one another.

I remember our first encounter in the Château de Bréville-les-Monts. Everyone was gathered in one large room: Men and women still wearing their ankle-length sarongs, couples of all ages, and children running all about. We had learned to greet them according to their custom, joining hands and bowing in their direction. We exchanged smiles, the only common language at hand. We discovered that, mixed in the same miserable condition, there were people of all backgrounds: A Laotian Prince and his family, an old minister, military people, even Hmong peasants who practiced slash-and-burn opium cultivation.

Several spoke French, and were able to interpret. The conversation became complicated when we had to use an intermediary tongue; for example, Hmong to Laotian, then to French, then responding back through the same path. When they told us their atrocious ordeals, it was always with a smile which seemed incomprehensible, but which, for them, actually showed utmost politeness.

I remember in particular this Cambodian couple who, to save their lives, had fled with an assault tank to Thailand, abandoning their children to the grandparents. They were inconsolable. Later, they had other children in France, but were always obsessed with finding those that they had left behind. Twenty years later, by dint of many sacrifices, they returned to Cambodia, and found one of their daughters. She could not forgive them for having left her, and refused to understand what had been the only way for all of them to be saved.

We had to arrive at an understanding of their manner of expressing themselves. When we asked a question, they could not reply "No," for it would have been impolite. So, when we tried to give them clothing, the response to "Do you want this?" was invariably in the affirmative. We had to guess the nuances of enthusiasm, to know if the response was actually positive, or only a polite but meaningless "yes."

The Far East has tonal languages; that is, a single word might be pronounced up to seven different ways. I personally was not capable of perceiving all these nuances, and they themselves sometimes needed the context, to help guess the correct meaning. Or, they would repeat the phrase and add a new one, to make the meaning known.

Among the Hmongs, there was a very nice man who had three wives and many children. They had invited us to celebrate a birth. The good fellow, who did not know how to read, had made up a touching speech, which concluded by saying that he now considered us as replacements for the parents that he had left behind.

It was my duty to explain that, under our present laws, he had to declare just one wife, and that the others would be considered cousins. But he did not wish to choose the one wife; he wanted me to do it. I foolishly believed that he was showing confidence in my good taste, and I refused emphatically to choose, saying that I did not know the wives well enough to be able to choose wisely. Only later did I understand the ploy—that my taking sole responsibility would have avoided protests from the other two. If I myself had been polygamous, I would have no doubt guessed that at once.

In midwinter, when the refugees arrived in France, we had to teach them to cover themselves when they were outside and to then take off the overcoat in heated apartments. They soon learned that water in France was not free, and that scaling fish in the sink inevitably blocked it up.

It wasn't easy to get the Hmongs employed in a factory, even as janitors. It seemed impossible for them to arrive on time, although they had been equipped with large wristwatches. Accidentally learning of the problem, I realized that they did not know how to read them. Yet another essential little lesson.

On each occasion that we visited the new families, tradition decreed that they would offer, under the name of tea, an exotic herbal drink. One day, they also suggested that I try a wad of betel nuts, which I helped to make. Since they brought me a chamber pot, I asked why. It was for spitting. So I refused this experience, because I couldn't picture myself spitting while conversing with my friends. I still had ridiculous prejudices...

Among the refugees was a Sino-Khmer most likely more Chinese than Khmer, who practiced acupuncture. The others had a tendency to keep him off to the side, almost as if there was some old collaboration going on. He was of superior intelligence, and had learned French very quickly. A little later, he found an extraordinary job as the personal physician of an emir, whom he followed in his travels. The Emir had offered him a large sum to accept the job permanently, but he finally entrusted him to one of his brothers, so that he could go open a restaurant in Quebec. He was afraid of being on the "oil time-bomb" in the Middle East.

There also was this Minister, a formerly unscrupulous profiteer of his country's old regime. Touched by grace, transformed by hardships, he had become a bonze,[*] and had converted a room in their housing unit into a Buddhist temple. He imposed a laying-on of hands and considered himself a healer, but I never really noticed an improvement. Perhaps I would have had to convert.

His respect for life was such that he couldn't crush a mosquito; he had to have it fly away. He no longer would drive, for that would risk killing someone. He had to employ drivers who did not share his religious convictions. The access to his paradise resembled the penalties for breaking the rules of the road; but we have the driver lose points.

Several years later, I saw him again, at the St. Lazare train station. He was shaved bald as an egg, and wore the saffron-colored robe. I was so happy to see him that I rushed to shake hands, forgetting the traditional greeting; then I noticed his embarrassment. I learned later that a bonze is untouchable. By the same token, when one offers a flower to Buddha, you may not smell it, for it must be given with all its perfume.

It is a widespread practice for young boys to spend several months in the pagoda, in memory of one of the deceased of the family. I really wonder how that influences their metempsychosis.[+]

I knew a refined, cultivated and educated refugee, a former pupil of the School of Agriculture of Angers, who used to say: "I would give six chickens for a snake!" Alas, he could no longer accord himself this pleasure since his grandfather had been reincarnated in the form of a snake. I was not bold enough to ask how he had discovered this.

---

[*] A Buddhist monk of the Far East.
[+] Reincarnation.

I must tell you about a certain young Hmong couple. The woman's father insisted on requiring a higher price from his son-in-law, because she was delivered to him in France. I had to convince them that he couldn't require reimbursement for a trip for which he had not paid and, under such exigencies, no young man would be able to marry her. Finally, everything was settled, and he found them a place to live. They were so happy to have a bathtub that they quickly used it, giving no thought to causing overflow for their neighbors, who came in to investigate, through the door left open by the couple.

During my involvement with the refugees, I met Michel T., a mixed race Franco-Khmer, whose father, a French officer, had been killed in their country. Michael had been raised in an orphanage in Cambodia. Being rather gifted, he had been sent to the city to pursue higher studies. He was a devotee of Cambodian civilization, and had come to see the refugees whose language he spoke. He was very generous towards us and, thanks to him, we soon were able to take a wonderful trip to Thailand.

Michel T. had married the daughter of the former ambassador of Thailand to Paris and, since he had to spend the Christmas holidays in Bangkok, we left with him. On our arrival at the airport, the Ambassador's car was waiting to drive us to a large hotel, where a room had been reserved.

Michel and his wife had accompanied us the first few days, to familiarize us with the city. Michel had even introduced us to an important bonze who presented me with a medal gilded with the image of Buddha, in recognition of the help that we had given to the refugees.

With them, we took our first "samlors." Imagine a three-wheeled scooter, the rear converted into a little truck with two benches, where you could stuff in as many as eight people.

For Christmas Eve dinner, we attended Mass in the gardens of the French Ambassador, and partook of the buffet organized by the Catholics of Bangkok. What a pleasant yet strange Christmas setting in this park without snow, where it was at least 30° C.*

I also paid a visit to the National President of the Society of St. Vincent de Paul of Thailand, who unexpectedly required us to remove our shoes before entering his home. Afterwards, he very kindly suggested driving us to a refugee camp. Since I could do nothing for them, I did not accept this offer, which would have seemed like voyeurism on my part.

In downtown Bangkok there was a site dedicated to the cult goddess Shiva. There, among many sticks of incense, the faithful left offerings of food. After its purification, the food was retrieved by the donors.

But the strangest experience of all was attending exhibitions of dancers in sacred costumes, paying homage to the goddess by moving to the sounds of xylophones. Pious customers hoping for certain celestial favors paid for granting such wishes as winning at the lottery or succeeding at an exam. If I were Shiva, my heart would not be softened by the posturing of these tired old women, who carried out their services without enthusiasm or conviction. I hope that in the special salons, where I was not permitted to go, the masseuses put more youthful vigor into their work.

Elsewhere, in a pagoda, people bought birds for the sole purpose of giving them their liberty. This beautiful gesture certainly was praiseworthy, but what of those who had caught them just to profit from their sale?

You could also get booklets of little gold leaf squares, to stick on outdoor statues of Buddha. At the time of the monsoon, shrewd persons would exploit the gutters of Bangkok like gold mines.

In Lop-bury, opportunistic macaques came into the pagoda, mostly open on the outside, and appropriated the offerings of the faithful. These unpleasant animals, protected by their sacred status, freely committed all sorts of disgusting acts.

---

* Fahrenheit = 9/5 Celsius + 32

In the pagodas, the Buddhists had at their disposal a cylindrical wooden box containing a handful of square blocks covered with inscriptions. After having prayed on their knees before the god, from whom they sought the oracle, they shook the box, threw out several blocks of inscriptions, and interpreted them.

One day, we ventured out without our mentors, to the southern island of Phuket, near Malaysia, so that we could visit the Bay of Along. We left the city and hailed a samlor, which assured group transportation. When they asked us where we wanted to go, we simply gestured "go." The more they asked where we wanted to go, the more our responsive gesture evoked laughter. They did indeed "take us for a ride"; finally, the samlor left the tarred road for a dirt path leading to a native village. They stopped before a house with wide-open double doors and two caskets visible inside. We had arrived with our traveling companions at their destination—a funeral wake.

After a tour of the village, there was nothing to do but go back to the tarred road to hail another samlor, this time knowing our destination: "Phuket!" The other travelers were wonderfully friendly, offering us some fig bananas. We appreciated these small, sweet bananas.

We had also been to Chiang-Maï, the capitol of the northern part of the country, where we were to meet the Reverend Father Mirco, the priest who ran a school for Karians. Over the centuries, these primitive animists had come from the Chinese mountains. They are morphologically very different from the Thais, having a round, flat face, with a small nose. Their lives are based on slash-and-burn cultivation, and we saw the fields of poppies that they tended. Their entire wealth consisted of the heavy silver bracelets and necklaces they wore.

Accompanied by the priest who served as our interpreter, we were received in one of their bamboo huts, filled with acrid smoke. On rocks in the center of the room, a small fire flickered, cooking the food. Above, strips of blackened meat were being smoked and dried. They do not use a fireplace, because the smoke chases mosquitoes and keeps parasites from breeding in the grass fiber roofing. For the most part, they are used to it--the smoke no longer stings their eyes. Not the case for us, we couldn't stay there very long.

On our departure from Chiang-Maï, we had to check our bags carefully, to be sure that they had not hidden drugs in them. Otherwise, the corrupt police could detain us en route, ostensibly fulfilling their duties, while the real traffickers were overlooked.

While looking for a new Departmental President for Réunion, I had the pleasure of meeting the Roches en route to their apartment in Paris. They were family friends from the period when my uncle was military governor of the Island. Together, my Aunt and Odette Roche produced children's radio programs. Following our conversation, Odette agreed to be a candidate for the Departmental Presidency. Yvonne and I went to the Island of Réunion to meet the many teams and to assess the work already done to organize and develop the *Conférences.*

Our National President, his wife and our Secretary General were to join us in presiding at the General Assembly. We stayed at the home of the H's, in a superb setting reached by a long path bordered with flourishing coconut palms. Madame herself had drawn up the plans of the house, a splendid single-story home with large, shaded bay windows.

Monsieur kept a wonderful collection of orchids, protected from the burning sun with a woven cloth. Being a multi-talented artist, Madame was an excellent musician, played several instruments, and devoted herself to the copying of icons. We occupied the guest room, which also served as her workshop, and we slept under the stern countenances of saints painted in gold leaf. Should we perhaps have put out the light before undressing, or turned the portraits to face the wall?

In Saint-André, we shared a lovely meal organized by Virapoullé, the Deputy Mayor, together with fellow Vincentians of the city. Each day was the occasion for pleasant, sometimes touching, encounters. Such was the meeting of a particular little group where I noticed that no one was taking notes. Their President, the only one who knew how to write, was in dialysis at the time. The illiteracy of the members did not prevent them from doing good works for others.

One morning, quite early, we took an extraordinary helicopter tour over craters and volcanoes, and descended into the *Trou d'Enfer,* a deep chasm with a magnificent waterfall providing the only possible access. We put down in the cirque of Maffat, where there was a little village with no access road. It was one of the former refuges of the *Nègres Marrons,* those slaves who were saved from their master's homes to find liberty in nature.

Our visit concluded at the Cathedral with Solemn Mass celebrated by the Bishop, the Youth Choir recital, and the awarding of medals by our founder at a General Assembly. I see again our National President and his wife, who had undertaken to shake the hand of each of the four hundred Society members.

Planning to return to Réunion several years later, I wanted to visit the *Conférence* of Curepipe, on the island of Maurice. This was the counterpart of our group in Bayeux. Hearing of this, the administrator in Bayeux decided to accompany me and bring his wife along. He contacted the President, who offered to house us himself in his villa on the slope of the volcano called *Le Trou aux biches,* which furnished a terrific view of the sea and the ragged volcanic mountains.

Another Society member took us on a three-day tour of this magnificent, interesting island of Maurice. Although the official language is English, brought by the last colonists, French is currently the most widely spoken language. The very beautiful avenue of Port-Louis is decorated with a bronze statue of La Bourdonnais, former governor of the French islands.

Since their independence, the economic situation is difficult, and dependent on sugar cane and tourism. Their dream is to become a new Hong Kong, as it was before the unification. For the moment, schooling--compulsory in theory--cannot be guaranteed by the State; several private, religious establishments substitute for State education. Our friends wanted to establish scholarships to help families of modest means to send one child per family for technical training.

The State hospitals function no better. Case in point, the story of the former chauffeur of our host: His son had broken a big toe while playing soccer, and had to be hospitalized. Despite the suspicious odor in the multi-patient room where he waited to be seen, days went by until the doctor came and declared that an emergency operation was necessary to stop the spread of the gangrene. Since the operating room was closed over the weekend (it was now Friday evening), he would either have to wait until Monday, or transfer to an expensive private clinic, where this doctor could operate immediately. Our host arranged the necessary transfer, so that, come Monday, they wouldn't face the very possible loss of at least part of the boy's limb.

In New Caledonia, I knew only the Vincentians who came to France from time to time, but they were so keen for us to visit that we finally decided to vacation there. Our flight, with just one stopover in Bangkok, took 24 hours. It was the shortest route--a trip of 18,000 kilometers instead of 22,000--past the United States and the Pacific Ocean. The trip seemed easier because of the warm welcomes of the Territorial President Raymond Page and Monseigneur Lambert, the Bishop of Vanuatu.

Parodying a funeral home ad, "Die, we will do the rest!" Raymond had written to us: "Come, we will do the rest!" And we must say that, together with the Society members, they were very much involved.

The airport of Tantouta is about 50 kilometers from Nouméa; Raymond was waiting to drive us to his house, where we would be staying. What can I say about this big, beautiful Page family, their four daughters and two sons-in-law? We felt as though we had been adopted. Bente and her daughters were delighted to have us taste the delicious dishes that they made.

We found New Caledonia to be even more beautiful than we had imagined, and the welcome of the Vincentians was extraordinary wherever we went. A carefully planned schedule balanced useful activities with pleasant ones.

We were received like family by the Mayor of Nouméa, Jean Leques. We met the Bishop and the President of Catholic Charities, who worked in close collaboration. Raymond brought us to the leper hospital, where several victims of Hansen's disease still resided; the psychiatric hospital, from which the mentally ill were too quickly released into a city offering no support; and some rare buildings, vestiges of the penal colony.

Member Jacqueline Broquet, Adjunct to the Mayor, took us to the shelter called *Abri Partage*, which she had created several years ago, with the help of our Society. In an immaculately clean setting, it provides about twelve men with short-term housing. With municipal subsidies, she will be able to double its welcoming capacity.

The parish priest of St. John the Baptist has raised the awareness of his parishioners; with their help, he is creating a sort of "Soup Kitchen." A new *Conférence* of St. Vincent de Paul is being born, under the direction of a young Vietnamese convert, a marvelously devoted and charitable priest.

Raymond also took us to see the squatters in the immediate suburbs of Nouméa. There are about 500 corrugated metal huts hidden in the luxuriant vegetation of the hills. These buildings, quite illegal, are set up at random and reached by trails hollowed out by the repeated passages of the occupants. For public health reasons, the Society of St. Vincent de Paul, at the heart of a group of humanitarian associations and official services, has tried to furnish drinkable water and establish liaisons among the administrators and the squatters, in order to avoid violence and face the issue of alternative housing.

Housing which ought to be reserved for the poorest is in fact used for those selected for their solvency, for there is no system of housing benefits. Workers who are tribal descendents, unable to pay high rents, find a convenient solution in these metal cabins, situated near their ancestral cottages. Further enticement for this way of life is that, if they were to return to their villages, clan law would require that they turn over their salary to the tribal leader, to use as he wishes. It is my feeling that the next few decades will see the end of the tribal system and the voluntary integration of the natives into modern life.

They took us to nearby Mont Toro; to the ruins of Fort Tereka, where cannons of the Second Empire endure; to Mont Kogui and its tree house available for nightly rental; to the zoological garden of Forestier Park to see kagus, the symbolic island birds, strongly protected from extinction. We also saw the exciting ethnological Museum, paving the way for our visit to Vanuatu. All this culminated in a visit to the historic city museum.

In Nouméa we were interviewed for the local newspapers, and by Radio Bleue. The five-minute portion of a news segment on France Overseas Radio seemed effective because, in the days that followed, people recognized me and addressed me in public.

Vanuatu, the native land of President Page when it was still called New Hebrides, is a volcanic archipelago consisting of 80 islands spread over 900 kilometers. One hundred fifty different dialects are spoken, and the official languages are Bichlamar, English and French. Raymond Page was delighted to again speak Bichlamar, the language of his childhood, and served as my interpreter and translator at the General Assembly.

Our Society had its seat on the island of Efeta, in Port-Vila, the capitol of Vanuatu. There were new groups totaling 130 members on the island of Malakula, and plans to create a *Conférence* on the isle of Spiritu Santo, as well. Unfortunately, the connections between the islands by small passenger-cargo ships meant several days of what we considered frightful discomfort. As for planes, their prices were prohibitive.

The strong faith and motivation of the members in Vanuatu seemed well suited to the particular conditions of their land. Our encouragement was especially important to them, because they felt isolated, at the end of the world. Their President confided that, having completed modest studies, he found himself quite alone when it came time to make decisions. Here also, we were welcomed with necklaces of flowers and shells, then by a song in our honor, a version of the one that they had sung for the visit of our Australian member.

We were invited to a grand barbecue, where all the women hurried about, dressed in mission dress.[*] Traditionally, guests eat first, then the women, then children, finally the men. The men, waiting their turn, drank Kava from a coconut half-shell. Kava is a light drug, calming and sleep-inducing. It is made from the mastication of roots by young people, who spit out the juice into a vase, where it ferments a little, before being consumed silently, only by the men, and far from the chatting women. At the seminary, where hygiene is more important, the roots are crushed with a mortar and mixed with water, before being drunk in a traditional cottage during the Saturday evening of relaxation. Our friend Page, who wanted to honor them by conforming to this tradition, found this brew particularly revolting.

We rented a car to tour the island with Joseph. In one place and another, there were remains of war supplies left by the Americans 50 years ago; Efata had served them as a base in the war against Japan. These rusted vestiges are now camouflaged by the vegetation, which has claimed its rights.

---

[*] A colored, sac-like dress imposed upon them by the missionaries, to cover their nudity.

In contrast to New Caledonia, the sea unfurls violently on this coast, unprotected by coral reefs.

At the end of our stay, I wanted to give a bottle of old whiskey to Monseigneur Lambert, so I went to an elderly Chinese gentleman whom Raymond knew well. As always, he was there, leaning on his elbows on the counter of his shop, where you could find anything. He was ready to sell me finely sculpted ivory, putting me at high risk with the authorities, but would not allow me to leave the least bit of alcohol, because it was Sunday, and he could have his shop closed down if it were discovered.

We treasure an everlasting memory of the friendly Bishop, who shared his meals with us. Reverend Father Célestin, with his beautiful frizzy Polynesian hair, drove us back to the airport for the return to Nouméa, from where we would soon depart for France.

We had just spent three dreamlike weeks with our friends. Yet when they drove us to Tantouta three hours in advance, for the checking of our bags, they didn't want to leave us for that long wait. They suggested another outing into the hillsides of the area, showing that they still felt a real desire to please, and that they weren't yet totally saturated with us!

Back home, in another world, we were surprised one day to receive a curious request from the National Council of France. Bob O'Reilly, one of the national representatives of our Society in the United States, would be spending a vacation with three friends in Normandy, seeing Rouen and Caen, and riding by bicycle from the landing beaches along the coastline to St. Malo.

We were pleased to have them stay with us, and we spent a very pleasant evening together. The next morning, our daughter Béatrice escorted them by bicycle towards the route for their trip. The following year, we accepted their invitation and went to St. Louis, Missouri. Bob wanted to know our entire itinerary, in order to have us stay with Society members in the different cities where we would be going. I did not accept this generous offer, because my knowledge of English would have greatly limited the conversation. We stayed just three days in St. Louis, "the Doorway of the West." We saw the famous arch, and it occurred to us that, for lack of a sister arch, it would be terrific publicity for MacDonald's.

With emotion, we saw the commemorative plaque placed on the wall of the Cathedral in 1945, for the centenary of the foundation of our Society in the U.S.A., while in the mosaics of the cupola, there was a portrait of Ozanam, our principal founder.

Of course, Bob O'Reilly was Irish. Every year without fail, since his trip to France, he addresses a St. Patrick's Day card to us, printed with his name and enclosing a ten-dollar check written to the Society of St. Vincent de Paul.

In later years, I have made other ties with Ireland. The government in Dublin sought out our National management, to insure that an Irish prisoner being held long term in Caen would receive visits. Furnished with this request, I applied for a visiting permit, authorizing a police report on myself. Since I was not considered too dangerous, I was granted the permit at the end of six months. When I found out that that the Irish prisoner had been sentenced to seven years in prison for drug trafficking, I was at the point of giving up my visits but, preparations having been made, went to see him, if only once.

He was a tall fellow with blue eyes and a jawline black beard, about 30 years old and pleasant in manner. At first, we conversed in English, but after a few months, in both languages, so as to encourage him to improve his French. I spent two hours with him every month, and became used to going through the barred doors and the metal detectors. We met in a large room with a little table on either side, and I placed my bilingual dictionary on the table.

Finally, he told me his story: He was the seventh child in a family of six girls and stalwart parents, who were pharmacists. As the last little one and the only boy, he was very spoiled, and had accomplished little in life. Unemployed, he had ended up in the business with his strict parents (they refused to sell condoms), but he did not get along with his father. On Saturday nights, he paid himself off with a joint of hashish as consolation, and made contact with a dealer who suggested a trip to Morocco.

So he had left with a girl and a small truck—both on loan—under pretext of camping. When he came back to France, they said nothing to him at the Spanish border but, about 20 kilometers further, the police accused him of having run a red light, as an excuse to detain him. With 170 kilos of hashish, the little car must have seemed abnormally loaded down.

His father died of a broken heart, and his mother came to see him once a year, with one of his sisters. We invited them to the house, but the Gaelic conversation of the older woman was incomprehensible to us, and the daughter's translation was in English.

After having served half of his sentence, early release to his country was suggested, but the customs office set a fine of one million francs. Not wanting to ruin his family, he remained there, saying nothing to them. At the end of six months, the thieving customs officers understood that they wouldn't get a centime from him, so they gave up and had him driven to the Orly airport. It wasn't worth the expense of feeding him.

Since then, every year, he sends me a greeting addressed to "The Association for Visiting Irish Prisoners Abroad." His mother also sends cards, and this year included a surprise gift, a certificate saying that she had made a donation for a novena of Masses to be offered, to assure my entrance into Heaven. She had surmised that I would surely need it!

FRENCH WEST INDIES: GUADELOUPE

SOURCE: Internet Explorer, *World Atlas CIA Map.* June 3, 2003.

CHAPTER XII

FRIENDS IN THE WEST INDIES

In February of 1974, going to the French Antilles was not yet a commonplace trip, and it was our first transatlantic flight in a Boeing 747. Today, I still marvel that such a massive piece of machinery can get off the ground and transport a heavy load for hours.

We arrived at Pointe-à-Pitre in the middle of a tropical storm. Since a similar plane had crashed on the volcano la Soufrière several months earlier under these conditions, our pilot decided to fly around a half-hour longer at reduced speed, before putting down at the airport of Raizet. We were terribly shaken by the air pockets, seeing the island first to the right, then to the left, and—since no announcement was made--wondering what in the world he was doing.

Guadeloupe is in the form of a butterfly leaning on its left wing. This region is called *Basse-Terre*, or "Low Ground." Although very mountainous, the summit of the Island (the volcano), it is called low, not for its average altitude, but for its proximity to the equator. The other half of the island, *Grand-Terre*, consists of a calcareous plateau, supplemented by little hills, the Mornes. The large tourist hotels are found on this small, drier segment. Our friends drove us to Saint-Ange's house by way of a magnificent and sinuous route. There we slaked our thirst with a Welcome Punch, generously ladled into mustard glasses. Beware of this delicious iced drink, decorated with a slice of lime; it goes down smooth as milk.

I have always had the greatest admiration for Saint-Ange. He was born into a large family, and his father was a shoemaker. When his father made a pair of shoes for a special occasion—a First Communion, a wedding, etc.—it was Saint-Ange who was responsible for delivering them.

Since he himself was barefoot, he would tie lianas of long flame-tree pods on the soles of his feet.

The Headmaster had educated Saint-Ange, his star pupil, the best he could. Therefore, he was prepared to present himself at the administrative examinations and enter into the Prefecture. As a young man in his twenties, he still sends me letters so perfectly handwritten that I am put to shame. I bought a computer, in order to answer him legibly.

` Having no children of his own, Saint-Ange has often provided two or three years of housing to youngsters from the countryside, so that they could pursue their education in Basse-Terre.

We were lodged at Maurice and Martha's house; in our honor, they had bought all new bedding. I can see, on the night table, a sort of little Breton lighthouse, to serve us as nightlight and to insure peaceful sleep. They didn't insist that we use this device, so we were happy enough with just the "Vapona," a bed-warmer which distills its vapors against anopheles, those mosquitoes that carry palydism, or dengue fever. I wouldn't have done without it... At night, we thought we heard birds, but it was the song of tiny frogs, the size of a fingernail, who live hidden in the green plants in the house and are agitated by the passage of tropical downpours.

In the Antilles, the wooden homes are all alike, situated on one level. On the street side there is a common room, closed off by glass-paned doors with louvered shutters. In back is a bedroom, similarly closed off towards the exterior. These two rooms are separated by a partition whose upper end is a trellis, allowing air to circulate in the two rooms. What this arrangement lacks in privacy, it compensates--thanks to the trade winds--with permanent natural ventilation. The kitchen is always built outside the house, to avoid the heat and the odors. The moment hurricane alerts sound, pieces of chipboard or metal sheeting have to be nailed over all these openings.

After hurricane Hugo, I returned to Guadeloupe, naïvely believing that only the lighter homes had been at risk. In fact, rusted metal roofs, not always solidly nailed in place, flew off quite easily, making enormous and very dangerous machetes. As soon as the third alert is sounded— the one announcing the imminent arrival of the hurricane— special precautions have to be taken: Stock up on drinking water and food, cut down any trees that could fall on the house and, after having sealed everything, stay inside, together, in the most solid part of the house.

Nowadays, they build "solid" homes, to stand up to hurricanes. The concrete slab is connected to the roof by metal on exterior wall posts. All openings are equipped with special metallic shutters. Nevertheless, poorly oriented houses can be very badly hit. If the wind enters one side, they have to open a window for it to pass out on the opposite side, or the wind force could explode the house. The volumes of water ripped from the sea do not fall from the sky, but are projected horizontally, destroying everything.

I have seen concrete electric posts twisted and broken, fences pierced, balconies broken down. Hugo lasted an entire night. At dawn, there was a great calm, punctuated by deathlike howls from dogs, driven crazy by the pandemonium. Their masters sometimes had to put them down.

Venturing outside, the inhabitants discovered a storm-tossed, disheveled landscape. The earth was strewn with debris and still-standing trees that were now leafless stumps, as if winter from a non-tropical land had fallen in one single night. All the harvests were lost. In the banana fields, they were forced to cut everything down, to get out of the area on foot.

Because of the hurricane, there was no electricity, no drinking water, no phones. It was difficult to measure the extent of the damage. In the port, people moved quickly to remove or cut loose boats that had been sunk, to re-establish access by water. Roads had been rendered impassable because of fallen trees and destroyed bridges. Everywhere there was desolation, on a spectacular scale.

Some disaster victims, who had built homes in off-limits areas, such as the protected military zone, or in the non-floodable gorges, would not have the right to rebuild them. Others had experienced such fright in their homes that they no longer felt it was safe to inhabit them. Those who had lost everything in the catastrophe would be temporarily housed for months in army tents, where the heat could be intolerable and sleep difficult, with the flap clanking in the wind. During a downpour, water would often seep in, and the earth became a sponge. We went with Saint-Ange to see disaster victims, but were unable to find a way to help them.

My friend had his car radio tuned to a local frequency, broadcasting burial schedules several times daily. Given the climate, the dead had to be buried within 24 hours. The radio station would designate the route of the buses chartered by families to drive to the meeting places.

In the West Indies, customs are unique. Funeral processions are impressive, and they block traffic for quite a distance. Caskets are covered with countless flower wreaths. The men wear hats and mourning clothes from head to toe; the women are enveloped in long veils, sailing with the breath of the trade winds.

The cemetery of Morne à l'Eau is very interesting, and highlighted by the guides. Most tombs are covered with slabs of black and white earthenware, bearing simple decorative motifs; some are hidden by heavy stone slabs, or the burial mound is protected with sturdy, insurmountable grillwork, to separate the living from the dead.

Some of the richer communes illuminate their cemeteries at night, for those fearing that zombies[*] might go out to haunt the living. In other parishes, the tombs are simply covered with giant conch shells, which the sun gently bleaches. Sometimes families even come to have picnics.

The city of Basse-Terre is built at the foot of the volcano la Soufrière, where a very steep road climbs bravely, to take one quickly to the cooler climate of Saint Claude. The Préfet and the wealthy of this administrative capitol live

---

[*] Zombies, according to voodoo cults, have the power to cast spells, whereas ghosts do not.

there. The port, destroyed by the hurricane, had not then been rebuilt.

The volcano on Guadeloupe's Basse-Terre is a real danger; it covered the city with ash several years ago, necessitating evacuation for several months. Consequently, the economy of Pointe-à-Pitre, on southwestern Grande-Terre Island, was reoriented profitably. Vast expanses of land were offered for the establishment of a modern city, the development of a sizeable port and warehouses, and the extension of the airport of Raizet, an increasingly important transportation hub.

France is trying to balance its investments between the two islands of Martinique and Guadeloupe, less than 200 kilometers from each other, but Martinique is developing more quickly. You see Martinicans set up businesses in Guadeloupe more often than the other way around.

I met some extremely generous West Indians, like Amalia, who couldn't receive a charity appeal letter in the mail without sending a needy person a check. She lived very modestly, but because of her repeated generosities, received a penalty for not being able to pay her taxes on time.

I'm thinking also of Lina, who had housed me above a henhouse occupied by a dozen crowing roosters. She reassured me that I wouldn't be hearing them much longer, because her husband was going to kill them all shortly. What slaughter, I thought, I hadn't asked for their death. But she said that, in fact, she had been raising them for three months for the banquet that would be given in my honor.

In the West Indies, I also had the pleasure of meeting unforgettable characters like Edward. One day, Saint-Ange had led us up into the Caribbean mountains above Vieux-Fort. The sharp slopes of this former volcano were now covered with a naturally seeded forest, with lush vegetation. There, at the bend of a path, we met a man in tattered clothing, strangely coiffed with a top hat cut halfway through on top in the form of a valve, to allow air circulation.

To my great surprise, Saint-Ange greeted the man of the woods respectfully: It was Edward. Saint-Ange introduced me, then asked permission for us to continue our walk on his land. We had just chanced upon the proprietor of this mountain area. He freely chose land in the clearings to cultivate roots, yams and manioc. In his forest, he knew where and when to harvest mangoes, guavas, papayas and the countless fruits that grow on their own.

But Edward's real fortune was in the exotic-looking wood taken from his forest. It had to be cut and brought down to the business route by the armload, where it could be taken away. Alas, he was getting older and his only son had become a famous Parisian physician, so he would never come to carry on the business, which made Edward unhappy.

I also made the acquaintance of Laïla, a woman of mixed Arab descent. In her turbulent youth, she had been an Independent, sentenced to jail for involvement with explosives. Later, freed before her sentence was up, she chose to join the Society of St. Vincent de Paul. She worked with a group of young people in Pointe-à-Pitre, to organize a Christmas party for the most needy. Then she came to be interested in the most pitiable of all, AIDS victims and crack addicts. With little support at the inception of her ambitious project, she succeeded by tenacity and courage in opening a welcome center to feed and care for them, and later house women with AIDS and their children. She received generous gift subsidies from the public and from established charities.

The people of Guadeloupe, like those of Martinique, often feel isolated on their island, where they seem to move in a circle. There is, in fact, a circular route along the coast, which conforms to the different elevations. Hunters may hunt only pigeons, because the iguanas are protected, although they devastate the small gardens of Guadeloupe. Aside from fishing, the pleasures of the beach or the sea, men may pass time around the pits, betting on fighting roosters. Moving from one island to another, or to the city, is expensive. So, the favorite pastime of the people is to have a party with friends or family, with a big meal and their rhythmic, loud music.

One day, at the end of a party in my honor, they began to sing a song composed especially for me. The refrain showed that they now held me in high regard. It went something like this:

> "You're not our color,
>   We don't hold it against you,
>   It isn't your fault,
>   It's your parents
>   Who made you
>   Like that!"

So I was completely exonerated, and amused that this had not occurred to me before.

CHAPTER XIII

TRAVELS TO ITALY: PART ONE

HER LANGUAGE OPENS THE DOOR

Se la vita è un viaggio
Viaggiare è viverla doppiamente.

[If life is a voyage, traveling is to live doubly.]
—Seen in the Monumental Cemetery of Milan

I love Italy, and consider it my second homeland, that of choice, where I have visited more than 30 times. I know it better than most Italians, from the chain of the Alps to Ericé, the extreme promontory to the west of Sicily. I have visited all the other islands, as well: Sardinia, Elbe, the Bay Islands of Naples, and those of the Archipelago of Eolie [in English, the Aeolies], with its wonderful, rough terrain.

I leave to *Le Guide Bleu** the business of describing the monuments to be admired and superb sites to be enjoyed, reserving for myself simply the pleasure of telling you stories that the single word "Italy" bring to my mind, as the name "Rome" could remind Fellini of his youth.

Despite my numerous trips, I've never been robbed in Italy—to the contrary, I've had many pleasurable, sometimes extraordinary, encounters, for which my knowledge of Italian paved the way.

I had studied Italian as a second language at St. Joseph's; the Chapter on school memories chronicles the modesty of my resources. Only within the country did I become taken with Italian, which opened the doors of a new universe. In the beginning, I tried to decipher public signs,

---

* One in the series of French guide books, an assemblage of maps and site information.

posters, newspaper headlines, etc. Traveling alone, it took a good two days to begin to break the silence and dare to speak with other travelers on trains, with the help in hotels, and with so many other people who asked only to chat with somebody, but especially with a young foreigner.

With particular fondness I recall my first trip, during the Holy Year of 1950. I had never dared venture into *Terra Incognita*,* and I had asked my friend Maurice to come with me. Frugal railroad workers that we were, we traveled by train, and my friend insisted on using his rudimentary camping equipment--a kepi tent and a gasoline stove of the latest style.

Through the window, we did not miss a scrap of the countryside. The first stop after the border bore a large sign reading « *USCITA* », which I took for its name. Since the following stations said the same, I finally got out my dictionary. It meant "Exit." In school, I had indeed translated *The Divine Comedy*, but in "Hell" the word "Exit" was certainly not used. I was ignorant as well of many other common words, and could not order from a menu without the help of a word list.

Because we were "Holy Year pilgrims," we were entitled to the *Bousta*, a booklet of multiple discounts-- notably, a reduced entry fee to museums and a list of registered restaurants where you could eat for the unbeatable price of 350 liras...

That was how I discovered *Pasta al Sugo*, the spaghetti dish covered with herbed tomato sauce and some pieces of meat, topped with a snowy summit of Parmesan, placed there sparingly and finely shredded, so that it does not solidify. In the finer restaurants, the cheese is generally left for the customer to handle, in a glass fitted with an adjustable lid, closing by gravity to protect the contents from flies. The assumption seems to be that this ingenious device, typically Italian, cannot be left at the disposal of people who visit the lesser restaurants; they might put more cheese in the

---

* Latin: [Unknown Territory]

plate than pasta. And if the party could buy just one entrée, they would be charged the supplement *Pane e copperto*-- bread and cover charge.

The first night with Maurice was spent "roughing it" at the edge of the Lac de Garde, in Desenzano del Garda, in front of a grandiose backdrop enclosed by the white peaks of the Alps. But we had to share our slightly muddy site with a lot of mosquitoes. We really couldn't complain; *they* hadn't come looking for us.

The next day we were in Venice, which suited me because of my interest in old buildings, and a latent passion for museums and their paintings. I promptly noticed that Maurice did not share my tastes and that, after the obligatory visit of San Marco and the Palace of the Doges, completed by a small boat tour (much less expensive than the gondolas) on the Grand Canal, Maurice considered that he had fulfilled all his obligations as a tourist.

The first time that I tried to change money at the Bank of the Holy Spirit in Florence, I had a difficult time explaining myself, and the employee said: « *S'il vous plaît parlez France si vuole che comprendre qualche cosa !* » ["Please speak French if you want me to understand anything!"] I was all the more mortified that he considered his broken French better than my Italian.

The tour of Florence had to be cut short; Maurice couldn't tolerate any more of the Galerie des Offices, where there were really too many paintings. I remember especially our dinner. That evening, he had insisted on making us a stew with oatmeal, but since his gasoline stove had spilt in his bag, the soup had such a revolting taste that I can still call it to memory.

In the morning, he was never in a hurry to get up, and devoted a lot of time to washing and dressing, grooming in particular a proud little moustache and the waves of a slicked-back hairdo. I forced myself to hide my impatience.

In Rome, after having visited the four major basilicas and a department store—to buy postcards—he felt that we had seen everything and could go back. I made the best of it, swearing to myself to come back one day without him, to visit everything that interested me. So, my passion for Italy was born, and I learned not to travel with just anybody. One should not cast pearls before swine.

That was how I met Vivina, a student in Architecture who was entering competition for an Embassy scholarship to study in France. She was very happy to meet me, to be able to speak French and prepare for her oral exam. We would meet in Rome, and she and her fiancé would take me sightseeing in the Eternal City. I promised to go with her to the Farnèse Villa, the French Embassy, to take the appropriate steps for her to travel to France.

Several days later, I met Ennio, an extremely cultivated and friendly architect, who introduced me to his concepts of Art by showing me what he had produced. The three of us set out for the historic old neighborhoods of the capitol, to see sights usually undiscovered by tourists. It was a real wonder! Foreign travelers cannot imagine the richness of all these old palaces and baroque churches, hidden in alleyways inaccessible to tourist buses.

Vivina taught me the secret of the Italian landscape, where they plant three cypress trees one against the other, to form a unique expanded spindle shape, which marvelously adorns the Roman countryside. The Italians are incomparable artists!

We happened to have dinner in a trattoria on the Lungo Tevere, which Ennio translated literally as "Long Tiber." Each of us ordered a pizza larger than the plate, and we were able to down an extra bottle of Dei Castelli Romani wine, since pizzas cooked to order take time. So, I discovered *Pizze napolitane*, which had not yet come across the Alps. The chef, in his high white hat, made the dough, twirled it on the end of a finger, covered it with tomato, cheese and condiments, and baked it before our eyes.

The feast of Corpus Christi is a holiday in Italy, so my friends had organized an outing with a friend, Olivetti. We spent the day in the Colli Romani, traveling in his car from Nemi to Monte Cavo.

They had found very well preserved remains of Roman boats in the Nemi Lake. The emperor Caligula used to visit, to rest in the clear air of the higher altitude, and to enjoy the coolness of the lake. These boats, carefully made with copper nails and tar, had been partially destroyed in 1944, when the Germans left. They had just re-opened the museum with what could be salvaged, completing the exhibition with models. That day, they were filming a documentary with about 50 assistants.

In the villages, the Romans enjoyed the holiday outdoors, on long benches at tables, where they peeled and enjoyed green Italian beans and drank Castelli wine. With my friends, I felt that I had become a true Roman!

To travel more comfortably, I had reduced my baggage to the absolute minimum, and everything was in my old briefcase. I would wash my shirt in the evening, to wear it again the next day. But being without a change of clothes was not completely without problems.

That was the case the day they invited me to go to Ostia, Rome's beach. While they were in the water, I had rolled up my pant-legs and was enjoying a dip. Catching sight of a beach umbrella pole, I thought I could lean on it to jump the waves. Unfortunately, the sand was washed out at the foot of the pole, my heels slipped on this surprise slope, and I found myself on my back in the water, up to my belt.

Quickly finding my footing kept my wallet from getting ruined, along with money and papers, but my only pair of pants was soaked. Fortunately, Ennio knew the person renting cabanas, who lent me a pair of pants. I can still see myself, night having fallen, walking the streets in Rome, wet trousers wrapped in a newspaper. But I felt good! At the hotel, the name of which translated as—I kid you not—The Inn of the Sun, on Paradise Street, I just stretched them out for drying. The next morning, I pulled them into shape—an ironing of sorts—and heard the grains of sand and salt bouncing on the tiled floor of the room, making little white points like microscopic pearls on the hexagonal floor tile, which had just been repainted in red.

Two days later, climbing the steps of the Greek theater of Syracuse, I felt a breeze in an unexpected place. The stitches of the seat and of one leg of the trousers had just given way.

Another year, in Padua, I was out early one Sunday morning, en route to visit the famous Basilica, when I noticed an extra-shiny sidewalk, in front of a shop where the curtain was lowered. I took one step, slipped, and sprawled with a second step. I was in front of an olive oil merchant, whose shop window had been broken, and the spilt merchandise had not been cleaned up.

All I could do was ask for help at the bakery next door, the only store on the street that was open. The baker woman called the Italian police and, at her request, I stayed in the bake house in my under-shorts while she tried over and over to soak up the oil on my trousers with talcum powder.

A pair of policemen arrived soon to take my deposition and arrange for the errand boy of a nearby tailor to bring me some pants to choose from. I took the least ugly one, whose stripes the color of goose poop gave me the air of a local fashion plate. Then I swore before witnesses that I considered that my damages had been compensated.

The baker lady brought back my partially de-greased pants, and the grinning cops declared: "It's a miracle of St. Anthony, that you arrived with one pair of pants, and leave with two!"

My new outfit seemed to put off the illicit street vendors of fake Parker pens and fake Rolex watches. Indeed, other foreigners were approached in the street by these vendors, who greeted them on the spot and spoke to them directly in their language, to suggest buying their wares. I marveled at how they could guess the nationality of a foreigner without having heard him speak. I learned that it was by their shoes and clothing that they recognized where their hoped-for victims came from, because Italian fashion hadn't yet reached all of Europe.

Before finding my modest hotel on the *rue du Paradis*, where I liked to return year after year and greet the same staff, I had tried different hotels. To overcome my natural timidity, I didn't hesitate to ask to see the rooms, so that I could refuse those that I didn't consider to be a good value for the price. On one occasion, I asked to see a room that I considered expensive. The owner told me precisely why: The room was for two persons. When I expressed disinterest because I was traveling alone, he further made it clear that his daughter came with the room. I had indeed seen the room, but I left quickly, without asking to see his daughter—which proved that I was not yet totally cured of my timidity.

In the fifties, you couldn't visit an art gallery without seeing artists, who seemed to be making copies of the masters. I had noticed that their paintings didn't progress very quickly, and each time that a visitor stopped to watch, they would pull out these adorable miniatures, already set into brooches, from a drawer in the easel. When you imagined the work that that represented, the low price was surprising. I was shocked that people would dare to sell such beautiful reproductions, even curiously made into a cheap piece of jewelry.

One day, I found the key to the riddle. In the train returning to France, a lady was very happy to show me a miniature copy of a magnificent head of the Virgin by Donatello. For this fine and detailed piece of work, the artists claimed to have used brushes made from their own hair. Doubtful, I let the daylight play over the surface of the brooch. Then it was easy to see that it was a pretty color reproduction, simply decorated with a painted ribbon and a few details, to lend relief. I admired it politely without revealing the trickery, to which, like so many others, she had fallen victim.

On another train back to France, I also made the acquaintance of a worried Italian, uneasy because he didn't know French. He was alone and going to Paris for the first time, to pick up women. Fortunately, he told me, he had learned Latin in school, and believed that he could use the language to get by in the Parisian quarter of the same name. To set him up for a surprise, I gave myself the pleasure of reassuring him. I could imagine the reactions of the street cop when he would ask directions, or a girl that he would try to pick up.

I covered thousands of kilometers by train. Italians love to converse, so it was an interesting and colorful place to meet people. I remember, in 1950, this anticommunist worker who was explaining to another: "You can go and see, the Americans eat pasta at all their meals, as much as they want!" This naïve description of the pleasures of the table in the USA was touching.

I remember also, in 1954, the hotel porter who, knowing that I was French, confided to me that he was going to vote Communist, but I must not repeat it to his boss. He must have read in *L'Unità*, the daily Italian Communist newspaper, that all French were Communists. I tried unsuccessfully to convince him otherwise.

That year, I was in Rome on May first, and the Pope was to celebrate a High Mass for workers. Feeling some concern about crowds, I arrived a little early at St. Peter's. I was not the only one to try this tactic. I noticed that the enthusiasts filtering in at the entrance had to present a yellow pass, just the color of an old museum ticket that I still had in my pocket.

I put myself in the middle of a group, and showed only a little edge of the smoothed-out ticket, to get through the cursory entrance procedure without difficulty. Luck had placed me in a group of Germans, who had reserved seats in a loft against one of the pillars in the dome of St. Peter. It was a choice area for seeing the Holy Father officiate, which he knew so well how to do. Interesting as his sermon was, I remember only that it was too long; not having breakfasted that morning, I was very hungry, but obliged to remain until the final Latin prayer, *l'Ite missa est* [Go, the Mass is ended].

To go to Sicily, the top-of-the-line trains used to clear the straits of Messina by ferryboat, while the other travelers had to take endless subterranean passageways to get to the boat and then take another train on the other side. This second itinerary was usually a race course, to try again to find a seat in the Sicilian convoy.

Going in the other direction, the island residents headed for the continent were encumbered with countless pieces of baggage, badly secured and of incredible shapes. They were transporting food—bread and local specialties— to consume on the trip, or to offer to relatives whom they were going to see.

Politeness decrees that, when you unwrap food and drink in the train, you offer some to everyone in the compartment.   To show good manners, one should refuse, but only to a certain point, that point to be determined. From what moment does a refusal become an affront? In his book *Conversazione in Sicilia,* Elio Vittorini is obliged to share the "picnic" of a sewage tankard driver, who claims to be a government worker in Milan, but whose scent bespeaks his real trade.

Being a traveler without baggage, I often helped these poor people carry their food sacks. I remember once, when the train was 24 hours late after a mudslide, I profited from their foresight.

Italy's unification is recent, and the regions are proud of their cultural differences. One of the big questions is where the true South of the country begins; according to primitive mores, this is the poor section of a country. For the Romans, Naples is the south.   The people of Florence include Rome in the South. As for the Milanese, they think the South is all sections of Italy below the valley of the Po River. I even had a discussion with a bookseller from Salò, who claimed that Milan was already the South—surely he exaggerated. Enio told me that, as a Roman, he felt closer to the French than to the Calabrese or the Sicilians. They are as the Arabs are to the French, he claimed.

For me, the dividing line is to the south of Rome. You only have to look in the trains—except for the first class high speeds—that are reserved for business travelers from the North, and for "Higher-ups" from the South. The convoys of the South consist of old cars, badly maintained and dirty. The floor of the toilet is normally so dirty that it consists of a thick grillwork cleaned by a water jet. There is a general relaxation of schedule, and trains are rarely on time.

Hygiene has made considerable progress in Italy since that far-off time when, in the South, they would paint on the walls of farm buildings, in large black letters: "DDT," followed by the treatment date--or, a dissenting message indicating that DDT had been refused.

I found the notes that I had taken during my first trip to Sicily, dated May 6, 1951:

> Yes, a real ferryboat, colossal, with three tracks to accommodate all the train-cars. Yes, the same as for England, a real ferryboat is at Villa San Giovanni waiting for us and, as soon as it finishes swallowing its heavy cargo of cars, it swerves, sets out to cover in one trek the 8 kilometers that separate us from Messina. Then with minute precision, giving us immense satisfaction because of its enormous mass, the vessel draws alongside the port, adjusting the train-cars to the millimeter, onto the end of the track.
>
> It's a great little steam machine, the kind they made in the last century, and we have adopted it. Blowing, whistling, it tries courageously to pull the coupling with that desperate force born of weakness. It's the Palermo train!
>
> Suddenly, leaving Messina, it's attacked by a long slope, the first turn of the Monte Peloritani. Then I really understand that it isn't like the other trains--they scoff at the tough terrain.
>
> Our poor little second-hand machine gives off heart-breaking sighs, in clouds of white steam streaked with the brown, acrid smoke of the peat fire in its stove. This is called the "express," covering the 230 kilometers in six hours. It's incapable of hurrying; accelerating, it hyperventilates. Then it meanders, stops indefinitely in a small station, waits for the train due from the other direction. Finally, it departs.
>
> Then it hurtles into a descent. Unaccustomed to this speed, the passengers are surprised, thinking that

perhaps the brakes won't hold. We're going to get up to 50 km/hour. Then, with a single quick movement, the train recoils when passengers least expect it, rears up, seems to hesitate—as people do when they suddenly think they have forgotten something back at the house. Then it stops out in the middle of the countryside between the fig trees of Barbary. Will it return? No! Finally, everything is fine on board, it can continue.

Everything is fine on board! The passengers shake their heads with relief, and their bellies settle down after the fear of faulty tracks. Oh, of course, they could get angry about this bumpy jolting, torturing them with its randomness. But no, they don't take it that seriously, they just bump their limbs against the rough wooden seats and spill the drinks of their traditional feasts on the floor.

Over there, in the last compartment, a kid is crying, his parents have just admitted that he's not on a real train, but only a sort of amusement park ride for adults, where everyone is having fun in this vibrating convoy. It's very warm, but there are so many tunnels and so much smoke that no one dreams of opening the rattling windows. Each new tunnel brings in air heavy with the greasy smell of peat, speckling its dust in the rivulets on their sweat-streaked faces.

Of course, somewhere in the train, there will be a cranky gentleman from the North, full of self-importance, complaining that he will miss a business meeting because of this "wheelbarrow" being two or three hours late. The Sicilians never complain—they're used to it and they know that here, time is valued differently!

The ticket inspector goes through the train at each station--the whole train--to show that he is indeed there, in his jaunty cap, white gloves in uniform pocket, checking first-class travelers' tickets. His hand is skillful with the hole-punch, using it with an automatic movement, his head turned and looking elsewhere.

During each passage, he approaches the passengers, asking in the kindest of voices: "Are there any among you who have tickets that I have not yet punched?" From time to time, he finds one who pushes the pretense that this is a real train, and pulls a ticket from his pocket; the employee punches it at random, while gazing at the scenery.

To people sitting next to sleeping passengers, he says: "No, don't wake him, I'll see him in an hour or two, when he's finished his nap." Happy, he goes on his way at the speed of a guinea fowl, shaking through the corridors.

In Palermo, I had found a trattoria with an illuminated sign in an alleyway a few steps from the piazza of the Quattro Canti. It was visible even in full daylight from the Corso V. Emanuele: « *Si mangia bene. Si spensa poco* ». ["Here you eat well. Here you spend little."] This proposal suited me perfectly. I had ordered a carafe of white wine with lunch. It was a sweet, strong wine, so delicious that I had called the waiter over, to ask what he had given me. "But sir, this is only our Sicilian house wine." A businessman settled down at my table, ordered a two-liter *fiasco*,* which he downed in little mouthfuls, complaining to have lost his appetite.

For breakfast, I had eaten rolls while walking, so I thought I'd stop in a shop where the walls were covered with barrels, and wash them down with a glass of Marsala, that very sweet, heavy wine. Unfortunately, I soon had to stop this pleasant diet; it made me nervous and I slept badly.

I had discovered a modest hotel in the heart of the old city, close to the pawnshop. While I was enjoying washing up after long hours spent in the smoky train, I was interrupted by a winsome servant girl, who had come in to ask if I needed anything. The following year, my arrival coincided with the same unexpected entrance of a maid; I then understood that I had lodged in a rather seedy establishment, although not "red-light."

En route to Rome another day, I had tried to phone friends from one of those cafes marked with a yellow face, signaling a public telephone inside. I used the token correctly and re-read the directions, but couldn't get connected, to the amusement of the customers. Finally they showed me a little cardboard sign overhead, where the word

---

* [a straw-covered wine bottle]

Guasto was written. My dictionary taught me a new word that I would never forget: "Out of order."

That year I had undertaken to tour Sicily by rail—not easily done, nor quickly. Many of the lines were fitted with one-way metric rails. One morning, I had to leave Agrigento at 5 a.m. At the proper time, there was only one train at the platform—without an engine—and I was the only traveler. I confirmed that it was the right train, but they didn't know when it would leave, because « *la macchina è guasta* ». I now knew what that meant, and the stationmaster advised me to take the Pullman bus, which left at 7 a.m., but would get to Sicily before the train.

To visit Selinonte, I had gotten off at Marinella station. At that time, it was a group of wooden cottages on a sandy path at the edge of the sea. I went to see the only little grocery store, where I met the Rocca Fiorita family. No, they said, there was no restaurant, but I could eat with them at 1 p.m. I left my briefcase and accepted their offer of a cold drink before going off in the direction of the Temples.

The official caretaker had a simple memory device for remembering the names of the three major Temples. This he repeated to visitors: « *A è Apollo, MI è inerva, CE è Jupitero* ». [AMICE means "friends."]

The Temple of Apollo measures 113 meters by 14; its columns have been there, toppled to the ground, for centuries--round and solid, more than 3 meters in diameter. I was astonished by such dimensions and by the immensity of the field of ruins, edifices lost here at the end of the world, dominating the sea in a splendid setting. In June, at morning's end, the thundering on the rocks was overwhelming.

I was dying of thirst. That particular day, I really understood the significance of the charitable gift of a glass of water. To me, a spoiled little Norman, the offer of a cup of water, as they spoke of it in the Catechism, had always seemed a bit stingy; now I knew otherwise.

I returned with pleasure to the home of the Rocca Fioritas, where the shade of the closed shutters gave a cool but false sensation. In the back of the shop, I shared the meager meal of this modest, barefoot family. After lunch, when I asked for the check, Rocca answered: "Here, travelers give what they wish, and they are free to leave nothing." He asked only that I write in his Golden Book, where foreigners praised Signora Rocca Fiorita's cooking in many different languages. Then they offered me a room for the siesta, and even suggested that I could stay there as long as I wanted, under the same conditions.

I would have had all the sand dunes and the splendid beach to myself. For an instant, I was tempted by this paradise, wanting to stay with these simple and generous people. But the pleasure of my vacation was, albeit foolishly, based on movement. Travel! Travel!

Twenty years later, having never forgotten Marinella, I came back with my wife, Yvonne. The town had become a beautiful seaside resort, like so many others of that particular style. When I recounted these memories to the hotel owner, he told me that Rocca Fiorita was still living, was more than 80 years old, and passed by on his moped every morning about seven, to buy bread. He stopped him the next morning for me. Rocca did not recognize me, but to prove that he was still mentally sharp, he claimed to remember Yvonne, whom he had never seen.

An iron fence now surrounded the town's vast archaeological excavation site, with a booth for entrance tickets. On the access road, vendors on scooters stopped us, selling counterfeit artifacts encrusted with dirt or broken and glued together to lend authenticity.

In the evening, having some spare time, and for the pleasure of conversation, I went by the police station—now that there was one—to tell them that it was a dishonor to their town to let naïve tourists be fleeced like that. They made sure that I hadn't come to file a complaint, because it was "too late" for that. They simply wanted to know if this attempted clandestine sale had taken place within the perimeter of the Temple area, because outside of that area was not their concern. They were well aware that the most important manufacturing of copies was several kilometers away, and this was a perfectly legal operation for Italy and for exportation.

Since, by my remarks, they discerned that I was a real connoisseur, they kindly recommended the antique shop *Da Alfonso*, where I could buy authentic votive lights with a written guarantee. I saw the shop window, and the lamps there were much more expensive, and of a style which did not inspire my confidence.

Vulcano (see map, p. 209) in Sicily, Italy;
elevation 1,600 feet.
The southernmost of *Isole Eolie* [the Aeolian Islands].

PART TWO: VOLCANOLOGY AND ME

Since my first trip to Sicily, my sole desire had been to climb Mount Etna; that active volcano rising to 3,300 meters set me dreaming. All the same, it seemed unwise to undertake this adventure alone. Luck would have it that I met two young Danish guys on the train and convinced them that this was a trip they couldn't miss. We shared the same room in a hotel in Catania and took the next day's early bus for the end of the road, the 1,900-meters-high Casa Cantoniera.

The weather was uncertain, with clouds passing by. Looking at the summit, we wondered if it was smoking or if those were thick clouds surrounding it. Although it was May, it was cold at that height. We had taken the cinder path and the bright spots diminished as we climbed. In the fog, the direction of the summit became increasingly difficult to observe.

We were not outfitted for this weather. I can still see the Danish fellows moving along in front of me, in their short pants. The clouds, transformed into snow, hung on the hairs of their calves like strange melting stalactites, contributing to the chilling of their enthusiasm.

I myself began to have doubts, owing to the real dangers of the expedition that I had proposed; my moral responsibility towards them was in jeopardy. For a quarter of an hour, we took shelter in a lava cave, before finally going back down, guiding ourselves by stakes that had been planted for the future ski lift.

Many years later, I returned with Yvonne to conquer the summit. The weather was sunnier, but a violent wind prevented the departure of the ski lift. We enjoyed going across the adventitious craters of that area, while waiting for the eventual departure.

Around 9 a.m., when it was decided that the ski lift definitely would not be leaving, a geology student at the University of Catania suggested that we go with him, to try climbing with a half-dozen enthusiasts. We were dressed for the cold, and had goggles to protect our eyes from flying cinders. The climb was without incident; nevertheless, 1,500 meters of uneven terrain took a full four hours to accomplish. We undertook this challenge courageously, before starting the tour of the crater. A swirling wind sometimes lifted the smoke, and we saw the interior of the crater, carpeted with sulfur and white spots of boron, and we noticed volleys of stones landing far off, from time to time. At other times, the wind beat us with suffocating sulfurous smoke, and we tried to breathe through a handkerchief; to make that work very well, it would have had to be wet. We made do with a halfway measure. Sometimes, the earth felt hot through the soles of our shoes, and sitting on the ground would have been impossible.

Halfway 'round the crater, we were surprised by a volley of stones more violent than the others. Our whole little group took off running in all directions, like a flight of starlings under the shots of hunters. We didn't stop running until we reached the base of the last cone, 300 meters below.

At that time, we met a group accompanied by a real guide. He had given up the ascent, saying it was too dangerous that day. Was it true? Had we been foolish? Or were the followers at the whim of a lazy guide? We would never know.

The entire next day, from Sicily's wonderful ancient theater of Taormina, we gazed from a distance of 30 kilometers at the summit we had conquered the day before; exhausted and full of aches and pains, we hardly had the strength to put one foot in front of the other.

In June 1983, we were to revisit Etna, under conditions which deserve to be retold. It was several months since the eruption, and the "No Access" signs had just been removed. We went to the Office of Tourism, but the offices had just closed. There was only one employee left, who took an interest in us when we spoke of all the other volcanoes that we had visited, in other places. She must have taken us to be more volcanologists than we were, because she suggested that we come back the next day to meet the Head of the Office and Deputy Mayor of Linguaglossa, who "certainly could do something for you."

Indeed, the Director put through a requisition for the minibus that was authorized to circulate throughout the lava flows and, since we had no car to gain access, he had two of his employees accompany us with their own vehicle. The employees were delighted with the unexpected chance to go up onto the volcano. They refused my offer to fill the tank, saying that their Department had paid; they accepted only a cappuccino.

We drove across abandoned towns, where the inhabitants had not yet returned since the eruption. Weeds had grown over the construction sites, rusty cranes stood near materials that had been abandoned for months. Sometimes a cooled lava flow had spilled onto the road, and had to be by-passed.

At the village entrance, for an unknown reason, the flow of lava had divided into two arms, forming a sort of islet between them, where trees had survived in the heat. Miraculously, the arm of lava extending into the village had only broken the wall of a votive chapel, stopping at the feet of a Madonna. "A true miracle!" emoted our companions.

Having arrived at the Casa Cantoniera, we saw the old hotel that we knew, half collapsed under a mountain of cinders. We were in a dangerous zone, under high surveillance of the police, firemen and military engineers, with a helicopter on permanent surveillance.

Our new friends quickly secured places in the all-terrain minibus, which drove us across the cinders towards 2,200 meters altitude. They had us get out and cross a cooled lava bridge, under which an incandescent river flowed slowly but inexorably towards the Valle del Bove, bringing scoria with bubbles of bursting gas that made soft little thuds: "Poof! Poof!"

Although the lava was no longer very bright red, its heat waves reached out several meters, making our cheeks very warm. A little devil, armed with a large metal pitchfork with two teeth, was pulling shreds from the fusing paste and depositing it in a metallic mold, to make original ashtrays for adventurous tourists. We still treasure ours.

Then we descended again, across beautiful high altitude forests, enchanting to our companions, who were not as used to green countryside as we. I wanted to invite them to have lunch at the first inn that we came to, but that was not to be; our meal was, it appeared, already provided for elsewhere.

At a lower altitude, we found a new route closed to traffic, with barriers on alternating sides, in order to make passage easier. They asked if we wanted to venture there; I answered that we were leaving it up to them. The road led to an abandoned winter sports area, where the ski lift was of no use.

Although we were far from observable volcanic activity that morning, a pocket of molten lava could open at any time in the face of the mountain, and engulf us instantly. Soon we arrived at the resort restaurant, where we were the only customers. They were expecting us.

I will not describe our feast to you, so that you won't regret *a posteriori** not sharing this risky situation. Everything was perfectly prepared, fresh and delicious, from appetizers to desserts, not to mention the best vintage wines of Etna. I must admit that I was afraid of getting a really stiff check when we left. But no, here again, we were the guests of the Office of Tourism. They asked only, as a favor, to let them drive us to Linguaglossa, where the Mayor awaited us with after-dinner drinks and a very rich tourist documentation of the region.

The Mayor was eager to show us how the hotels were connected by screened-in passages, which meant that the tourist guests would be led directly to them. We could thank

---

* Latin for a decision made after all the facts are known.

him at our leisure for this unforgettable day; he simply wished that I would furnish him with an article on our impressions—I could even write it in French.

As you can see, volcanoes have always fascinated me, and from Etna to Vesuvius, I know all those of the Archipelago of the Aeolies,[*] and have visited them several times. These islands owe their name to the god of the wind.

In Milazzo, I had bought a ticket for Lipari, the most important of the islands. At that time, before the storm had hit and people had fled their homes, there was an old steamboat servicing the archipelago, Very early in the morning, the sun was blazing hot over a sea of steel. My boat stopped en route, at Vulcano, to let off a few local people. When I saw the extraordinary palette of colors from this smoking volcano, I rushed to catch the shuttle boat. But the captain intervened: "Here is not for tourists. You have a ticket for Lipari, you have to go there."

Lipari, the capitol of the archipelago, had a bad reputation. Malaparte had been held there, with several undesirables connected to Mussolini. There was the Hotel Nizza and the Pensione Salinas;[+] I checked into the Pensione. My room had the appearance of a monastic cell, where the rays of the lighthouse swept through its narrow little window, on a regular nightly watch.

For the meal, the whole barefoot family surrounded its sole guest. The carafe of wine enthroned on the table was protected from flies by an inverted cone of newspaper. The owner stood and watched me eat. He was eating a cucumber, which he cut in thin slices, offering me a taste.

After the midday siesta, the heat was usually still unbearable. I couldn't go out until 5 p.m., and at 7 p.m. it was already dark. It was my first trip to the south, and no

---

[*] Also spelled Eolies, and referred to as the Eolie Islands.

[+] A *pensione* is a boarding house; i.e., you pay for a room, and meals are included.

one had warned me that we were in the period of Sirocco,[*] which transforms the country into a furnace.

The next morning, very early, I left to discover the unforgettable panorama of Quattr'occhi [Four Eyes], towards Vulcano. Then, I wanted to see the obsidian flows, the *vetri neri* produced by the geothermic transformation of silica.

Obsidian was a highly prized bartering commodity of prehistoric peoples, and many traces of it remain. There were also open-air quarries of *pietra pomice*, with the mysterious name missing from my little dictionary and which no one knew how to translate into French: « *Della pietra pomice = della pietra pomice* ». I learned only that this volcanic substance [pumice] was rendered into a hundred different grades from the raw material, and that they use it to make scouring powders, abrasive pastes, laundry additives, etc.[+]

This pumice forms a gigantic cliff looking out over the sea. The exportation process is powered by bulldozers, which push the cut side directly toward chutes, where gravity guides it into the holds of the boats that take it to worldwide points. Strangely, the oblique blade of the machinery, constantly in contact with the powder, gives off an intense luster. When stones escape and fall into the sea, they float towards the open sea, like little corks.

On the heights of Lipari, I was intrigued by the sight of astonishing fields of concrete. They were intended to cap the pluvial (rain) waters, to store them in an immense subterranean reservoir. Today, the area is rutted by earthquakes and disuse, and water is shipped by tankers from Calabria.

On the other side of Lipari is the former home of the god Vulcain. Called Vulcano, it was completed many years ago by the strange appendix of Vulcanello, that little volcano

---

[*] A hot, oppressive, wind from the Libyan deserts of Africa. It blows on the northern Mediterranean coast chiefly in Italy, Malta and Sicily.

[+] Pumice is often shaped into an oval "stone" that can be held in the hand and used for scrubbing, with a sandpaper-like effect.

that grew from the sea and attached itself by a narrow tongue to the low land. Foolhardily, people built houses there, and they were swept away by the next tidal wave. Sensational headlines followed, of course, and this made all cottage dwellers nervous!

Nowadays, Vulcano has a real port, where boats and hydrofoils come in. Just next to it, where you clear a labyrinth of multicolor rocks through a tortuous passage, you fall upon a strange pond near some drying clay statues wearing sunglasses and hats.

These are incurably ill people, drying themselves in the sun after having entirely covered their bodies with the clay carpet of the pond bottom. Later, shod in thickly soled sandals, they will go to the boiling jets in the sea, to remove the clay at a comfortable temperature. This will leave the skin very soft.

We tempted fate ourselves, by spending a night in one of these bungalows at high tide, before starting out very early to climb and tour the crater of Vulcano. We had left a little too early, and had to wait for sunrise in order to find the trail. Presently, we were involved in a strange exchange of light signals between a yacht and a car, whose worried driver came to ask what we were doing there. What illegal cigarette traffic were we about to interfere with?

As soon as there was enough light, we took the path, led by a yellow mongrel dog, typical of the archipelago. He accompanied us up to the crater and left when we started the tour, because the sulfuric gases bothered him more than us. In the rising sun, through the smoke curls, the vast landscape had a magic, unreal quality.

How well I still remember that young woman in the motel restaurant. She had a terrible nervous tic that made her wink and blink constantly. There was another woman with a pockmarked face, who came every year for the cure, without realizing that this radioactive clay could be inappropriate, even harmful, for her.

From there, we left on a mini-cruise with Salvatore, a fisherman who had converted his skiff into a tourist boat--a new, more lucrative undertaking. He drove us to the Grotta del Cavallo, an immense porch of lava frozen into place, with the sea rushing in. He suggested that we go to Panarea the following day, to have lobster with some others who were interested.

We took that outing, but found ourselves restricted to the rear of the vessel; the bridge in front of the captain's piloting cabin was reserved for the over-all tanning of a well-preserved countess and her muscular gigolo. These companions didn't bother us, and the captain seemed to consider it our entertainment, but the young cabin boy was too distracted, and irritated the captain.

At 10 a.m., our captain offered refreshments of fruit from his garden and wine from the grapes of his vineyard. Later, he provided a rope ladder, for those who wanted to swim in the sea. Then we traveled to a promontory of Panarea, to see the remains of Neolithic Age circular huts. He also tried to organize a fishing party, but the arrival of a shoal of dolphins—protected animals—quickly put an end to the fishing. Salvatore, a bit of a drinker, was aggressive, and negotiated good meals for himself and his clientele in an isolated inn in Panarea. He acted as commander leading his soldiers.

From the terrace where we had lunch, we were close enough to Stromboli to see the periodic eruptions and explosions, preceded by a feather of black smoke and a few seconds' delay.

Yvonne and I have climbed Stromboli twice. The first time was in 1973, with a guide also named Salvatore, the pre-destined given name. Leaving late in the afternoon with about thirty tourists, we had to scale 800 meters of uneven terrain to get above the erupting openings.

In the setting sun, you could see the volleys of rocks shooting very high and then falling back into the crater or onto its exterior side facing the sea; there they rolled noisily and sent up dust clouds. As darkness fell, the stones became red bombs, and then there were great lighting effects.

Around 10 p.m., from the crest at the top of the crater, we saw five incandescent openings.   They were blowing gas jets, screaming like jet engines and intermittently transforming into light fountains.

We had with us a tourist who, transfixed by this extraordinary show, repeated constantly: "To think that it comes from the center of the earth!"   She was just beginning to realize that her geography book was not make-believe.

MAJOR VOLCANOES OF ITALY
SOURCE: USGS/Cascades Volcano Observatory, Vancouver, Washington. June 3, 2003

Salvatore had positioned us well, where a steady wind allowed a good view of the spectacle, without the strong fumes. We stayed there spellbound, outside of time and everyday contingencies, waiting for the next incandescent puff to manifest itself.

Sometimes, after minutes of waiting, several fires would explode simultaneously, causing a truly dazzling illumination. The sparkling sprays, coughed out by strong gas pressure, shot high above us into the sky, to fall a distance away—fortunately! When they touched the earth, the glowing bombs pushed down the slopes into the sparkling flows.

After midnight, we had to start back. Taking advantage of the magnificent full moon, Salvatore had us schuss down through a very steep cinder flow. We glided more than descended, filling our shoes and stirring up dust clouds that enveloped us in an eerie fog under the moonlight.

At the hotel, sandwiches awaited us and candles were burning, to compensate for the loss of power from the electric generator--turned off to economize, or perhaps broken down. So, with no water in the sink, we washed with a wide-mouthed pitcher, depositing most of our cinder coating into a washbowl.

In Stromboli, except for the little white painted houses that are whitewashed every year, everything is black: the mountain rocks, the sand on the beaches, the cinders blown helter-skelter across alleys just wide enough for a saddle-backed donkey to pass.

In front of the town, about twenty minutes away by boat, Strombolicchio rises up, a sort of landmark volcanic fireplace, appearing to have been thrown up by the sea. A staircase was put up to allow access, but it is now forbidden.

When we returned ten years later, still captivated by the memory of that volcano, Salvatore was dying, his lungs ruined by the Stromboli's vapors. But we made the climb again, by ourselves, leaving one morning at dawn. As before, the path presented few problems, but could be called an endurance climb. At the top, we found some young people who had spent the night. They had stayed very late, watching the displays, and ended up wrapping in blankets to sleep. Exhausted and oblivious to the noise of the volcano, they had slept protected from the wind behind low walls formed by volcanic rock falls.

Upon our return, we were given a hero's welcome. From the town, they had watched with binoculars, surprised that "old people" would dare to make a climb they had given up long ago. I remember the head of our pretty landlady, who must have washed and dressed very briefly; she had a "hemline" of fine black grime around the curves of her ears. Here water was scarcer than wine, and black soot was waiting everywhere!

We then returned to Lipari by air. The sea had become too rough to take the usual boat; with its two skis lifting out of the water with each wave, those crossings were extremely difficult and barely safe. Knowing that traveling by sea can be impractical for long periods, the natives lead their lives accordingly. For example, pregnant women leave a month in advance to give birth in Milazzo, and avoid medical helicopter evacuation.

In Lipari, near the little port of Marina Corta, we had found a cave cleverly renovated from a pirates' refuge into a restaurant called *I Pirati*. The waitresses were dressed as lady pirates, and presented the menu as a parchment, which you had to unroll. Everything was seasoned with pirates' sauce—it was « *Zuppa dei Pirati* », « *Spaghetti ai Pirati* », etc. There was something "Pirate" on each line, and the girls were instructed to use that word more than usual.

The cashier's post was an old rum barrel, and the bill was presented in a sort of miniature pirate's chest, where the customers had to place their money. The cave walls were decorated with old pistols and blunderbusses.

To keep the mussels completely fresh, they were in a net, hung over a banister and submerged in the sea. It was there that we were present at the feast of an octopus, which had managed to open the bivalves through the mesh of the net.

The owner had insisted that we come on that particular evening of the dinner-show. Three fellows sang Sicilian songs in an incomprehensible (to us) dialect, emoting about hunger and suffering, accompanying themselves on the guitar. The owner had come over by me, to translate the words into Italian.

Then one of the performing artists grabbed a decorative blunderbuss from the cave wall, and threatened the guests one by one to deposit tips into the hat held by his accomplice. Each guest complied graciously. The landlord then remembered that he had proposed this show to his diners, and the performers were obliged to pass the hat once again, asking, "Who gave this bill?" and giving everyone back his share.

The proprietor of *I Pirati* also owned a hotel, the Augustus, where we were staying. Alas, the barking of the dogs kept us awake and, upon his tardy return to the nest, we also had to listen to the noisy reproaches of his shrew of a wife. The poor devil pleaded work responsibilities, but she suspected that he had been under the charms of one of his piratesses. And goodness knows, they WERE pretty!

One Sunday evening, we had driven to the extreme western point of Sicily--Erice, towering 750 meters over the city of Trapani. We were there one Sunday evening, to see the sunset. Well, this idea had also occurred to many inhabitants of Trapani, who had parked their cars in complete disorder.

At nightfall, everyone wanted to leave at the same time, causing an indescribable traffic jam. I knew right away that my Citröen, wider-bodied than their vehicles, could not leave unscathed. So, I tried to substitute myself for the absent traffic cop, in order to open up the village.

By some miracle, they obeyed my gestures, without guessing that any discussion would have disclosed a funny accent. In less than an hour, I could take my turn at backing out, without any risk, and Erice was freed.

Actually, this stand-in role was not any funnier than the one that I had fulfilled several years earlier, at Vesuvius.

Our whole family was there with the Renault R8, when we came up to the entrance to the toll road, leading to a huge parking lot under the crater's edge.

The official tried to sell me advance tickets for a guided tour of the summit.   I refused, explaining that we were there just for the view.   After parking the car, we looked at the landscape and noted that the guides were taking their customers onto a real mule track.   When we tried to take that path, the guides hurried over to keep us back, brandishing a framed municipal stop order from Naples. One of them explained in Italian that the city guaranteed the qualifications of the guides.   The tone was heating up when, after complimenting them on their credentials, I pointed out that the high quality of their tour in no way prevented me from entering the path without them.   When I asked the name of the guide who was blocking our ascent, I felt a certain wavering; so, I pointed out that, since I was a guide at the highest peak of Chamonix, their path would pose no problem for me.

I had just offered a means of saving face.   They began to holler « *E college !* » ["He's a colleague"!] Apparently accepting me as one of theirs, they tapped me on the shoulder and offered each family member a walking stick—which led the other tourists to believe that we also had been taken in.

I left by the access path at the edge of the crater with our two oldest children, Elisabeth and Béatrice, and was rejoined soon by Yvonne, with the younger ones, Agnès and Laurent.   Four-year-old Laurent was already a great climber for his age.   The path encircling the crater was wide enough to allow people to pass each other easily.   It was dangerous only in that an inside lip, several hundreds of meters down, was giving off fumes.   We had a magnificent view of the Bay of Naples.

About ten years later, we were to make another climb, this time in Calabria, and it was to end in very strange company.   Since we were very warm on the highway, we had decided to cool off with a little foray to a higher altitude, by stopping in a mountain village recently created for winter sports. From there, you could take the two-person ski lift. At the top, we found out that the upper lodge restaurant was open in summer, and the prices were good.

After a morning walking on the crests, we came back around noon; they informed us that the meal began at 1:00 p.m. We used the time to rest and gaze out at the view.

By a poor dirt road, a group of men came along, and alighted from half a dozen black cars. You might have thought that it was a business luncheon, if the members of the group hadn't looked so dissimilar. Some had lively eyes and seemed very confident; others had low foreheads, like henchmen. They all went into a reserved room, where they talked in loud, ringing voices, in a dialect incomprehensible to us.

At 1:00 p.m., we went into the restaurant to choose our dishes from standard menu. The Chef himself, in his tall white toque, came out immediately to suggest the following: "Today only, if you like, I can prepare a tasting menu of local specialties, for the same price." And he completely transformed our choices. Noticing that I already had a carafe of wine that I had just ordered, he added: "This is Cirò wine, that we used to give to the Olympic champions of antiquity; it is excellent. But allow me to offer you a vintage bottle, which you will find much better."

The meal was extraordinary; I can still see him, coming out again, to beg us to make an effort to taste a delicious cheese in the form of a pear, encased in butter— which we have never found anywhere else. Since we had drunk half of the carafe, as well as the bottle, I was more prepared for a good nap on the terrace than for getting back behind the wheel.

Naturally, this sensational lunch was identical to that prepared for the group of men that we had seen arriving, and who joined us in the dining room before the end of our meal. Who could they be, now speaking in normal tones? I could have suspected a Mafia group, had it not been that there were only two routes of access to this isolated spot: the very limited-capacity ski lift and a long dirt road, which would have allowed sufficient warning—if the police had wanted to follow—to disperse into the area.

Two years later, I told the story of this strange meal to my colleague from the Transportation Ministry of Rome. He showed me the newspaper report of a recent decision to cut off the ear of Paul Getty III (the then-hostage grandson of the oil magnate), in a mountain resort in Calabria. The date was very nearly the same as the date of our climb. I leave the probable conclusion to you, but assure you that we had no vote on the matter.

One particular day, I had come to Rome to make the acquaintance of my colleague Biffarini. His office assistant, who accepted the bottle of Cointreau that I had brought for the occasion, explained that, as a boy, Biffarini had learned a little French in France, while offering tourists his services as a guide.

The Ministry is a monumental building, erected under Mussolini on one of the seven hillsides dominating the eternal city. Biffarini hastened to take me out on the terrace, where we had a wonderful view. He was delighted to show me all the important buildings--buildings that I had learned of long ago. I let him tell me, thinking that it must have reminded him of his youth. He asked me the exact nature of my job with the SNCF. Since he apparently over-estimated it—I sensed that he had taken me for the Head of the Transportation Division--I was careful to keep it in soft focus.

At my request, he took me the next day to see the Computer Center of the Italian Railway System, installed in a non-functioning station. Their computer was more up-to-date than the SNCF's. He could give me information that ours could not access, and I could do the same for him. Our getting together was therefore positive and productive.

Since this computer also managed the personnel, it was fun to go into its memory to see if there was an agent with my name, or if another Italian railroad worker also had his name. No, mine wasn't there, and he was the only one under his name. The whole story of his career appeared on the screen, and I learned that he had been in the Ethiopian War. With certain access keys that everyone seemed to know, they could have shown me the salary of the CEO. I kept myself from asking!

He then told me that when they first installed the computer, the Transportation Minister was so taken with its power that he put in his own question: "How's the weather?"   Surprise!   The machine was prepared, and the answer appeared on the screen: "Don't ask stupid questions!"

Biffarini must have considered me pleasant company, because he invited me to his home for a "simple" lunch the next day. The table covered with fine lace, his wife decked out as though for the Feast of Corpus Christi, his little girl-- learning French, but too shy to say a single word to me— plus the fabulous meal served, all gave the lie to his "simple" invitation. I was the first foreigner that they had invited to a meal, and I felt that they wouldn't have made such a fuss for other Italians. Had he taken me for a Director of the SNCF?

When we flew for the first time in a 747 to the Antilles in 1973, a friend who heard our enthusiasm asked if we preferred the Antilles to Italy. I didn't like this dilemma, because one can like strawberry pie and coffee-flavored éclairs; love of one doesn't rule out the other.

We have taken many other trips throughout the world, each more beautiful than the others. Each country has its own charms, which must be discovered more than compared. But when all is said and done, I personally have to say: « *L'Italia soprattutto* » --"Italy above all."

CHAPTER XIV

WORKING ON THE RAILROAD

My father worked in administration at the Railways, exactly where I would make my debut later. When I was very young, I sometimes had the treat of accompanying him to the "Big House," a four-story building accommodating the Regional Lines of Lower Normandy, Hauling, Tracks and Buildings. At that time, it was a building of some import in our city. The workers called it, with fearful irony, the "Palace of the Monkeys," for that's where the big bosses were found.

The first time I went with my father to his office, my eyes barely cleared the tabletops. The smell of tobacco mixed with aniline ink pervaded. Perched on a chair, atop huge bound documents, I amused myself by applying multiple stamps, which I could not read, on recycled paper.

The office had just been gifted with a new, vertical file system, which allowed access to three floors of documents. This was accomplished easily by rotating it, and without even rising from one's chair. This unique type of merry-go-round delighted me; I would make it turn faster and faster, until centrifugal force, to me an unknown phenomenon, spread the papers throughout the room.

Despite my interest in this experiment, I was exhorted not to duplicate it and, from that point on, there were firm admonishments to touch nothing. I learned that Mme Garne had spent an entire afternoon re-filing papers that had been scattered in an instant.

The employees were shirtless, and put on worn jackets protected by cotton over-sleeves, held at the elbow by a rubber band. I remember an agent who had taken up the bad habit of scraping the point of his pen on the left inside flap of his jacket, which was then spattered with violet scars. In the office, the feminine contingent was rare. Each man wore, hooked to his shirt, a detachable celluloid collar, finished off with a "regulation" tie, whose perfect knot never had to be redone.

The "pencil-pushers"--whose status did not entitle them to the armchairs reserved to management--modified their straw-bottomed chairs with a leather pad or a thick seat-cushion, to reduce the painful effect of long, perspiring sessions of sitting.

There was great respect for the pecking order: Only the office managers were allowed to submit current business to the Chief Engineer or to one of his two assistants. For that, they removed their cotton over-sleeves, or changed their jackets. On New Year's Day, theirs was the honor of going to the home of the Head of the Arrondissement,[*] presenting their good wishes and those of the personnel. On this occasion, they were offered small cakes and a shot of porto.[+]

At this time, the hoi polloi envied the privileged status of the railway workers. Their list of benefits read: free medical care, two weeks of paid leave, retirement at age 50 or 55, trips by train at unbeatable prices, group discount prices for home purchases on installments, guaranteed employment, and other lesser benefits.

After World War I (1914-1918), the Railways were obliged to reserve jobs and employ veterans and victims of war, who unfortunately were usually minus something--an arm, an eye or a leg. They were accepted after a simplified exam, without always having the required skills, but having often kept from those heroic times a notable taste for strong drink.

Our office's administrative personnel had been rounded out with "victims of Dautry." This famous Director had been appointed in 1936, at the inception of the SNCF, to put its house in order. We lost count of the "victims" transferred for professional irregularities, such as having been surprised while fishing or enjoying themselves in a café, on company time.

---

[*] Administrative district within a city.
[+] Port wine, wine from Portugal.

The exploits of Dautry were the talk of the town. One morning he had kept watch at the door of the restroom in the locomotive depot, to distribute medical advice to agents who entered at the start of the workday, declaring to them: "You must be sick to need to come here already!"

There was the story that, while he was traveling incognito on the Caen to Paris train, a chatty woman passenger had confided to him all her complaints about the Railways. Passing the town of Evreux, Dautry discretely sent word to the Chief at the platform in St. Lazare, so that, upon their arrival, the flustered and confused lady was presented with a magnificent bouquet of flowers, compliments of the Director.

When I was little, my father often had funny stories to tell about the railroad workers. When I didn't want to eat my very hot soup, he would begin to imitate Darbon, a deep-voiced fellow from the South who rolled those French *r*'s to declare: "The best way to quench your thirst is to eat boiling hot soup."

He also recalled a colleague who was a former pilot in the war of 1914. On his way to the Flying Club of Carpiquet, he had bet that at low tide, he could pass his plane under the swing bridge of Ranville. To the admiration of his companions, he succeeded in this exacting feat.

My father told us the adventures of Baccoco, an artist who also played several musical instruments, and excelled at both music and art. One day when Dad was traveling with him, Baccoco, who was from Corsica, deplored the fact that in Normandy you see only cows in the meadows. Dad asked him to draw a cow's ear, but even though they prolonged the conversation, they waited in vain to spy a model. By the way, do you know the ins and outs of a cow's ear?

Drinking wine on the job was forbidden, but some would go to the coat closet before four-hour break time, and discretely take the appropriate "medication" from their lockers. All eyes were closed to that. Baccoco, their supervisor, must not have liked drinking alone, because he took up the morning practice of clinking glasses with the office guys in their corners. This happily erased the barrier of the chain of command.

Informers promptly got to the Head of Personnel, the terrible Gaillard, who chose the known break time to show up unannounced to see the "boys." There they all were, glasses aloft, the draftsman with a bottle of white wine, pouring for each one in turn. Gaillard had caught them red-handed. Assuming a ferocious air, he began to shout: "Oh, Monsieur Baccoco! I do not like this! Not at all!" Untroubled, the guilty one answered with a large smile: "Sorry, Monsieur Gaillard. Today, I have no other choice of wine to offer you!" The boss, surprised by this witty repartee, could only retreat as suddenly as he had arrived, so as not to burst out laughing in front of them.

Poupie, the corporal among the office guys, was a veteran. One day he came to ask in the Personnel Office what he had to do to get the military medal. This hatched the idea of sending him a false summons from the 43rd Artillery Division, to report to establish the necessary dossier.

At the first military office where he reported, the officer, not convinced by the letter, took it lightly and sent him on to another office, where he was sent off again to yet another, and so on and so on, until finally all the administrators of the Regiment were in on it. The joke was on us, when the extraordinary result was that the military personnel believed in our farce, and awarded him the coveted medal the following National Independence Day, July 14.

Poupie was always ready to glean the least advantage—a suit, a coat, a pair of shoes, etc., with a 30 per cent rebate from the SNCF. His *modus operandi* amused everyone, and one day earned him an indelicate sort of joke. While he was walking through the Personnel Office, someone called out to Madame Jude: "Does Monsieur Poupie have permission?" Poupie leaped over towards her and asked: "Permission! Permission for what?" The response had been prepared in advance, and was prompt: "To kiss my rear, idiot!"

We were far from the era of modern reproduction. Multiple copies of documents were made by a lithographic procedure and, for duplication, the mail was written up in a beautiful, easily read script rendered in aniline ink. Copies were obtained in a manner laughable by today's standards. At designated times, the office boy came to get the letters, and placed them under a hand press, between sheets of moist blotter paper and a yellow silk paper. The aniline text came out onto the colored paper, which was read as a transparency. That was the formal proof that a document had been sent, and it was kept in the schedule of due dates or in the dossier.

You might say that there could always be the sly one, asking after the fact for "the yellow" of a letter never sent, in order to hide his negligence. That involved the complicity of the office boy, usually negotiated with a bottle of red wine. Actually, this dishonest practice was infrequent. The "yellows" disappeared as typing became more common.

The years following the Liberation were extraordinary. The Americans wanted to re-establish the rail line from Cherbourg immediately, to provide supplies for the front. They used a very simple signal system: From the last car of the convoy, a soldier intermittently poked into the network of burning magnesium fuses of the stub axle. Their reddish glow could be seen even in full daylight. The last luminous cartridge enabled the mechanic of the following train to estimate the distance separating it from the car in front, in case of a sudden stop.

The Department called in a professional photographer to take snapshots of ruined bridges, tunnels and other SNCF buildings. He was accompanied by Deville, who supposedly spoke English. In spite of Deville's explanations, the Allies took them for spies and locked them up without water in a freight car. There they remained for twenty-four hours before we noticed them missing, and were able to free them.

One quiet afternoon in the Caen Division, only the artist, in his white blouse, was still there when a young female candidate for grade crossings gate-person presented herself for the required employment physical exam. Because of the white jacket, she mistook him for the doctor. Since she was nice-looking, this sly character followed through with the mistake, for the pleasure of having her undress. Of course, she had to come back the following week, in order to be seen by a real doctor.

In 1947, when I myself had to pass that physical, it was more procedurally correct, but not without incident. Henri, a one-eyed veteran of the war of 1914-1918, drove the applicants to the offices of the various specialists downtown, so they wouldn't get lost in the destroyed areas of the city.

He took this as an occasion to have bowls of cider served at the Bar of the Orne. This ceremonial Communion must have been, for the initiates, a portent of their new life. In memory of my father, he wanted to break tradition and offer me the Welcome Drink himself. My polite refusal, however, did not keep him from drinking to my health— which was the important thing.

Thus it was that, five years after the death of my father, I found myself in his old office, with agents whom I already knew by reputation. One day, I had the very poor judgment to ask Poupie: "Does Poupie have permission?" He remembered it all, hurled himself furiously on me, hollering: "You stupid little jerk! Want me to break your neck?" So it was confirmed that he had more memory than sense of humor.

Couflet, my Dad's former right arm, was still in his office. He always wore a black leather pouch on his left eye, making him look like one of the *Pieds Nickelés* cartoon characters. Every day, he would ask: "Did you see the headlines in *Franc-Tireur*?" I always wondered what fascination he found in the aggressive headlines of this newspaper born of the Liberation. He was the only one who read it, and it ended up disappearing, headlines and all.

Gaillard , a tall old gentleman just beginning to stoop, was still Office Supervisor. He tinted his thick, bushy eyebrows deep black, and his gaze beaconed out above his glasses, perched on the end of his nose, in readiness for their sole purpose—as a reading aid. He wasn't a bad sort, but he played the role of tough boss over his former colleagues, a role he had landed by dint of his devotion and many unpaid overtime hours on the job.

His status was not easy to maintain, in the midst of a wine-loving team, who maintained that it was his own poor health that kept him dry. Maurice and Henri were never quite tipsy, but always pushed the issue. After they had both disappeared briefly, you knew by the singular way that the one-eyed called out noisily to the one-legged: "Hey, Maurice, whaddaya think of that?" and the retort: "Whaddaya know, Henri, old man?"

The Office Supervisor was especially careful not to cross swords with Maurice, a former district chief who had been demoted, had known him "back when," and never failed to remind him: "Hey, you didn't used to be such a big deal back when you would come to the office in your little boots, right off your mama's knee, with your snack packed in a little basket." These touching memories of his youth humiliated Gaillard and he took flight, which no doubt was the desired effect.

Gaillard reigned supreme over all the office supplies. He kept them under lock and key, to validate his authority. I can still picture myself as a young beginner, going to him to timidly request a new pencil. He required that I show the old one, so that he could judge for himself its degree of wear, before generously furnishing me with a "stub-holder," a sort of metal-tipped sleeve where one inserted the pencil remainder, in order to use it up to its very core. The stub-holder was more expensive than a new pencil, but we were bound to the thrift code of the railroad workers. Gaillard's triumph reigned over a rookie who dared not protest.

When, finally, a pencil was so small as to be non-serviceable, even in its holder, we had to present it to him.

Since he never thought to then take it, we kept the same defunct stub and showed it each time we wanted a new pencil.

The son of a humble gate-person, Gaillard had passed his Certificate of Primary Studies brilliantly, and expanded his vocabulary with a dedicated reading program, consisting of the *Petit Larousse illustré*,[*] including the pink encyclopedic pages. Thus, he could use words that he considered rare, including an occasional inappropriate Latin phrase.

He built up his conversational repertoire by diligently reading the Vermot Almanac [similar to the *Farmer's Almanac* in the U. S.], and by recounting some of its stories, but never crediting the source. He loved acting important and heading up office events. I will always remember the first election of personnel delegates, which I attended as the youngest magistrate's assistant. He had handled it like a movie production, to assure that everything went smoothly. The voting office was to close for *le déjeuner* [lunch] between noon and 2 p.m. He had sealed the urn with a quantity of wax and large seals, and had even doubled the chain with a cord that was also sealed.

When service resumed, Gaillard had the perfect condition of all the seals verified for the union representatives. Alas, Jeannot then showed him how, with a simple nail, you could force the axis of the hinges and open the urn from the other side. The Office Supervisor, who had so proudly positioned his seals, was appalled. Finally, after going through the documents, the union representative allowed the vote to stand validated. They could be magnanimous and forgiving; they had received the usual number of votes.

When Gaillard got too bored in his office, where he surveyed us through a wide glass, he would come out and tell stories. We came to know them all, but he was so happy

---

[*] The classic, highly respected French dictionary (French to French definitions, not bilingual).

to retell them that he forgot to puff on the old, poorly rolled butt that dangled moistly from his lips, and it ended up extinguishing itself. He had a very animated story-telling style, and there were favorite themes. There were "medical" and "scientific" recitations. We made a game of eliciting the retelling of certain stories, for we knew the words that would launch them.

He also talked about his garden, casting himself as an expert. The day that he had boasted of his superb velvety red roses, one appeared that afternoon in Mémaine's vase. Alas! Instead of quietly enjoying this discrete gift from her boss, she was so flattered to have been chosen (from all the women there!), that she called out loudly into the corridor that she recognized it right away as one of the roses of which he had spoken. Gaillard knit his tufted eyebrows and took off, under pretext of a phone call, his face scarlet as a schoolboy's.

Everyone agreed that Mémaine was nice-looking. She always glanced around while getting up from her chair, and re-positioned her girdle while letting her well-proportioned buttocks slap down. She must have thought that it excited all the male office personnel. Who knows? Her face was nicely made up, and she scented herself with "Bandit" by Robert Pignet, a product fashionable at the time—but from her peasant background she had kept the loud intonations of her people, the natives of the *Département de la Manche*.*

As a new hire, at an age when most girls of that era thought only of marriage, she was installed in an office facing that of Loulou, a pretentious youngster who believed himself assured of a brilliant career in the SNCF. He was preparing for all the required advancement exams, but she had no problem troubling his virginal innocence, and they were soon married. They were provided lodging in a temporary barracks not far from Caen, along a secondary rail line.

---

* The territorial division near *La Manche*, or the English Channel.

During the war, when game was not hunted, it had become abundant on the embankments of the rail lines. One day, Loulou had the idea to do something out of the ordinary, and placed traps along the tracks. He rather considered these tracks as his property. A splendid full moon illuminated his first steps as a poacher. He had already placed about twenty traps when, hearing a noise, he saw two shadows in a thicket on his pathway.

Petrified, and believing that he had fallen on some game wardens, he hurried to the foot of the embankment and hurled his remaining fistful of snares as far out as he could. For a long time, the scene was frozen in the cool, clear moonlight of the January night. Around 1 a.m., Loulou was thinking that he couldn't stay there indefinitely, that his young wife would be worried and perhaps would even call the mounted police, which would have been a disaster. So, like a jack-in-the-box, he leaped onto the trail. The others did likewise.

When they met, he claimed that he was putting up the sides of a bridge that was under construction. The others assured him that they were keeping watch over a signal lamp, where kerosene had been stolen. Each pretended to believe the other's story, before going home, relieved just to be over a good fright.

Since Mémaine wanted a « *Pomme d'amour* » [Jerusalem cherry plant] on her desk, a kind colleague gave her a radish seed, which she potted and conscientiously watered for several weeks. She marveled at its curious growth pattern, and the others asked her daily how it was doing, before concluding: "Given that she is an expert in *Amour*, the plants must have taken gardening lessons from her."

Mémaine generally arrived about ten minutes late for work, and later took pains to tidy up her desk and ready herself well before closing time. This irritated Gégéne, the Assistant Office Supervisor, and she got sharper and sharper reprimands from him. A couple of days after the latest lecture, Gégéne approached her again to point out that she was not heeding him. She exploded: "I'm not the only one to be ready. Why do you always pick on me?" In a moment of madness, he lost his cool and laid the back of his hand across the pretty little face, where his signet ring left a nasty mark.

She ran into the hallway crying and yelling, "That wild man was going to kill me!" No doubt she exaggerated, but she had placed herself in the best position to be seen and consoled by everyone. Those who wanted to get on her good side, or who had their sights set on the assistant's job, advised her to get a medical opinion and file a complaint.

The "slapper" spent three sleepless nights. He had just bought his house, and risked being transferred as a disciplinary measure. Mémaine wasn't a bad sort, and the bosses wanted to avoid a scandal. The Chief Engineer's assistant calmed them both, and the guilty party gave his excuses. Mémaine modestly exploited the situation by arriving yet a bit later and leaving a bit earlier, knowing the office assistant would never say anything to her again.

Gégéne was a plodding little fellow. He had begun his career as a clerk in the small Breton station at Banalec, carrying out single-handedly all the chores: Loading the animals; maneuvering the cars onto the pointed metal device (*la pointe*) so that he could move them a short distance; issuing tickets; and--as soon as he had passed the required exams--taking responsibility for train security.

He told us that we didn't realize our good fortune in the Rail Service, whereas with the Operations Service, demands for written explanations rained in every day. "Why did the 4702 leave two minutes late on July 7?" The agent would receive a written reprimand or, worse, an official warning in his dossier, sometimes with a reduction in his bonus. All of which were just minor penalties. Often, they underwent inspections, their knowledge of protocol was verified, the cash-box was checked and required to be not one centime over or one centime under the asset amount. Woe to he who might have given change from his pocket! When the inspector was seen in the train, the previous station agent, in announcing the convoy, "This is Quimper 7:32 a.m., I'm sending you the 1709," might add, "Watch out, it's loaded!" Then his colleague understood that trouble was on its way.

Through him, we learned something of the rough life "on the job": The snow-laden switches that jammed up halfway through the trip, the poorly oiled funicular transmissions that froze up and sustained an open signal past the safety point. This last was one of the most serious security breaches.

Gégéne's wife, who had taken him as her second husband, was a skillful seamstress. She had remade her first husband's clothes to fit his small build. Learning this little secret, we couldn't help thinking that it was fortunate that she hadn't married them in the reverse order.

On days when he was in a good mood, he sang the French ditty: "She had a wooden leg, and so that it wouldn't be seen, she put a rubber cushion under it." This, of course, was easier to sing than the main aria of *La Tosca*. In response, Roulette would whistle the refrain of « *A Joinville le Pont* », which included Gégéne's name—a sort of Homage to the Office Assistant.

To liven up his weekends and bring in a little extra money, Roulette played saxophone in the Zénon Orchestra. In the office, his typing speed on his old "Japy" was surprising. I have never seen anyone type so fast. Once in a while, to humor me, he would hum the air from The Norwegian Dance of Lalo, setting off the rhythm with his ruler on the metal cover of his typewriter.

As the older workers left one by one on retirement, the office became more and more lively. At 10 a.m. and again at 4 p.m., Harel, Roulette and Jeannot would go to urinate in concert, conversing joyfully. The boss, seeing them go by, nicknamed them the synchronized bladders.

When one of the directors would call and ask for Madame Garne to come to his office, she would leap up from her chair and run across the office. Jeannot made up a fake speed limit sign, for 30 kilometers* per hour, and would brandish it under her nose, to avoid her causing traffic accidents.

Jeannot was less prudent when he "fought" with Roulette, under the most trivial pretexts. They would roll around on the floor under the tables, bumping into furniture. It ended the day that Roulette's brand new pants caught and ripped on a post of our "centrifugal" metal file.

One beautiful spring morning, Harel accepted Jeannot's dare to break an egg on Jeannot's head. His very long hair was dripping with mixed white and yellow, an authentic egg shampoo.

Jeannot was a card-carrying conjurer. In the fifties, he used to go with other railroad workers--would be strolling musicians--to perform with the Young Artists of the Railroad and liven up the evenings of the Norman peasants. In the office, for want of knives to swallow, he absorbed rulers and pencils. It was there that I finally discovered that particular magic secret. He also made scarves disappear, and carried out a thousand other fantasies.

His "Magic's Son" card allowed him to stock up in Paris specialty shops where only professionals could buy. One day, on his way to Paris by train for such a shopping trip, he prevailed upon the mechanic, a friend, to let him ride in the locomotive. It was an old 231, burning three tons of briquettes between Caen and Paris, pulling the convoy at 120 kilometers per hour, enshrouded in clouds of smoke.

Jeannot was delighted. His buddy had lent him goggles to protect his eyes from soot. It was wonderful to go at top speed through the Tunnel of la Motte, where the darkness was all the more opaque because the smoke of earlier trains lingered there.

In Evreux, the mechanic had suggested that he go back into the passenger section, to wash up. His face was all black around white circles left by the goggles. After an hour

---

* One kilometer is 5/8 of a mile.

of cleaning up, he arrived at the St. Lazare station in a barely presentable state.

During the day, he noticed several times that people looked at him strangely. Finally, one of the merchants of conjuring tricks, who knew him well, asked what had happened to him. He looked in a mirror, to see that sweat had pulled long rivulets of coal smut from his hair down onto his face.

Jeannot was outrageous in some personal eccentricities. At work, I saw him soaking his feet under the table, treating his corns; and when he woke up too late in the morning, he sometimes shaved in the office, using hot water from the radiator drain.

While we were training in Paris, he had bought a bottle of Chouchenn, and decided to spend the evening in a cabaret where you were expected to keep on buying drinks during the show. At the end of the first hour, he realized that his champagne glass was empty and that another would come at a steep price. Taking advantage of the dim lighting, he secretly refilled his glass with the Chouchenn, whose color, in the half-light, could pass for champagne. Having to repeat this several times, he found his way back to the hotel with difficulty and an empty bottle, and didn't awaken until noon the next day.

Taking on the role of healer, Jeannot had brought back from the St. Marcouf Islands a young gull with a broken wing. He fed it herrings or whitings, which the creature swallowed in one gulp. One day, he brought it to the office to demonstrate. We could see the gull's throat swell as the fish slipped down its gullet. Spying us all standing around staring, the bird became agitated and began to leave droppings everywhere as it jumped from one table to another, to avoid being captured. In the midst of general hilarity, Madame Garne followed it around, wiping up the traces.

Jeannot spent all his vacations in his villa at Quineville, and reported his adventures to colleagues at work. Since he knew that the postal worker was reading the postcards, he tried to amuse and interest her. Once, he had announced on a card that he was going to send something quite unusual. The next day, he showed up at the post office with an oblong-shaped package. It was a dried-out, dessicated beef tibia that he had found in a field. The postal worker made up all sorts of "informational" questions, to discover the contents of this strangely shaped parcel. Jeannot answered discretely, so as to be sure that she would open it in secret.

The following year, he had announced that he would send, by overnight delivery, a small surprise in a big envelope, and warned his colleagues to open it very carefully so as not to lose the contents. The next day, he himself brought the envelope to the post office, along with a letter explaining how to care for the flea that was included. Understand that he had not put a flea in the envelope; however, we found one when the envelope arrived. And everyone died laughing, thinking of the trouble that the postal worker had gone to, in order to include the insect that she believed she had lost, through her nosiness.

At that time, the ticket agents had no bank accounts, so they would receive their salary in an envelope. Each agent would verify the amount in the presence of the accountant, who answered to the strange nickname of "Four Paws." He had small bloodshot, runny eyes and, since he slobbered a little also, he always had a handkerchief in hand. His daughter had married a British soldier after the landings, and he had tried once to go to England to see her, but renounced it for good, because you could drink only in pubs, and only at certain times of the day. Those English had absolutely unbelievable customs!

For the monthly payroll, he and a pistol-carrying colleague would tote a large briefcase to withdraw funds from the Central Cash Office in the train station. This little walk was also the occasion to pass by the Buffet. Having gotten accustomed to the routine, they forgot the danger and the seriousness of their mission so completely that, one day, they came back to the office without the bag. It had been left on the moleskin booth of the bar. They went flying back, crazy. It was still there; no one had thought to steal that grimy old satchel, which, appearances aside, held the monthly salary of one hundred people.

At the accounting office where salaries were handled, we were served by Madame Caron, a tall thin woman. She had been marked for life by her early career as a clothing salesgirl at Delaunay's. She smiled so, and was so friendly that, at the end of the conversation, we always expected her to ask: "Can I wrap that for you?" Every day, she lunched on potato puffs; the gossips explained that she had to share them, one by one, with her pudgy husband, who ate the potato part while leaving her the puff part.

In Research Studies, there was Garne, a small, very clean old guy, if you make exception for his skin condition, which made his hands peel onto all the dossiers. He had such polite, refined ways that he would go out into the corridor when he had to pass some gas, or spray his throat to combat an asthma attack. He always had a pencil in hand, to make note of the smallest details, and to underline passages, while pronouncing: "Seen. Seen," in a very intent manner. This must have been some sort of memory device.

Despite Garne's culture, he had not gone past the rank of Assistant Head of Research Studies. One day when I announced that I was going to vacation in Florence, he engaged me in a conversation on Savonarole,[*] whom I had not yet heard of. In his eyes, I must have appeared to be a real ignoramus.

He was so cultivated and circumspect that, by trying to balance the pros and cons of a situation, he would become incapable of a decision. This did not please the higher-ups, so eventually they called a simple draftsman up from the ranks, and replaced Garne.

---

[*] Jérome Savonarole (Girolamo Savonarola in Italian), a Dominican brother born in Ferrara, Italy (1452-1498). An impassioned preacher, he tried to establish a Constitution in Florence that was half theocratic, half democratic. Excommunicated, he was burned at the stake for heresy.

Our Division boss, M. Ruge, had the officious habit of never announcing himself over the phone. He simply said, in his most serious, no-nonsense voice: "X...Come in here!" One day, some jokers called Loulou several times, imitating the booming voice: "Come in here!" The poor guy had already been fooled before, and had gone needlessly to the boss, at a loss for what to say. But this day, being indisposed, he had responded: "Tell Monsieur Ruge to go to h...!" Whoa! It was no joke, and the Arrondissement boss couldn't have been more directly informed of the feelings of his underling in that regard.

Monsieur Garne was immediately called in by the boss, who wanted to know if Loulou had lost his marbles. Garne, very embarrassed, was obliged, with all the circumlocutions of his flowery discourse, to confess the story of the bad jokes, and countered with: "He has absolutely nothing to do in your 'Studies Office'! It's time to put him to work!"

In reality, "Research Studies" was a sort of plant nursery, sprouting designers well known for their dilettantism; art conforms badly to production. This affair, added to others, did not improve the reputation of the office.

That April first, the joke was a rotten conger eel's head, complete with bones, balanced on the entrance door of the office. But before the chosen victim had arrived for his fake phone call, M. Gaillard, the terrible Head of Service, entered unexpectedly, and took the fish full-face.

I carried away the unforgettable memory of the retirement departure of M. Garne, an unexpected event that upset the established sequence of steps. How many of these retirements had I seen, always with the same ceremonies? The prospective retiree is there for the occasion, dressed in his Sunday best, emotional, often accompanied by his wife. The boss's speech retells his whole career in a nutshell, with all its transfers and promotions, expressing the gratitude of the administration "for his good and loyal services" and, following the sacred ritual, the boss then offers the chosen gift bought with donations solicited from the other workers.

To carry on with the predictable pattern, the recipient often has prepared on paper his little spiel of thanks, which he reads with feeling, and sometimes a tear in the eye--while everyone waits only for the moment when they can fall on the tables prepared for "knocking back the last shot" of friendship.

With Garne, all that was not to be. It was Cresse, then Arrondissement boss, who had to give the speech. Actually, he had begun working twenty years earlier, as a young Attaché agent on trial basis, after having left a Grande École. He had been with M. Garne, and had forgotten nothing of his first contact with the particulars of his service, so he began to paint a cruel but colorful picture of the Studies Department, where the agents used to exchange slides and hide them in the drawer at the least alert. For effect, he exaggerated the facts. It was very funny, and all the designers and draftsmen would have had a good laugh, if they had not felt that the boss was profiting in a cowardly way from this solemn occasion in order to give them a lesson, showing that he hadn't been fooled, and knew all about their "extra-curricular" activities.

M. Garne, sacrificed as a burnt offering, went up in smoke, his prepared speech no longer appropriate. Despite his gifts of improvisation, what could he say after that? As their immediate boss, he felt humiliated before his agents. With his wife there as well, he was at a loss for a reaction to this brutal shock. He just invited those who had the heart for it, to have some drinks with him.

I remember regretfully another retirement, where, at the conclusion of his thank you speech, the District Head had asked the boss to let the agents leave work a little early for the reception at the station eatery. The favor was granted. At the agreed-upon hour, we all left our desks promptly. To save time, the prospective retiree had already prepared a large horseshoe-shaped table with plates of cake and champagne poured into glasses. Only three showed up around the District Head. Trying their best, they still couldn't eat and drink it all, and separated with difficulty.

Like the others, I had thought that my absence would not be noticed. I had gone home, never thinking that I would be remorseful for the rest of my life.

Later, I attended yet another extraordinary retirement, that of Sincent, a Centralien, or graduate of the *École des Arts et Manufactures*. For reasons unknown, he had not been promoted to the level that he could legitimately expect from the Railways. Considering his post, the Regional Director had made a special trip from Rouen to deliver the departure speech. He recalled his career, and gave him an unusually large bouquet of flowers. Then he read the General Director's letter, which proclaimed him Honorary Engineer, and gave him the letter.

With an extraordinary sense of humor that we had never ascribed to him, the recipient opened the Pandora's box of his rancor, hidden for so many years. It was the wittiest and the funniest speech that I have ever heard. Everyone laughed to see the departing figure of the Regional Director, who, with this turn of events, left without waiting for the friendship toast, of which he, no doubt, no longer felt worthy.

For personal reasons, I had never wanted to leave Caen. Avoiding transfers is quite an accomplishment for a railroad worker. I had accepted several changes of office and even of job description, to end up in the restructuring framework of the SNCF of 1973, as an Inspector in a service of decentralized General Management in Caen, called the Office of Transport. Here I managed international exchanges of merchandise rail shipments from the EUROP park to all of France.

I was brought in to replace M. Hébert, a nice fellow retiring from the Electrical and Signals Service. Hébert had passed all his life at this post, and knew every thread of its details. On his desk, he kept an old, grimy desk blotter that was abnormally domed in the middle. It held all sorts of useless and outdated newspaper clippings. His most treasured clippings were from an old 1927 paper, because on that day there had been no piece of bad news. He could re-read them as often as he wished and rest assured that nothing unpleasant would turn up.

He loved playing the horses. For sure, this "hobby" had never ruined him financially, but the condition of his summer home in Meuvaines, held together with props since the Landings, hinted that he had never landed one of the big, famous prizes, such as the *Prix d'Amérique*.

Hébert had warned me: "Don't let yourself get messed up by listening to this one or that one. Here you have just one boss--the Head of Inspection." This person was from Marseille, and had kept that regional southern accent. Dealing with colleagues who gave him problems, he would swear, but without acrimony, and he always ended up working things out. When he wanted to tell me something, he always began with: "Hey! Well! Little..." I admired him and loved him like a father; he was simplicity itself. To some extent, he treated me like the son he had never had.

He had been an artilleryman during the last war, and had lost three fingers from his right hand. This obliged him to hold his cigarette between his thumb and little finger. He must have been even more inconvenienced by an abnormally frequent need to scratch himself across his pants. He managed with his two fingers, by twisting his arm discretely; no one seemed to notice.

Every morning, to begin the day, I went to the Command Post to make note of any abnormal occurrences attributable to our service during the past 24 hours. It was an imposing office, where two agents were recording live the movement of the trains, phoned in from the stations. They traced in ink all the operations of the trains, on the sheet prepared in advance, where an abscissa gave the time in minutes and sequenced the stations. At the background of the board all the possible operations of regular and special trains were pre-printed. The steeper the slope of the traced line, the faster the train was going. Horizontal dashes marked the places and the stop times. In case of accident, they had the authority to stop a convoy in a station and re-load it on a train with the right-of-way. On one-way tracks, they could, if necessary, change the crossing station foreseen on the diagram.

When a train was late, I had to immediately question the local person responsible, to inform the Arrondissement Head and my colleague Rimove from Paris, who then informed the Head of Service.

Rimove was a charming man, the expiatory victim of a cruel fate. As a young Centralian Attaché, he had begun his career as District Head in Conches, when the terrible catastrophe of Saint-Elier, between Conches and La Bonneville, took place on October 25, 1933. Although the actual causes were never clarified, they needed a guilty party, and it was he. They transferred him into offices where he could never derail a train. He stayed on, and only later came to understand that he should have left the SNCF. Phoning him every day, I used to think about the cruel humor of the destiny that made him spend his life investigating incidents that others could have provoked.

Along the tracks, we had aerial lines for security and telecommunications. Burying them in troughs was definitely a step forward in eliminating frost damage, although sometimes rats would chew through the cables. Generally, their punishment was death; we had only to find their execution site, in order to repair it.

Sometimes in the fall, tiny flies would swarm into the warm interior of the electric clock, in a mass so compressed that the flies interfered with the works, provoking strange faults in the reporting service.

Before the widespread use of the Automatic Block,[*] there was the Rodary System, which meant that an agent had to manipulate devices at the proper time, to confirm the train's passage. Otherwise, the following convoy would stop at a closed signal, instead of maintaining its speed. To avoid

---

[*] Electrical security system closing the signals automatically, if a railroad car is on the track in the zone protected by the signal.

the consequences of this negligence, they had to establish an electrical contact inside a sealed electro-mechanical device. One smart aleck discovered that, by sliding a bicycle spoke into the device at a certain point, you could establish contact and free up the track, to hide the mistake.

During the investigation of the accident, the inspectors found a bicycle spoke in the semaphore post, and asked why. The poor guy naïvely explained how he had used it, and illustrated with a demonstration, which he presented almost as a brilliant invention. I still have this spoke, which had been affixed to his dismissal dossier. In the SNCF, you don't fool around with security!

Later, to improve the security of the convoys on the line from Lison to Lamballe, they installed the Automatic Block. Since the Director was to come expressly to help when it was first put into service, the draftsman had prepared a great explanatory chart with diagrams, to allow Paupol, the one responsible for the signal system, to carry off a clear rendition of the system that would be understandable to a non-specialist.

Paupol was a short chap, pot-bellied like a tobacco jar, charming but very timid. Under the eyes of the big boss, he was nervous. The Arrondissement Head must have foreseen trouble, and had carefully studied the file himself. Coolly, he pulled Paupol off to the side, and took over the daunting task.

We experienced a problem with the Automatic Block between Caen and Cherbourg. The first railcar of the morning went by after a long period without traffic, and condensation from the night before had caused a thin layer of rust to build up on the rail, which the short convoy couldn't always rub off. The conductor, seeing the signal out rather than lit, as it should have been for his approach, would put on the brakes. This improved adherence onto the rails, correcting the situation. Since we couldn't modify the timing regulation in this zone, which would have become too sensitive, we finally let a merchandise train pass before the Rennes railcar.

My duties were multiple, and quite diverse, so I was assigned to handle instruction for the invention of Clolus, a worker in mechanical signals, who earned a bonus for somehow reinventing the tackle block. In order to lower the heavy weight of the large oscillating ribbands, or side-pieces, that workers had to contend with, he had thought of multiplying their efforts with a system of pulleys. He was authorized to install an experimental system. He had attached to his dossier an extensive collection of photos to demonstrate the facility of the maneuvers by "the Father of Madame the Gate-person." We saw a little old moustached gentleman smilingly manipulating the pulleys, then "the lovely daughter of Madame the Gate-person," who opened the route by lifting a load three times her weight.

Our Service was a breeding ground for inventors, so we had Inspector Bajoc trying to perfect an electronic detection pedal for traffic passages. Along the tracks, there did exist electro-mechanical pedals, intended for announcing the trains. They were equipped with a little steel arm very close to the rail, which, upon passage, sunk into the fender of each wheel. These repeated blows meant that there were frequent replacements, a real gold mine for the pedal merchants, who were protected by patents.

In the early 1960's, Bajoc proposed replacing this fragile material with a solid steel plate that would be grazed by the wheels, sufficient to allow a high frequency, weak current to be amplified as with radio receivers. Unfortunately, it arrived too early for the necessary electronic material to be on the market. He had also created a battery-powered system of amplification, with lamps and a re-chargeable battery—unsuitable to the severe conditions of the terrain.

The perfection of this invention brightened the final years of his life. It was to have an enormous market, for tens of thousands of electro-mechanical pedals were out there. A contact in Installations put him in touch with a pedal manufacturer. While the SNCF was offering him a laughable bonus and the right to use his patent only in the subway system or abroad, our traditional supplier of electro-mechanical pedals received him like an Oil Magnate, at the George V, a restaurant of quality and elegance unknown to our Bajoc. He was offered a large sum for his invention.

Bajoc was delighted, and ready to conclude the transaction, which seemed to assure his glory, when he discovered that the manufacturer's goal was to nip his idea in the bud, so that it would never come to light, and he would then be able to continue indefinitely selling his own. Our simple, honest inventor was scandalized by these bad intentions. He refused, choosing fame over money. He had neither.

Today, when I notice one of the many electronic pedals on the tracks, "born" thanks to transistors, I think of him, the father of them all. While in the neighborhood merchant shops, his widow still tells the story of her husband, a brilliant engineer and famous inventor at the SNCF.

The typists were grouped together in one room, under the surveillance of Mère Barbelette, who launched them onto the urgent tasks and was to keep them from chatting—mission impossible, since she herself had a particular gift for gab. When I had to bring over something to be typed, I took a pleasant moment or two to catch up with their chatter. In this pre-television era, we had to listen to Lulu tell all about the movie she had seen at the theater the night before--all the funnier when it was a well-known classic which her account transformed beyond recognition.

When Lulu's second husband had bought a car, she explained how he had cleverly made a funnel to top off the motor oil level through the gauge hole, this accessory not having been furnished at the time of sale.

Young, inexperienced driver as he was, he did not dare cross the street with his car, so he convinced Lulu that his car could not be turned to the left. He had driven from the Renault garage to his home by a complicated itinerary, which avoided secant movements towards the left.

It was at the office of the S.E.S. (Electric and Signal Service) that I met Nénésse. Without really understanding his plight, he arrived one beautiful morning, like an angel fallen from grace. Before that day, he had been responsible for administration at Cherbourg, but he had become so deaf that he no longer could even hear the trains passing by. And so, the Arrondissement Chief had dismissed him from that administrative service—the worst humiliation for a field agent.

They had required him to use a Sonotone, which, at the time, came with a box the size of a flashlight. In the office, he had become the punching bag of the Great Riton. When the Great One starting regaling him with unpleasant curse words, Nénésse would make a show of cutting the current to his apparatus, shouting: "I won't use up my batteries to listen to your b...sh... Sometimes it's a blessing to be deaf!" Five minutes later, Riton would noisily slap the desk with the flat side of his ruler, hollering: "Plug yourself in, Nénésse, I have to talk to you!"

When his co-workers were making rounds and there was some quiet time, Nénésse, a born storyteller, enjoyed telling me tales of the Cotentin, where he had had responsibility for the signal system of the lines of northern la Manche.

There was the story of the Maritime Station of Cherbourg. Even during the cold nights of winter, there were carloads of goods to be moved. As long as the loading agent was swinging his lantern, the mechanic had to reverse the train, and he had to stop as soon as the lamp was raised and immobilized.

That night, what had happened? The man on the platform, had he mechanically continued to swing his arm? Had the mechanic forgotten to watch the lantern? A huge splash, and a car had fallen into the river basin, where it disappeared completely. After forceful mutual reproaches, they decided: "We just won't say anything!"

But then, fearing that the hull of a ship would be demolished at dawn, they warned the stationmaster. He sent the rescue crane with a deep-sea diver, to put the car in a sling and reposition it properly on the tracks. Having barely reached the bottom, the diver had himself brought up, and opened his helmet to ask: "Which one do you want brought up? There are three." So, it wasn't the first time in Cherbourg that unscrupulous workers had drowned railcars!

Cotentin North is an end point of the world, surrounded by sea on three sides, so that exchange with fellow humans is relatively rare, and traditions are more likely to be conserved. So the wooden barriers that enclose their fields have kept a particular form. The vertical post on the hinge side extends quite a bit above the pivoting framework, and from its summit hangs a long scarf, intended to hold the opposite side of the gate, to avoid the bottom rubbing the soil.

Nénésse corroborated the local traditions as well established, by supplying a wealth of personal stories.

When, at the beginning of their marriage, he learned of the death of Alphonse, he was not unduly affected; this was an uncle on his wife's side, whom he had seen just once, among the one hundred fifty guests at their wedding. But his wife had just given birth, so he himself had to attend the funeral to represent the family and fulfill the customary obligations.

The gathering took place in a little village with a name ending in –*ville*, like so many others in Normandy. Fortunately, it was accessible by train. Leaving the station, he noticed the funeral procession crossing the square, so he all but ran to catch up and reach the church.

They had seen him arrive from the station, and a woman heavily veiled in black invited him to the post-funeral meal. This, according to custom, was expected. The tomb was blessed, the men retreated to the café and assembled around the big table that the women had prepared. While eating, they spoke, always in the *patois* [dialect] of their region, of everything and of nothing: Of the seasons that "are not as they used to be, because they've disrupted the weather with their TSF,"* of "the dryness of the meadows," etc. Then they spoke of the deceased, whom they criticized only in veiled terms: « *Ch'eutait teu'de mé' un tschacré lapin...* » ["All the same, he was quite a guy with the ladies."]

At the end of the meal, after a lot of wine, these people don't sing, said Nénesse, they show their social grace and manners by telling good stories. Those who had drunk the most laughed the loudest, to give the impression that they had understood. Nénésse had kept his sobriety, for he was watching for the train arrival time. On the stroke of 4 p.m., he left the group, shook hands with the men and again embraced the ladies, who all said: "We'll have to get together again, we'll have to see each other soon!"

He got back home pretty late, but his wife had waited up, to hear all about the funeral and the gathering afterwards.

--They invited you to the meal? Was it good? There must have been a lot of people. Wasn't he deputy mayor of his commune? Did they have a good speech?"

--Hey, no. Maybe they didn't want that.

And his wife, persevering, asked:

--Did you see Uncle Crouillebois? He and Uncle Alphonse wouldn't have anything to do with each other after their father died.

--Oh, you know, there were a lot of people there. I don't remember his face.

--Oh, but you know, he's the one who gave us that awful cracked vase that broke right away. And his wife, Aunt Adelaide, the big redhead who wore a green dress at our wedding, and it was so low in front that the staff-bearer in the procession blushed, and couldn't take his eyes off her. And at dessert, she even sang some pretty off-color songs.

"As for the Uncle, I couldn't swear to it," said Nénésse, "but the Aunt, she wasn't there, I would have

---

* [*Télégraphie sans fils* = wireless radio]

recognized her, even in black, with her bust like a wet nurse at a flower show."

"They weren't there!" she exclaimed. "You can say you won't have anything to do with each other, but you still go to the funerals... Who did you see of the people that were at our wedding?"

This gave Nénésse much pause. He thought again, put it down to the crowd there, and the emotion...but suddenly grabbed the announcement. He had indeed been in a town whose name ended in –*ville*, but not the right town.

Later, he was invited back:

--*Faudra qu'on s'r'vé !   Faudra qu'on s'r'vé !* ["We'll have to get together again!"]

In the Normandy countryside, maybe because there is still some illiteracy, they continue to use "Announcers" for burials. Any other method of giving a death notice is not considered proper. In each family--in the tribal sense of the word--it was usually established that one among them, always the same person, would go to learn the funeral information, and would be the Announcer.

Among the relatives of Nénésse, it was cousin Ugène who was traditionally charged with this mission. Being a small farmer, he was somewhat out of his field [!] in this role, but it was true that, fatigue aside, certain rewards were part of this task. Being asked to "announce" is not a service that can be refused. Taking the time to drink a cup of coffee, learning the name of the deceased, the place and the time of the burial, and obtaining the list of people to notify—these were his duties.

Ugène organized two or three bicycle routes, comprising about thirty kilometers, to inform everybody. Recurrent as this scenario became, when people saw him coming, they knew the kind of news he was bearing. The formulaic greeting, in *patois*, was always the same:

--*Euh ga's comm'nt tieu va?   E'co' eune m'vais' no'vel'.   C'é qui qu'é mo't ?* [Hey guy, how are ya? Another piece of bad news. Who died?]

--It's cousin Casimir. The Mass will be in Siouville at 10 a.m. *à l'ancienne.*[*]
--You can't just go back like that. Come in and have a coffee.

And they exchanged news of all the family, keeping the ties strong, for they saw each other only on major occasions. Ugène drank his *jambinette* (half coffee, half Calvados). If it was wintertime, he had to warm up; if it was summer, he had to dust off and, everyone knows, emotions parch your throat. Then he would leave on his old bike, towards new funereal libations.

That particular evening, he had arrived at Nénésse's rather late, and the day had been rough. His legs felt shaky and the road was long, while the bike tended to drift constantly from one side to another.

--I bet that you're coming to announce another piece of bad news. (Nénésse expresses himself in standard French, while Ugène continues in *patois.*)

--You bet, he's dead, it had to happen to him, the same as to all of us.

--But, Ugène, who has died?

--You know better than I do!

Ugène collapsed into a chair, but not from grief. He was no longer held upright without his bicycle. In spite of everything, he was waiting for his "Calva coffee," while repeating like a litany: "You know better than I do!"

Along with his fatigue, the absorption of a little more alcohol didn't help, and he couldn't unleash the least memorized scrap of information. He just kept repeating: "You know better than I do!"

Nénésse then tried another method to learn who had died; he reviewed all the relatives of an age likely to "pass on." But Ugène shook his head "no" at each new name suggested. Oh! Without contrariness, you could see clearly

---

[*] [old style], meaning solar time, which was dropped after the advent of the radio and TV, but still used here—the author says, "so as not to confuse the cows." They needed to be specific, to avoid confusion.

that he himself was sorry that he was powerless to express more on the subject. He consoled himself by repeating tirelessly: "You know better than I do!"

Which was only all the more irksome.

Then Nénésse tried to localize the ceremony: When and where would it take place? But he really couldn't "announce" anything more; they knew the news much better than he.

Nénésse's next idea was to suggest that Ugène spend the night, hoping that things would come back to him with the light of day. But he couldn't be detained any longer. Ugène made his way towards his bike, saying: "Thanks so much, Nénésse, I'd really like to stay, but it's impossible, I still have too many people to see, to make the announcement."

Not all of my co-workers were as funny as those I just wrote about in this chapter. And not all had stories as colorful as those of Nénésse, who knew how to tell them so well.

For my own retirement, in addition to the traditional reception on the premises of the SNCF, I had invited about a hundred friends, from the Service as well as from the neighborhood, for a dinner-show in the parish hall. It was an excellent occasion to celebrate the 75th birthday of the curé, the Reverend Father Lesieur, at the same time as my retirement.

We had begun with a huge quantity of sangria flavored with rum from the Antilles. This had immediately set the ambiance, and I had enough talented friends to offer a quality show. Jeannot received double billing: As Magic's Son, he carried out several magic acts, including the famous sawing in half of a woman locked in a crate. As filmmaker, he showed several old films of neighborhood festivals, then those he had made at work at different times throughout his career.

Mémaine, who wasn't used to drinking, had let the sangria get to her. Seeing the old film, she hollered louder than usual: "Hey, Bajoc, well, he's dead! And the little bald guy whose name I don't remember any more, well, he's dead, too! And that one wearing the trousers with creases, he's dead, too," and the funeral parade continued. She spotted them immediately among all the others, bringing them to mind in an instant.

It was very comforting to find myself still living, after the mention of all those employees of the SNCF who had died on the job. At least, I had held up, and I would be able to savor some of that time, that much-talked-about retirement, while all those poor guys had paid into it for so many years of their lives, riding on the merry-go-round without catching the brass ring.

CHAPTER XV

MY OWN UNITED STATES
OF AMERICA

In "Madeleine," that famous song by Jacques Brel, Madeleine's trembling lover, ever-patient but waiting in vain, sings, "She's America to me."

When I was young, my concept of America was like that-- out of reach, attainable only in my dreams. Only much later did I discover "my own United States of America"—not found in any guidebook, written only in my memory and in my heart.

Armand Idrac

Before the war, our parents had driven us one day to Le Havre to see the *Normandie* that extraordinary ocean liner that could cross the Atlantic in five or six days. I can see myself, very small, at the end of the dock, looking up and down the wall of window-pierced steel plates. That wall was as insurmountable for me as the ocean that the great ship crossed so easily. On that particular day, it was not open to visitors, which further heightened the mystery.

In those days, we encountered very few Americans, and they were striking in their different modes of dress: The Texans kept their ten-gallon hats on their heads, the women of a certain age continued to dress in vivid colors. We admired their outward signs of wealth and assumed that, since they could make such a trip, they were rich, and represented all Americans.

Only at the time of the Liberation did we really encounter Americans—soldiers who ate white bread, chewed gum, gave out chocolate and smoked Gauloise Blondes cigarettes. They restored our broken-up roads with powerful, unfamiliar machines that we could only call by their own names for them, such as *bulldozer* and *cater-pillar*. With those wonderful Belley engineering bridges and their elements assembled like pieces of a giant robot, they replaced the destroyed works of art.

Hitchhiking had become a normal means of getting from one place to another. The soldiers willingly took us aboard jeeps, trucks, and even enormous amphibian vehicles, for the price of the perilous climb aboard. So, we saw the thighs of the young and pretty girls—for no one else took on the challenge.

Since it snowed a lot the following winter, I enjoyed a snowball fight with some black American soldiers. In my young ignorance, it surprised me that they didn't mind the cold. It didn't occur to me that these men had, no doubt, never experienced Africa.

I will never forget my first visit to the American Military Cemetery at St.-Laurent-sur-Mer. Planners were still laying it out. From the mound of earth destined for the main monument, I saw thousands of wooden crosses aligned and extending endlessly to the sea. There, wreckage still emerged from the ships that would never take them back to their country.

Thereafter, I've returned regularly to this place of remembrance, but never have I been as deeply moved before so many graves.   In this now very beautiful setting overlooking the sea, the landscape has ceded its cruelty, for, despite the wind-borne sea spray, the Cemetery's French grounds keepers have cultivated trees that stay green all year. The trees create an optical limit to the immense field of resting places.   The poor wooden crosses have all been replaced with crosses or stars of David fashioned in Carrara marble—a beautiful white veined with green.   They are aligned perfectly in every direction.[*]

Around the superb center monument, symbol of resurrection raised to the glory of the fallen soldiers, the names of those not found are engraved on the wall. On the tombs of unidentified remains one reads the simple, laconic

---

[*] Approximately nine thousand American soldiers are buried in the American Military Cemetery above Omaha Beach.

inscription "UNKNOWN," throughout entire square regions. On other tombs, the engraved name is inscribed, with two dates, the grade, the regiment and the State of origin. Only Franklin D. Roosevelt's son is modestly set apart, with a gilded inscription.

At the other extremity of the terrain stands a round temple of elegant simplicity, open to all beliefs. Although there are many visitors, it is a place of silence and meditation.

The flagpole bearing the starred banner is reflected in the water lily pond. Morning and evening, the colors are raised and lowered to the strains of the national hymn, played by an invisible, ghostlike orchestra, the sound of which floods the site. It is then that the American visitors are set apart: They stand still, right hand placed over the heart for the duration of "The Star-Spangled Banner."

Very moved, I think of all the young men come from so far for an ideal of liberty--dying on our land, a place unknown to them. There are those who came from Pennsylvania, Iowa, Idaho, New Mexico, Texas, Colorado, Florida, and other states. Reading the names, images of states that I have come to know parade through my head-- from the sumptuous, calm forests of Maine, to the majestic Rockies, to the splendid settings of the Far West. How could they leave the wonder of all that?

Quelle connerie la guerre!! [What damned stupidity war is!!]

Some years after the War, I learned of The Experiment in International Living. This is an American association created by veterans, to foster friendships among young people of all countries, in the belief that a better knowledge of others will help prevent wars. During the years that we received these American students *en demi-pension* [lodging and two meals per day] in our home, they followed courses for two months at the University of Caen, and on weekends we took them on outings in the region.

In this friendly family ambiance, they considered us as their adoptive French parents, giving rise to wonderful conversations with our children, who saw very soon the usefulness of knowing foreign languages.

I can't possibly write of the score or so of guests that we hosted, cared for, loved. Alas, very few have continued to keep in touch! But realistically, we would have had trouble following a correspondence with each of them. Some have come back with their parents, their spouse, their pupils. We have even been able to respond to some invitations to visit, when we traveled to the U.S.A.

It's a pleasure to recall for you those guests who left the most vivid memories.

Chris was our first student, and he stayed for the entire school year. His group had been poorly prepared. They arrived at Le Havre by boat, then took a bus for Caen. At each village on the way, they wondered anxiously, "Is this Caen?" To prepare for their trip, some had asked advice of veterans of the Landing, who gave them out-of-date information. One young girl arrived with 50 pairs of nylon stockings, others had brought a six-month supply of boxes of chocolate breakfast mix.

Chris was a very well brought up boy, pleasant to live with and meticulous in his grooming, but more interested in grooming than in his studies. We loved him very much, and he was very kind to our four children, who were still small at the time.

He was full of wonder the day he discovered that we had an electric knife, because he had not yet seen one where he came from.

He was there for the momentous events in Paris in 1968, when the news media reported that brutal police repression of student demonstrations had led to strikes. Within days, ten million workers were on strike, many occupying their factories. The political implications were enormous.

All this left Chris completely indifferent; he became worried only when he received no more letters from his girlfriend, and no money order from his parents. He wanted me to predict what was going to happen. I told him that I knew nothing about how it would turn out, since it had never happened before. My remarks did nothing to reassure him. In spite of a very modest level of language skill, Chris succeeded in becoming a French teacher. He returned several years later, on a trip to Paris with three of his pupils, to whom he wished to introduce his French family. Exhibition aspects aside, it proved that he really liked us too, and thought us worthy of being "shown."

Another time, the large bedroom was occupied by two friends, Lana and Dona. Dona had a very white complexion, while Lana was more *café* than *lait*. Lana's father was mayor of a large American city. The girls were very gifted, and together they had quite a profitable stay.

Allison, another student, had strange eyes, with violet-colored irises such as I had never seen. She simply wore colored contact lenses, as yet unknown in France. As a joke, my children would call her « *Ali sonne à la porte* » ["Alli rings the doorbell"], which she disliked intensely.

To fill in for a host family that went on vacation, we had the pleasure of receiving Joanne. She was an extraordinary student such as we had never seen. Already a teacher, she was older than those whom we normally hosted. She did not hesitate to ask us: "You used such and such a word; please, how is it written? What is the exact meaning?" And she wrote in a little notebook, which never left her.

The following year, we had the joy of opening our door to the parents of Joanne, my translator/editor. Now retired, her father had landed at Omaha Beach as a Navy medic on D-Day. We took them to see the city; then, with my aunt, we drove the thirty kilometers to Falaise to the castle where William the Conqueror was born. While I went into the keep with *monsieur*, we left the two women resting, seated on a bench. How stupefied I was to notice upon our return that they were happily conversing, each in her own language, each acting as though the other understood! True, under those conditions, it would have been impossible not to be of the same opinion; but all that mattered to them was the discovery that they liked each other.

We also hosted Mary, a tall, very supple girl who studied dance, like our daughter Agnes, which gave them something in common. She had close-set eyes, giving her an unusual appearance. We speculated as to her heritage. Indian, perhaps?

Mary-Lou was a beautiful blonde, with thick hair, always very happy, with a cascading laugh that sounded like a bag of walnuts rolling down a staircase. She worried us quite a bit one day when she felt ill to the point of asking for our doctor. She believed that she was having a return bout of mononucleosis from the previous year. When our doctor informed her that it was a self-immunizing disease, impossible to contract a second time, she got up immediately—cured! How important the psyche is when you're sick!

Now that she's an airline attendant, we can imagine her announcing any emergency to her passengers with bursts of laughter in her voice. From her we learned that a seat-belt extension is provided for plus-sized travelers, and that they have to pay for two tickets, or go first class. She did not like taking care of the luxury passengers, because their hands wandered more, and she was obliged to find a delicate way to break away.

We also received Anou, an Indian princess who was studying in New York, and had been able to join the Experiment group and come to France. Once she had wanted to treat us to her country's cuisine, and ordered spices from India especially for the meal. We had left her the kitchen for the preparations; when we went back into her "laboratory," we were all overtaken with multiple sneezes. We had invited Indian friends from Caen to this dinner, and all the women were wrapped in magnificent saris.

Anou confided that she was uprooted by choice, but proud of her heritage. She did not wish to melt into American civilization, but neither did she want to return to

India and fall back into antiquated family traditions.   Her family had already chosen a husband for her.

Ritchie was a fine little woman whose parents lived in New York.   She had been admitted to the University of Cornell.   She was a very intelligent girl, with a fantastic memory.   She knew everything on all sorts of subjects—a real *Pic de la Mirandole** in a skirt.   But not unaware of it…

Later, we had the pleasure of seeing another student several times.   This was Nancy, who would bring her students to France every other year during spring vacation. We always spent a day together, whether she came to Caen or we met in Paris.

Long ago, when I began to work at the SNCF, my office was next to rail lines from Paris to Cherbourg, so I could see the trains going by.   At that time, the "Queens"[+] stopped over regularly at Cherbourg, between sailings from Southampton, England to New York.   Normally, there were three trains for each transatlantic crossing.   This gave me something to daydream about.   I wanted to go to the U.S., but the trip by sea was costly and too slow for me; my vacation time was too short for a round trip of ten days or so by ship.   And there was the risk of getting seasick.   What means did that leave for the trip?

Then, it all became possible with the advent of the 747s and charter flights.

Yes, America was far, and it was big.   For a long time, I tried to devise a trip as complete as possible, to discover this country that we dreamed about.   The solution was simple: Several trips had to be planned.   And that is what we did.

The first time, we took the train to get a Lakker's charter flight in London.   You couldn't reserve, and you had

---

* Giovanni Pico della Mirandola, 15th century Italian humanist, distinguished for his precocity and wide range of knowledge.   He became the symbol of erudition.

[+] The British cruise ships the Queen Mary and the Queen Elizabeth.

to line up to pay right before leaving--but the one-way ticket was only 450 francs, or about $90.

On that first trip, we arrived in Boston. Mary met us there, for an overnight stay at the townhouse of some friends, who had left her the key. What a pleasure, how happy we were to see Mary again, after so many years!

The first contact with the old city disappointed me a little—in America, I had not expected to see red brick buildings with English style sash windows. But then she soon took us to a wonderful museum, where we found a little of everything.

The models of Niagara Falls and Colorado's Grand Canyon were so faithful to reality that our sense of surprise was somewhat diminished later, the day that we discovered them on our own.

In one glass case, there was a normal lung next to that of a smoker, designed to disgust people and discourage them from smoking. Our poor friend began to weep, because her mother had, in fact, died of lung cancer due to smoking.

Further on, on a slice of an enormous sequoia tree trunk, the growth rings were marked to show the dates of the birth of Christ, the discovery of America, and several other important historic events. Elsewhere, a live porcupine was being presented. What a strange creature!

But above all, what surprised us the most was finding such a diversity of subjects in the same museum.

Mary took pity on us with our limited English; she ordered our tickets for Denver, and reserved a car and hotel, because we would be arriving at nightfall.

The weather was very beautiful in Denver, and from our small plane window we could see vast expanses that seemed desert-like, but embellished with large green circles or beautiful verdant rectangles. These were cultivated areas, appearing that way because of their mode of irrigation.

At the airport, the car rental agent suggested driving immediately to our hotel, and pointed out the location on the rental car map. Oh, my! After several kilometers, we did find the avenue, but it seemed like an abandoned suburban area, with dirty townhouses in poor condition—unlikely to be near the three star hotel where we had reserved. It was already dark, and people were afraid to open their doors to us. Finally, we found a brave woman with a large dog, who responded and went so far as to take out her car and drive us there. We were particularly touched by so much kindness. What would we have done without her? The large avenue where we had found ourselves was under construction, and the different sections were still disconnected. The hotel was indeed very close to the airport, but from our location, a long detour was necessary. Without her efforts, we would never have been able to find the hotel. Americans are really very nice, and take pity on wayward strangers in their country.

The next day, we proceeded westward. There were wooden huts everywhere, grouped into villages. We found a place—I dare not say a restaurant—to have an American breakfast, with eggs, pork sausages and "home fries." All in a setting of doubtful cleanliness, suited to gold-seekers who still hadn't found any gold.

It was the complete scenario for films of the Far West. Sometimes we crossed paths with men on horseback, who, like all cowboys worthy of the name, hung the requisite lasso on the saddle. Of course, we met up with Indians as well, recognizable by their bronzed faces. Since they spoke English and were not aggressive, our images of feathered warriors were put aside—but thoughtfully.

In the course of our travels, we saw Indians in their villages, seemingly still carrying on the old traditions. On the other hand, some were perfectly assimilated into contemporary civilization, ready to exploit the tourists with no bias as to their origin. But this didn't prevent us from venturing into their camps, where they had all the necessary commerce and businesses, from service stations to Superette grocery stores—even motels, which would one day render us a memorable service. Here is the story:

So that we had more freedom to move around, we never reserved a hotel; instead, we were careful to arrive before 5 P.M., to look for a place. We noticed that, on the main routes, especially where they intersected, there usually were motels.

On this trip, we had been rolling along for some time in the Florida Everglades; it was dusk, and we hadn't found lodging. Then, in the middle of the Seminole Indian reserve, by the side of the road, appeared an enticing, brand new little motel. It was too late to dine in their restaurant, but nearby was a grocery store with everything we needed. There, the boss, like the customers, was Indian.

The next morning, we went to see their tent-covered, enclosed camp, where they were in costume and selling crafts to visitors. They had big American cars like everyone, but discretely hid them outside the commercial zone, so as not to ruin the exotic appearance of the market. They suggested sky tours of the swampland, but our innkeeper had already offered a discount special for his lodgers.

Because the swamp was very shallow in places, they used flat-bottomed boats equipped at the rear with a powerful motor. It pushed using an airplane propeller protected in a cage, to avoid hurling the tourists out into the greenery with the alligators.

That day, we had an unforgettable tour of the full swampland, among tall grasses and the panicked flights of egrets and anhingas, frightened by the terrible noise of the motor. We finally arrived at a group of straw and cob huts, elevated on the terrain. We were in an authentic Seminole village where they used to raise poultry and small alligators in separate areas. They enjoyed handling the alligators, for our pleasure. Only much later did we taste this animal, at the entrance to Shark Valley, amidst the Miccosukee Indians, on the way from Miami to Naples.

They offered menus with fried frogs' legs and alligator steak. Actually, we didn't find the flavor unusual; it seemed to depend on the preparation. Then they gave us an excellent address about twenty miles from Miami. By exchanging land parcels in the reserves, they had managed to build an enormous casino with 300 rooms, the "Ramada Limited Miccosukee Resort." The exterior was reminiscent of an enormous, garish green and pink cake. The parking lot was so large that transportation was provided to the front desk. Inside, the luxury was extraordinary, so we stayed for a week. Every evening, we could eat all we wanted for $10, or have the chef's choice for $7. This was served in a subdued setting, with a small candle on each table. For this price, they offered a very large plate with steak, vegetables and a small rock lobster. We had made friends with the headwaiter, and he confided that the personnel were forbidden to gamble, and the restaurant operated at a loss solely to keep the players, who let themselves be fleeced by the slot machines and other attractions designed to win their money. One evening, we paid a "thank you" visit to all those poor guys who were allowing us to dine so well for so little. So passionate were they for these "one-armed bandits" that they seemed not to notice as we passed close by. On the whole, they didn't look like big winners.

In these immense, artificially lit rooms, daylight did not penetrate, and there were no clocks. Time stood still, all was flooded with mind-boggling, loud music, just allowing you to hear the noisy spill of coins into the metallic jackpot slot.

Since there was an army of six elevators serving the rooms, we would bet between ourselves on which one would arrive first. Every morning, we found the local newspaper on the thick carpet in front of our ninth floor room. Even on Sunday, when it weighed a kilo and cost $1.00, it was free.

The magnetic key to our room also accessed the special direct elevator down to the heated and attended swimming pool, to the sauna, and to the sports area. These special pleasures were for hotel guests only.

In the bathroom, the bottles of toiletry were renewed regularly. Complimentary herbal teabags were set out. Only the mini-bar carried a fee. Two queen beds, cable TV, VCR with videocassettes and games added to our pleasures.

Plenty of towels, plus bathrobes and slippers were provided, not to be spirited away in the luggage, but available for sale.[*]

An all-you-care-to-eat breakfast buffet came with the room. We had never seen such a vast buffet: meats, cold cuts, eggs, all sorts of bread and cakes, and fresh or canned fruits from all four seasons. There was even a soft ice cream machine with many flavors, to make cones in what Europeans call "Italian style."

The floor was thickly carpeted in vivid motifs, the walls decorated with frescoes of the modest lives of the Indians' ancestors. In those times, they had lived in huts made of branches and had found nourishment in frogs and alligators.

From the resort, we took a beautiful excursion into Shark Valley, on a pretty little train with cars on pneumatic tires. There were speakers in the cars, to more easily point out the fauna scattered in this extraordinary marsh of the Everglades. This zone was relatively dry when we visited in winter, when the swamp is fed by brackish seawater. In summer the abundant rainstorms irrigate it with fresh water. This implies a very adaptable blend of vegetation. The outing ended in an observatory overlooking the zone. At our feet, scores of alligators warmed themselves peacefully in the sun, among egrets, pink flamingos and anhingas—all seemingly unafraid of the alligators.

The roads are marked with special warning signs where alligators and brown bears cross—and this is no joke. We saw some, and were told that, in Florida alone, about sixty plantigrades[+] are killed on the roads every year. So, even in clear weather, they recommend driving with the headlights on.

---

[*] Editor's note: Armand gives details, because such personal luxuries are not common in hotels in France. Most European hotels focus outward, on the history and culture of the region, rather on hotel amenities.

[+] Animals that walk on the sole of the foot, with the heel touching the ground, as opposed to digitigrades, those that place the toes on the ground and walk with the back of the foot more or less raised.

Another day, we took a motorboat side trip into the "10,000 islands" near Naples. There, you need to avoid hurting manatees with the propellers, because these large sea cows have no fear of man. Like land cows, manatees eat only vegetation. At the back of the boat, seagulls in flight caught pieces of bread thrown by tourists. On the highest branches of the mangrove-covered islets, nesting American eagles lifted their white heads to watch us pass by.

The funniest outing was the trip to Flamingo. The captain had suggested a boat to view regional fish and birds. After a half-hour, we were already pretty far from the coast, and still hadn't seen anything other than a couple of kinds of seagulls. He passed around plastic laminated cardboards with pictures of the promised animals, their names and characteristics. No one complained. Hadn't he kept his word? No claim had been made that we would see live creatures.

I must admit that in America, the customer generally receives more than what has been promised. So, when we followed the gold miners' route in California, we also visited, not far from Sacramento, a restored ghost town abandoned by pioneers of the last century. All the homes and businesses were inhabited by characters dressed in 1850's style. The grocery was decorated with timely ads and boxes of merchandise of yesteryear. The door of the barbershop was ajar, open for business. At the far end of the village, a boy was panning for gold, sifting the muddy water of a stream, and trying to rent pans to others with a spirit for gold-seeking. To draw passersby, he showed three stoppered bottles with little specks of gold soaking in water. These he claimed to have just found. When I walked by again, two hours later, he was showing the same bottles and the same three specks of gold.

We were able to extend our visit with a stagecoach trip, using ticket facsimiles of that time period. Yet another "extra" awaited us on this ride in the countryside: At a turn of the road hidden by a tree bough, the stagecoach was attacked by masked bandits on horseback who, menacing with their pistols, appropriated jewelry, watches and wallets—which, naturally, were given back further along on the route.

The day of Prince Charles' wedding, we were staying with Mary-Lou's parents and we all were curious witnesses to the broadcast of this interesting ceremony. We thought it was treated rather ironically, because only the beauty of Lady Di was featured. I still remember that it was very warm that afternoon when our host proposed drinking to the health of the wedding couple. He must have had abstinence scruples, for we had to wait until dinner, when just the men—except for our seventeen-year-old son--sipped modestly on one glass of beer each. Hmm, not astonishing that a marriage so cursorily toasted ended as it did.

In my mind's eye, I see again the shop window of a practical-minded merchant who, exploiting the news of the day, promoted coffee cups of Prince Charles' head, with one of his super-sized ears serving conveniently as the handle.

From there we ventured into Death Valley, and not without trepidation. Our friends had passed through on their honeymoon trip, and a sandstorm had taken all the paint off their new car. The lowest point of this desert is 86 meters[*] below sea level. Here you'll find Badwater, a small lake so salty that it never dries, even during the worst heat waves of 57° Celsius.[+] During the last century, convoys of twenty mules used to pull wagons loaded with white gold, or boron. They had reconstructed a convoy without mules, to show the tourists this impressive caravan. The rocks eroded by sandstormsfas hioned bizarre forms. Every evening the trails

---

[*] One meter is slightly longer than a yard—approximately 39.37 inches. At 282 feet below sea level, this is the lowest spot in the Western Hemisphere.

[+] Fahrenheit = 9/5 Celsius (Centigrade) + 32. The hottest air temperature recorded in nearby Furnace Creek, Death Valley, was 134° F (56.7° C.) on July 10, 1913. This is second only to the world record recorded in Africa. Badwater itself is reputed to be hotter than Furnace Creek.

are checked, to be sure that no one is lost in this desert. This must have happened at some time or other!

Since we were lucky to come out alive, we still wanted to try our luck and continue on the road to Las Vegas, no more than 200 kilometers away.

I remember that on the nightstand of all the motels, even outside of Nevada, we found enticing publicity booklets for the hotels and casinos of Las Vegas, at unbelievably low prices. Moreover, these establishments presented extraordinary attractions, from the medieval castle of Excalibur to the pyramids of Egypt, passing by the pirates of the Caribbean, where the volcano awakens every evening at nightfall. At the Caesar, we arrived just in time for the entrance of Cleopatra and her magnificently costumed entourage, in the atmosphere of Roman pomp that the lavish scene required. Actually, I wanted to see Siegfried and Roy's magic show, but they were on vacation just then.

From numerous invitations, we accepted that of an Armenian family whose daughter we had received at our home. They lived in Palo Alto, California, on a splendid hill overlooking San Francisco Bay. Their all-wooden house had been made earthquake-resistant, and included an automatic turn-off gas system. In their huge yard were does and a raccoon who, despite the lure of some bait, refused to come out to see us. We were lucky enough to see some elsewhere.

These friends took us to visit San Francisco. We toured from the pretty little fishing port with yachts that made us think of the south of Italy, to the Chinese quarter where we thought we were in Asia. On this port is a well-known French bakery, "Boudin," coincidentally the name of our sister-in-law. Gourmands came daily for croissants and French baguettes. In the back of the bay, you could see Alcatraz, which moved me to exclaim, with the air of a former convict: "Oh, Alcatraz! My wasted youth!"

Further on, an old "Queen" ship in the port had been transformed into a shopping center. At the foot of the gangway was a popcorn vendor dressed like a captain; unemployment must have led him to seek another career.

We not only got to ride the famous cable cars, but our friend procured a visit to their depot, a strange, late nineteenth-century brick construction.

One evening, he invited us to dinner in an Armenian restaurant, where the table was ready and waiting and a perfect menu planned. On the way back, he stopped in the highway emergency lane so that we could see the city with all its lights. He took the precaution of opening the hood, to feign engine trouble and avoid problems with the police.

We went over the Golden Gate Bridge. To encourage car-pooling, crossing was free if you had at least three persons in the vehicle. The gigantic bridge cast its shadow on the arm of the sea down below. Later, we enjoyed surveying this bridge and the magnificent bay, from the sky.

Following the coastline in our car, we soon came to the immense urban area of Los Angeles, which managed to have traffic jams, notwithstanding six-lane city highways in each direction, and the "Stack," the impressive four-level interchange.

We were especially keen on visiting Hollywood, the gigantic Disneyland and Universal Studios. Then, we stood in front of Grauman's Chinese Theatre and saw the imprints in cement of the hands and feet of the greatest movie stars, who had found here the coveted recognition of their achievements.

Being French, we thought it our duty to go east from San Francisco to visit the "Vineyards and Masson Winery" of the Napa Valley. Amidst the vines was a warehouse, extraordinarily clean and equipped with stainless steel vats. Of course, they recommended that we "drink only the true California Champagne, and beware of French imitations." The visit ended with a tasting of their products, and a receptacle provided for spitting out the mouthfuls of wine that was tasted. Since it was not required, I did not participate in the spitting. On the whole, we thought their wines were excellent, but too young; I have a weakness for the Chardonnay vine.

Although my passengers didn't agree, I followed the coastline to the south, to enter Mexico and see Tijuana. I had naïvely imagined that the proximity to the USA would enrich this city. Not so. The hills covered with miserable housing did not beckon visitors. Oh! We had blithely entered without customs or the police, and were disillusioned on the return trip, detained for two hours and then seriously questioned.

I still remember the humor of the police officer who verified the French passports and asked if we preferred the U.S.A. or Mexico. Seeing our enthusiasm for his country, he assured us that we were not the only ones to share this point of view.

Another year, we had the pleasure of again seeing our friend Joanne, who guided us brilliantly in Philadelphia and its region. Philadelphia is a superb city, with numerous and rich museums. With a mentor like Joanne, we were very fortunate.

Naturally, she took us to Independence Mall, to the famous cracked Liberty Bell, then to the Schuylkill River to visit the USS Olympia, former flagship of the Mexican War and today a superb Naval Museum.

So that we wouldn't suffer from the heat, her mother had lent us her own air conditioned car to see Valley Forge, where George Washington camped with his troops that terrible winter of 1777-1778, during the extraordinary events of the War for American Independence.

Another day, we drove out to a farm run by the Amish, who live today as they did in olden times, without machines or electricity. I was moved to say that they cheat a little, by calling on neighbors who drive and, not being of their convictions, agree to carry out the more difficult tasks with their own tractors. Today, you can still meet up with Amish on the road, in black, horse-drawn carriages from another age, and unique, button-less clothes. I pity the children, constrained by these pious beliefs.

During this visit, we were invited to lunch in the wonderful lakeside villa home of Joanne's aunt and uncle. Here I swallowed the solid silver knife of which I spoke in another chapter.

There is so much more that I could write about the awe-inspiring United States, but I'll conclude with some final impressions.

On one trip, we stood at the Canadian border marveling at the famous Niagara Falls, one of the most impressive sights in the world;

The natural parks of the West, one more beautiful than another, must be mentioned, although I don't intend to compete with the Michelin guides. Here are just a few of my unforgettable memories of their beauty:

- The indescribable marvel of the Grand Canyon, with Colorado split into a furrow 1600 meters deep;
- In the upper course of the Rio Grande, Monument Valley, with its striking rock formation, the natural background of so many films;
- Salt Lake City, the "Mecca" of the Mormons, with its gigantic copper quarry open to the sky;
- Mount Rushmore, sculpted into colossal heads representing those four famous presidents of the United States: George Washington, Thomas Jefferson, Theodore Roosevelt and Abraham Lincoln.

A "special mention" award goes to Yellowstone National Park, situated in Wyoming at an altitude of 2400 meters. This was the first established National Park. It is as big as France's island of Corsica. Yellowstone has more than 200 geysers, including the celebrated "Old Faithful"; all sorts of volcanic evidence; lakes of different colors; immense agglomerates of snow-white chalk; canyons;

abundant waterfalls 150 meters high and audible kilometers away.   While hiking there, we chanced on various animals—bison, deer, brown bears, and grizzlies.

If today, health reasons prevent me from enjoying the USA, I have come full circle, for America has once again become, as in my youth, an inaccessible dream.   But now I have these unforgettable memories of a country so close to my heart.

APPENDIX: THREE SHORT STORIES

INTRODUCTION

As the author states in the Preface to his Memoirs, he has placed the "Three Short Stories" as an Appendix. He wrote them during the war, when he was about fourteen years old; their form is one that he would have liked to develop further. Indeed, the stories epitomize the longings and emotional fugues of the young adolescent, with feelings of loss and idealization of the loved one that are not alien to adults.

Who has never felt removed from reality in the midst of noise and gaiety, while suffering a very private agony, as in "Eleonora"?

"The Story of the Little Soldier Who Went to War against the Russians" captures, almost as in a short film, the effects on tender, young hearts caught in the life-altering events of early World War II.

As for "*Amo Josiam*," who among us cannot identify with the broken-hearted sweetness of this youngster? He mentions, incidentally, that the bombs were dropping—just a backdrop to the war fought as teenagers begin to grow into the adult world. The lyrical expression here is the most fully developed of the three stories.

J. S. S.

Essay of Poetry in Prose

As a member of the children's choir for years, I heard the following gospel read many times at the end of Mass.[*] Through repetition, I committed it to memory and, from that young age, learned to love the charm of poetry with words that repeat like a refrain.

ARMAND

In principio erat Verbum, et Verbum erat aput Deum, et Deus erat Verbum. Hoc erat in principio aput Deum, Omnia per ipsum facta sunt : et sine ipso factum est nihil, quod factum est : in ipso vita erat, et vita erat lux hominum : et lux in tenebris lucet, et tenebrae eam non comprehenderunt.

Latin: [In the beginning was the Word, and the Word was with God, and the Word was God. He was in the beginning with God ; all things were made through him, and without him was not anything made that was made. In him was life, and the life was the light of men. The light shines in the darkness, and the darkness has not overcome it.]

New Testament, John (1: 1-5) (1114)

---

[*] At this time, before the modernizations and reforms of Vatican II, the Mass would have been said in Latin.

Eléonora

It's the Feast of Palermo. And you are no longer here! The music thunders, thunders over the city; the boys are winning and shouting, the girls are flirting and rolling their big eyes.

My gaze passes over the swings, the round group flying by on grotesque monsters. The man with the twisted hard mint, the merry-go round horses and the suckling pigs turning and turning—and you are no longer here!

"Drive in the nail...Three hammer strikes!" cries the girl at the last stand. I saw her hands, festooned with real gems, struggling to stir up the crowd. And the country folk striking, striking, twisting the nail ends...For a moment, the ticket-taking girl looked at me, she looked at me...There was no more noise, no more husky people, no more swearing men, missing the strike. Just her face, your face, a single face...

She recognized me, and she gestured. "Monsieur, three hammer strikes!" And I found you, Eléonora, my far-off Beloved. In her eyes, I saw my reflection: "Keep it up, keep it up, Monsieur!" I hit, I hit, without looking, without hearing. I had found you...

No, you couldn't have been pretending. When, trembling with tenderness, you closed your sky-blue eyes, to embrace me, and asked very softly: "Do you really want me, Rinaldo, do you really want me?"

The wind on the pebbles plastered waves onto the point of Corso. Air-rifle shots--I heard their crackling--like the night before you left, when I begged you to let me go with you, even to the end of the world.

Why did you refuse? Why did you insist it was impossible? My need to live comes from you. I'll die if there's no hope of being with you! Oh, my Love, take me! And she said: "No." Her curls shook against her shawl:

"No, no, no." If the tale was not possible, why had I fallen in love?

The girl at the stand caught the money in mid-air, shrugged her shoulders, and I took off at random into the side streets.

Eléonora, my far-off beloved, would you believe it? Without thinking, I had come back to the "Magic Village" of the French, where we had been together. Do you remember? The villa looked at me with the big empty eyes of its deserted windows. Then, aimlessly, I entered, and all the doors opened before me, all of them...

The room breathed the perfume of a deceased countess...

Under my fingers, the piano could not repeat the sounds that you asked for. But again, I pressed you against me, and your small unforgettable voice, the voice that I still heard at the Festival, your small, soft voice still murmuring: "Do you really want me, Rinaldo, do you really want me?" A creaking door interrupted my thoughts...

For you, I worked; for you, I submitted to my father, for you, I put up with the hot sun on my neck. Sometimes now, in the early morning, when the net weighs heavy under my arms weary from a long night of fishing, I feel that I can't do any more. But in the gleam of the catch, I imagine you, you. And in a single haul, I lift the trawl.

Will you never come back?

Wait, I see you, Eléonora! Wait! A blond with a small face passes by, and it's you. She's the vision of you-- angelic and blond--the sun rising again over Palermo, transfiguring the Conca d'Oro for me. Monte Pelegrino reels before me. I want to catch up with you and ask you again: "Will you come with me to La Favorite?"

You will say yes, as she will, and on the long road there, I'll murmur in her ear, "Please, take my arm, Mademoiselle!"

She will laugh and laugh—all girls are happy to be loved. Her cheeks will take on the tint of ripe prickly pears.

Yes! Blond girls will pass by at dawn, still more will go by in the evening. But I won't speak to them, I won't ask anything of them. Nothing other than that they remind me of you and of my Love—this immense feeling growing, always stronger, as if that could still be possible.

A sailor of the Royal Navy offers me a cigarette; it was you again, the smell of your cigarettes, those "Players Navy Cuts" that you would smoke down to the end, the smoke yellowing your fingertips.

As a child on the beaches, I had searched for a long time for the most beautiful seashell; one day, I found the wonder: gilded, pearly, perfectly chiseled.   No other youngster in Palermo had found one as pretty. I loved it more than anything.

Then, I wanted to know if it was reciprocal, and if this marvelous little thing that I possessed also owned me. I set out for the extreme point of the jetty, and tried to guide my shell to the bank by hopping and pushing it along in the water. The sea was high, the seawall long and rimless and, for the shell, the distance was quickly covered…The little trip went well, and I began to believe that it had an attachment to me, as well, when suddenly, it took off, veered three or four times on itself, and plunged straight to the bottom.

Why did I have to take a chance with my Happiness?

I bent over the water, losing myself in it, but it was out of sight. How I looked for it, how I cried for my shell, never come back to the bank, never again. My golden shell, it was so much like you.

"Rinaldo," said my mother, why don't you whistle barcaroles* any more? You don't sing on the way back from the Punta di Priola, like you used to. I don't hear your voice in the sea wind. Rinaldo, why?"

--*E partite Eléonora!* [Eleonora is gone!]

---

* An Italian boat song, characterized by alternating strong and weak beats in 6/8 time, imitating a rowing rhythm.

--*Figlio mio* [My son], what difference does it make if the foreigner is gone, the girls in Palermo, aren't they beautiful to look at? *Figlio mio,* sing the barcaroles again for me.

Then, I tried to start singing again, so as not to cause her pain; but in a breath, I recognized--I'm sure of it--I heard your little voice murmuring again: "Do you really want me, Rinaldo? Do you really want me?"

THE STORY OF THE LITTLE SOLDIER WHO WENT TO WAR AGAINST THE RUSSIANS

Recipient of the Diploma of Honor
Jeux Floraux of Tunis 1951

I was twelve years old; twelve years of my unhappy childhood had made me grow old, if you only knew! One winter night, coming home from school, I had noticed him playing under a porch ledge. Maybe he had been playing under this porch for years. Maybe I had been noticing him for years, in the evening, on the way back from school. But this evening, while he was waving an arm and calling to me, "Mirella! Mirella, *Buonasera* [good evening]!" I suddenly understood that I loved him, and that this vague, indefinable feeling that I felt upon seeing him, had to be Love.

Saying nothing for a long time, hardly daring to look at him, I met him regularly in the evening on my way home. I associated him with all my dreams and all my escapes from being an unhappy child. This must have gone on for months, perhaps years. I no longer remember, nothing remains outside of this feeling, which kept me silent. I thought: "As long as he doesn't know that you love him, as long as you don't get to know him better, he is like your dream, as you wish him to be, as you yourself make him; if he knew your feelings, he might disappoint you!" So I kept quiet for years...

It rumbles around in my heart, like a little bell, the memory of the day when I spoke to him. Spoke with words that lived in my soul. He shook my hand with so much strength, so much tenderness...His eyes looked at me, so big, so big, they drank me in...

Why hadn't he embraced me?

"I want our Love to be pure as a diamond, so that it will last...You will be all mine, soon, later; today I want only your soul, nothing but your soul, your whole soul."

And as I watched him leave, he turned around often on the road; at the angle of the street, he sent me a kiss, just one, very small, so vibrant, a word of Love in telegraphic style.

Then he left to fight in the war against "the Russians."[*] From the frozen front, he sent me letters for a long time: enthusiastic, tired, gay, desolate, joyous, impatient, bored, but always loving me with all his soul, writing with the hand that had sent me the kiss, writing in ink, in pencil, tucked into envelopes of blue or gray, all violated by the censure...

My eyes would search in vain on the maps for the nameless steppes where he was fighting, where he was living, where he was writing from, where he was while thinking of me.

In the black and white of the letters, I pursued my Love Story, my grown-up little girl's novel, that pink library book written with my life.

When the postman left letters in the mailbox, I sensed from the rustling of their small envelopes against the compartment, whether I had his. My letter, the only one that mattered, there after unimaginable delays en route, carrying his Love so deep, from so far, like a perfume. A love from somewhere in the Far North.

Then, I received no more blue envelopes, and no more gray ones. But tonight the mailman will come back, and tomorrow he'll come by again, burdened with his open box, sowing in his path the seeds of joy, pain, love, sorrow, overflowing happiness or the dashing of hope for girls in love.

The spokes of the mailman's bicycle turned with the noise of a lottery spin. Just once, just one letter, so that I'd

---

[*] At this stage of World War II, Russia and Germany were still allies, and therefore enemies of France.

know what was happening, and the reason for this long silence. But it was a lottery that I lost every day, and gradually I gave up the hope of again receiving news.

Was he taken prisoner? Wounded? Dead? Rather than this silence…I wept…

I wept in my room, where I took refuge to keep from weeping. I saw my young girl's face in the mirror of the armoire. It had become so ugly that the hideous bonze[*] on the bookshelf was laughing and showing all his teeth. It was so ugly that the fantasy on the blue China vase hated it through its eyes of jasper, strange eyes that followed me everywhere.

I hid the wet cheeks of the now-ugly Mirella in the hollow of the pillow, so that I couldn't see the laughing bonze, couldn't feel the ferocious look of the porcelain-- when suddenly, I heard the clock sound, breaking the silence. The rhythmic noise of its constant presence was an outrage to my vigil; and then, the full song, this cadence which marked the ridiculously slow passage of time until the next delivery of the postman. The tic-toc suddenly became weightier, like a horse's pace…Yes, that was it—the horse of a messenger, the one bearing his news; but the beast advanced so slowly that I heard his shoes one after the other. Without moving, I waited a long time, the sound of the steps still far off and unhurried. Was this messenger mocking me?

The half-hour rang "Yes!" The fading of the tones reverberated "Yes!" Yes, it was mocking me. I threw the clock onto the tiles of the foyer. But by some cursed force, the hammer began to strike before dying out—striking again and again: "Yes! Yes! Yes!…" And I never received another letter…No, he isn't dead! No, that's not possible, I would have known it somehow.

The thousands of soldiers gone to war against "the Russians," and from whom there is no news, haunt the hours. From unknown camps of misery, where one would hope them to still be alive, their thoughts and dreams are able to

---

[*] Buddhist monk of the Far East.

escape. The lovers capture these invisible messages in their secret hearts, hear the whispering of their voices in the rustling of leaves, dream of their lives, dream of their smiles, dream of their return. They'll come home soon--tomorrow, perhaps? Tomorrow... Always tomorrow!

Mirella lived an indefinite life of signs and omens: "If the wagtail stays on the cherry tree until I count to ten, then he's alive and thinking of me." The bird would stay or not stay, but, if it could glimpse the total happiness or total despair held in its wings, I believe that it would stay frozen on the branch for a lifetime.

With the war over, the prisoners began to come home; Mirella went to wait for every train and, not seeing him, ventured to ask the lucky ones:

--*Avez-vous vu Ennio ?* [Have you seen Ennio?]

--*Ennio ! Connais pas ! Connais pas !* [Don't know him, don't know him.]*

And they again embraced wives and children. Their joy at being reunited was unbearable.

--*Avez-vous vu Ennio?*

--*Ennio! Non lo conosco! Non lo conosco!* [Don't know him, don't know him!]+

At the angle of the street with the two butcher shops, closed up in a niche in the wall, is "The Madonna of Hope." Mirella believed in nothing, but she began to keep up a watch with the icon, sending her kisses when passing by. The Madonna would smile sweetly at these prayer-less devotions, as she smiled at all devotions and all blasphemy. The calm smile of the statue told Mirella to wait, still wait...

One day, when the war long over, the government decided that the soldiers who had not yet returned, and of whom there was no word, would be dead. They were dead. At first she couldn't believe it, because people don't die by ministerial decision.

---

* (Some respond in French.)
+ (Some respond in Italian.)

Then the other girls cut their hair, put on long dresses, went dancing.   Mirella, who looked at them unseeingly, understood neither their laughter, nor their songs, nor the sunlit town square. From that time, she began murmuring in a low, weary voice that would make you cry: "I was twenty years old, twenty years of my unhappy childhood made me grow old, aged me, if you only knew."

AMO JOSIAM[*]

With half shut eyes, I lightly inclined my head, but I couldn't really see her face any more, her little girl's face that was lost during the war. I only remember her eyes, blue eyes like sweet almonds. I no longer recall her child's face, but I seem to still hear her thin voice, taking on the inflections of a young woman, to confide to me: "You know, I'll be in *sixième*[+] when school starts up, and I'll learn Latin."

For me, the simple fact that she would learn Latin was a wonder. I imagined her already speaking the strange language of my Mass book, and the simple idea of learning Latin must have surprised and moved her, as it did me.

I must have been in love with her for a very long time, perhaps since the day when, pressed on the same chaise lounge, we listened to her brother tell the story "The Adventures of the King of Gold." I couldn't have known her without loving her, and I had known her for such a long time that I must not have existed before knowing her.

Saying « *Bonsoir* », I took pleasure in pressing her little hand very firmly between my two hands, and I held it there for a long time; but she, unlike me, hadn't read bad books, and no doubt understood nothing by this gesture, which to me seemed an unspeakable lover's audacity.

On Sundays, as a choirboy, I didn't take my eyes off her, and each time that the priest pronounced the word "love," I signaled her with my eyes. My burning cheeks took on the color of my cape. I could see Josée look at me like that sometimes, too, because my place was in front of her.

Her indifference to these thousands of little nothings threw me into despair. Day by day, I was increasingly taken

---

[*] Latin: [I Love Josée]
[+] In the U.S., approximately sixth grade.

with the desire to make her feel more strongly towards me. Often, I would dream that she came softly, placing her arm around my neck and pressing her mouth to my ear, telling me words of love that I had awaited for such a long time. Waking, I would caress the spot on my ear that her lips had chosen.

We were playing in my yard. When it was her brother's turn to wait for us to hide, I told Josée to follow me, I knew a good place. I pulled her behind a grove of spindle trees, and whispered: "I love you, Josée." She screamed "Idiot!" as she did when she stuck herself while sewing for her dolls. Her brother hollered, "Ninety-nine, one hundred," in the distance.

--And you, do you love me?

--Maybe!

Doubtless, she had never been asked the question.

I came out red-faced from the ordeal and, fearing embarrassing questions at home, I passed a wet handkerchief over my face. But I was in such an anxious state that the remedy proved worse than the sickness. It felt as though my cheeks would burst, like over-ripe tomatoes.

The next day, her brother reproached me severely. She had told him everything and this brat--a year younger than I--laid a reprimand on me that started like this: "I kid you not, if it weren't for me, Josée would tell our parents."

I couldn't convince myself not to believe him; I went cold at the very idea of the catastrophe that he claimed to have spared me. Moreover, I had lost all his respect with this one act.

One of my naughty friends, in whom I foolishly confided this misadventure, took a superior air, and declared: "You know, you must be crazy; you have to tell this little girl that you love her, in Latin: « *Amo Josiam !* » He had a way of saying "this little girl" in a scornful, bemused tone that reduced my idol to nothingness. I admired his scorn at the same time as it bothered me deeply.

Sometimes, when we would see Josée in the distance, he would order, in his rough, already-changing voice: "Go on, guy!   Go on!   Holler to her: « *Amo Josiam !* »   I trembled, fearing she would hear.   This « *Amo Josiam* » from his mouth seemed like blasphemy.   The lout, he couldn't love her like I loved her.   « *Amo Josiam !* » he would call out to me in the street.   « *Amo Josiam !* » he would holler into the open doors of the echoing corridors.   I suffered painfully from his game.   « *Amo Josiam* », I caught myself murmuring, like a prayer.   « *Amo Josiam !* »   Like a sob without a tear.   « *Amo Josiam !* »   Sweet, but cruel.

I happened to see her every day, on the way to school.   Loving to eat, she enjoyed my vitamin cakes; the simple fact of pleasing her comforted me enormously.

Then I discovered, in a big red book, the immortal sonnet of Arvers:

> My soul has its secret, my life has its mystery
> An eternal love conceived in one moment...

He translated my feelings so faithfully that it astounded me.   I plagiarized him immediately, with the aplomb of a forger confident of impunity.   We met alone and I gave her the sonnet, saying offhandedly that I had written it for her.

Josée seemed very moved.   She must have found it so beautiful that she let her inseparable friend read it.   The friend came up to us, read through the paper and declared promptly, in a detached, cultivated tone which took me aback: "That's funny, I've already read that somewhere!"   It was some time before I dared to again see Josée or her inseparable friend.

World War II was in progress, and the bombs were going off every night.   Josée's parents decided to leave for the countryside until the war was over.   On the eve of her departure, I went to say good-bye to my friend.   She was alone, gathering flowers in the garden.   For an instant I believed that our good-byes would be emotional.   I wanted to keep the memory forever.   She reached through the flowers and held my hand and, without looking at me, said a simple

« *Au revoir !* » [Good-bye!] as if I were to see her tomorrow. Then she resumed humming, "As the blue bell mounts the hill..."

I turned around, heavy-hearted with all my scorned, neglected love. Passing the rose garden, I heard her again, her voice still humming, "As the blue bell mounts the hill..."

Pain from disappointing good-byes, scent of roses, songs, I tasted it all on the road of my exodus, to the tune of this miserable German tune that I whistled, "As the blue bell mounts the hill..."

A tune, the smell of roses, the memory of my beloved seen through the flowers—these haunted the sleepless night of the last attack, when we thought that we would surely die under the shells of the tanks. Fool, I had tried to think of her the whole night, to be sure that I would die thinking of her...

In the aftermath, waiting hours for the distribution of water from the cistern-truck--which never did arrive--I encountered Josée again. She seemed even more beautiful to me in the midst of so much misery, so much horror.

When school resumed, we had classes at the same times, and we had to take almost the same route to school. We saw each other often, and these renewed encounters drew the envious mocking remarks of my classmates. But the pest that I hated the most was Bastuccio, a spindly kid who was at least four classes younger than I. Every time he saw me alone, he would run up, to walk the route with me. His manners were so refined that I would have been rude to rebuff him. He never failed to ask me courteously for news of « *Mademoiselle ton Amie* » ["Mademoiselle, your friend"].

I would always fashion my response, through a sense of modesty that I consider poor now, so as to give the impression that « *Mademoiselle mon Amie* » was rather insignificant to me. But he wasn't deceived, and it seemed to me that he foolishly enjoyed making an "older person" take the trouble to try in vain to fool him.

« *Mademoiselle mon Amie* » had shown me a photograph of herself, in a romantic pose, and I begged her to give it to me. "You can't be serious!" she said. Then she promised to ask her mother's permission. The next day, warning me not to say anything about it, she gave me her picture.

It was a gift of herself that she gave, and I was transported. I forgot the time of my class, the snow, the frozen earth. Again, I see myself entering class late, into the midst of chilled pupils. They began to tap their feet in the freezing room, hollering louder and louder: "Light a fire, some fire!" I didn't feel the cold, but I remember precisely that scene, of which I wanted no part; I pressed her slender silhouette, in an envelope, against my chest.

A pale winter sun illuminated the windows, frosted with softly melting flowers. They called to me: "So you're not cold, you're not stomping your feet?" No, I wasn't cold, and no one else in my place would have been cold. No, I wasn't cold, the melting ice held all the sorrows of my unhappy Love. But they were melting, and only joy would remain, all the joy of my Love burning in the sun. I started to tap my feet, too, so as not to appear cowardly, but while they were hollering: "Light a fire! Some fire!" I thought I heard them all exclaim, with that same verve: "Josée! Josée!"

I hid her picture in the covers of books and in my notebooks, between sheets of folded blotting paper. I couldn't do without her image, as I couldn't do without her. This passion was my happiness, while it also threw me into confusion. It was all the greater because it remained uncertain, fragile, incomplete.

Josée! There were days when you made fun of me, when you cruelly enjoyed describing the lover of your dreams, that nebulous being that you always described as having different features from mine. I was tall, he would have been short. I was brunette, he would have been blond. And you were mean and laughed at this cruel game. And your friend laughed, too. It did me no good not to believe in the game; it hurt me terribly, with the sharp pain of a physical illness.

There were also days when you loved me! Days when you helped me brush close to ecstasy, when you let me believe that you would never hurt me again. One Thursday, when I was passing in front of your house, you glued your little pink nose against the windowpane. I could just make out the direction of your gaze, and your nose was pressed so hard against the glass that it appeared as a little white, round spot. I will never forget that little nose glued against the pane, and you, looking at me passing by...

Another day, when we were reading the same book together, I ventured to put my arm around your shoulders. I pressed you softly against me, and I could feel the wildest of your locks tickle my cheek. I had only to turn my head to kiss you. I was sure that you would like that, too. At that moment, your brother came in. Why did I never again put my arm around you?

I put up with your spoiled little girl whims, and ended up all the sadder because you plunged me from pain to joy, and back again. Then, when I couldn't take it any more, one day I had to confess all this. Before your hasty leave-taking, you quickly murmured with those adorable little lips: "Let's be friends, I don't love you!"

I never saw you again. Never again! So you became the magic fairy in my childhood picture book. With time, this shadow self became still more beautiful, incredibly sweet. I had clarified it little by little in my sorrow, from the souvenir of the Josée who had given me so much joy and done so much harm, in order to have from this adorable little girl only the memory of her eyes, with no memory of her face. The memory of a childhood Josée who therefore had never truly existed.

Il mondo è uno spettacolo: Vieni, vidi, e te ne vai.

(Italian): The world is a show: You come, you see, and you leave.

Read on the bottom of a plate in San Gimignano, long ago

REFERENCES

BIBLIOGRAPHY

Asselin, Gilles & Ruth Mastron. *Au Contraire! Figuring Out the French.* Yarmouth, Maine: Intercultural Press, Inc., 2001.

Carell, Paul. *Invasion—they're coming! The German account of the Allied landings and the 80 days' battle for France.* Translated from the German *Sie Kommen!: die Invasion 1944* by E. Osers. New York: Dutton, 1963.

Céline, Louis-Ferdinand D. *Voyage au bout de la nuit.* Paris: ©Editions GALLIMARD, Collection FOLIO N° 28, 1987.

Cretzmeyer, Stacy. *Your Name is Renée: Ruth's Story as a Hidden Child. The Wartime Experiences of Ruth Kapp Hartz.* Brunswick, Maine: Biddle Publishing, 1994.

D'Este, Carlo. *Decision in Normandy.* New York: E. P. Dutton, Inc., 1983.

Ghiglione, Margaret & Carol Pouchol, eds. Charts. *AAWE Guide to Education.* Paris: AAWE 6th edition, 2003.

Hastings, Max. *Overlord: D-Day and the battle for Normandy.* New York: Simon and Schuster, 1984.

Keegan, John. *The First World War.* New York: A. Knopf, 1999.

Mayle, Peter & Judith Clancy, Illustrator. *A Year in Provence.* Vancouver, WA: Vintage Books; Reprint edition, 1991.

Platt, Polly & Ande Grchich, Illustrator. *Savoir-Flair: 211 Tips for Enjoying France and the French.* Skokie, Ill: Distribooks, 2001.

Ryan, Cornelius. *The Longest Day: The Classic Epic of D-Day.* New York: Touchstone Books, 1994.

Zuccotti, Susan. *The Holocaust, the French and the Jews.* New York: BasicBooks, 1993.

PERIODICALS

"France Takes the Lead in the Study of Volcanoes." *News from France.* Vol. 03.06 May 21, 2003.

Galanti, Marie. "Waiting for a Nibble." *France Today.* Vol. 17 No. 4, April. 2002.

Normandy's Conquering Spirit: The 50th Anniversary of D-Day. Spec. issue of *FRANCE Magazine.* The Maison Française: Washington, D.C. No. 29, Winter 1993-94.

"Ten Reasons to Study in France." *France Today: Educational Issue.* Vol. 15 No. 5, 2000.

"Words of the Day: A Collection of Letters from D-Day." *News from France* Vol. 03.07 June 11, 2003.

VIDEOGRAPHY

Au Revoir Les Enfants (Good-bye Children). Dir. by Louis Malle. Perf. Gaspard Manesse, Raphael Fejto. Orion Pictures Corporation, 1987.

Faces of the Holocaust. (Marcel Jabelot) French with English Subtitles. Exec. Producer, Barbara Barnett. Producers, Martha Goell Lubell & Sharon Mullally. Dir. of Photography Toni A. Banet. 1995.

The Hawaiian Volcanoes: A Force for Creation. Producer, Director, Camera & Editor Jay Harada; Producer, Cyril Akashi; Scriptwriter, Barry Hampe. Harada Productions: Hilo, Hawaii, MCMLXXXIX (1989).

The Longest Day. Dir. Ken Annakin, Andrew Marton, Bernhard Wicki, Darryl F. Zanuck. Perf. John Wayne, Robert Mitchum, Henry Fonda, Richard Burton. 20th Century Fox, 1962.

Saving Private Ryan. Dir. Steven Spielberg. Perf. Tom Hanks, Edward Burns, Tom Sizemore, Matt Damon. Written by Robert Rodat. DreamWorks Pictures and Paramount Pictures, 1998.

WEBSITES

Badwater Death Valley geological field trip. <http://www.aqd.nps.gov/grd/sgsnps/deva/ftbad2.html> Accessed July 8, 2003.

La Conférence de Saint Vincent de Paul. <http://www.vincenter.org/tree/svdp/index.html> Accessed June 27, 2003.

Death-Valley.US Climate. Accessed July 8, 2003. <http://www.death-valley.us/climate.html>

Les Etats-Unis de A à Z. Outline of French Educational System. <http://www.amb-usa.fr/irc/faq/scsystem.htm> Accessed June 4, 2003.

FrancePress, Inc. <http://www.journalfrancais.com> <http://www.francetoday.com> Accessed July 6, 2003.

French Embassy Press and Information Service. <http://www.ambafrance-us.org> <http://www.france.diplomatie.gouv.fr> Accessed July 7, 2003.

The French Tutorial. frenchtutorial.com, Hervé Foucher, 1999-2002. Accessed June 3, 2003. <http://www.helio.org/education/french/vocabulary/learning_system.html>

Italy's Volcanoes: The Cradle of Volcanology.
<http://boris.vulcanoetna.com> or
<http://stromboli.net/boris> The volcanoes of Italy, their
geology, activity and hazards; frequent updates on
significant eruptive events. Accessed June 5, 2003.

Major Volcanoes of Italy. Map.
<http://volcano.1pgp.jussieu.fr:8080/guadeloupe/capture
video.htm> USGS/Cascades Volcano Observatory,
Vancouver, WA. Topinka, 1998; basemap modified
from CIA map, 1997; volcanoes from Simkin & Siebert,
1994. Accessed June 1, 2003.

World Atlas.com. Map.
<http://webimage/countrys/namerica/caribb/ciamaps/
gp.htm> Accessed June 12, 2003.

World War II Online. Playnet Inc.
<http://www.hq.wwiionline.com/journal/
war_story_5.shtml> Accessed August 3, 2003.

INDEX

ABOUT THE AUTHOR

Armand Idrac was born in Normandy in 1928. His early childhood, schooling and family life were not atypical of that era. In 1942, his father suffered a fatal coronary attack and, through an unspoken agreement, 13-year-old Armand became the head of the family. Trusted by his Mother and little sister, it was he who decided to flee their home when the Allies landed on the beaches of Normandy and the battle for Caen heated up. Severe food and water rationing followed, with bombings, machine gun volleys, helping the wounded, and burying the dead. They were forced to share living quarters with German troops in the various châteaux where they took shelter. But the family survived to lead productive lives.

Armand's love of life, humor, practical jokes and travel has been a powerful force in his fascinating life. He and his wife Yvonne still live in Caen, in the house where they raised their children, just a few feet from his ancestral home. Today, they continue to help other city residents through the Society of St. Vincent de Paul, and they enjoy traveling in northern France to visit children, grandchildren and friends.

Armand's life's work was with the French railroad, but his avocation was construction. His buildings are still strong, as are his many friendships.

BEACH LLOYD PUBLISHERS, LLC

Web: ***http://www.beachlloyd.com***
E-mail: ***BEACHLLOYD@erols.com***
Phone – (610) 407-0130 or
Toll free 1-866-218-3253, Ext. 8668
Fax - (775) 254-0633

P.O. Box 2183
Southeastern, PA 19399-2183

QUICK Order Form

🖳 **Fax orders**: 775-254-0633. Send this form.

☎ **Telephone orders**: Call 610-407-0130 or
toll free 1-866-218-3253, Ext. 8668.
Have your credit card ready.

🖳 **E-mail orders**: BEACHLLOYD@erols.com

🖃 **Postal Orders**: Beach Lloyd Publishers, LLC
Joanne S. Silver, Mgr.
P.O. Box 2183
Southeastern PA 19399-2183

Please send the following books and other products:

_____

_____

Name: _____

Address: _____

City: _____ State: _____ ZIP: _____

Telephone: _____

E-mail address: _____

Sales tax: Please add 6% for products shipped to
Pennsylvania addresses.

Shipping by air:

U.S.: $4.00 for first book & $2.00 for each additional book.

International: $9.00 for first book & $5.00 for each
additional book (estimate).

Payment: ☐ Check   ☐ Credit card:

☐ Visa   ☐ MasterCard

Card number: _____

Name on card: _____ Exp. Date: _____